To dad—from whom I inherited this obsession.
And to mom—who put up with it.

Mets IN 10s

Mets IN **10s**

BEST AND WORST OF AN AMAZIN' HISTORY

BRIAN WRIGHT | *Foreword by Jerry Koosman*

THE
History
PRESS

Published by The History Press
Charleston, SC
www.historypress.com

First published 2018

Manufactured in the United States

ISBN 9781467139687

Library of Congress Control Number: 2017963227

CONTENTS

Contents

FOREWORD

My journey from the farm in Appleton, Minnesota, to the mound at Shea Stadium almost never came to pass.

I was drafted into the army as a nineteen-year-old in 1962, the same year the Mets franchise was born. It was an honor to serve, but baseball was my ultimate dream.

Stationed in Grafton, Illinois, on a Nike/Hercules site after my basic training at Fort Leonard Wood, there were no facilities to pursue such a dream. But luckily for me, my dentist at the time happened to be a commanding major general of the Minnesota National Guard, and he assisted me in trying to get transferred to a base down South where I could hone my pitching skills.

As a contingency plan, I took and passed the officer's candidate test to become a helicopter pilot. Had I pursued this ambition and completed training for it, I would have eventually been put on orders to go to Vietnam. However, my transfer came through from my dentist, and I was off to Fort Bliss in El Paso, Texas. My destiny changed forever.

There, pitching for the army's baseball team, my catcher was John Lucchese. In a fortunate twist of fate, his father was an usher at Shea Stadium—the brand-new home of the Mets. John told his dad of my talents, who then passed that information along to scouting director Joe McDonald.

Soon after, Mets scout Red Murff came to watch me pitch. In the game he observed, I struck out eighteen batters. On August 27, 1964, I officially signed with the Mets organization. After enduring the trials of the minor leagues, the majors came calling in April 1967. I pitched only 22.1 innings that season, but the next year would be my big break.

I was part of the starting rotation for 1968 under a disciplined manager, Gil Hodges. Little did I realize how important he would be to me and the team's success in the near future.

After shutting out the Dodgers in my first outing, I went into my next start—the home opener at Shea versus the Giants—filled with confidence. But quickly, in the top of the first, I found myself in a nobody out, bases loaded situation.

Up to the plate stepped Willie Mays, a player I idolized and imitated as a kid.

How did that farm boy from western Minnesota end up in a fix like this? But I was able to strike Willie out, get Jim Ray Hart to pop up and fan Jack Hiatt. My confidence reinforced, I went the distance, and we had a 3–0 victory.

That '68 season was special for me, as I won nineteen games and narrowly missed the National League Rookie of the Year. But 1969 proved special for all of us and all of New York.

It was a year when everything came together. We caught and passed the Chicago Cubs in August, taking the division with one hundred victories, taking the pennant and defeating the Baltimore Orioles in the World Series.

I started Game 2 at Memorial Stadium in Baltimore and had my best stuff, taking a no-hitter into the seventh inning. Although I allowed two hits that let the Orioles tie it, key ninth-inning singles led us to even the series heading back to New York.

We won the next two on the strength of Tommie Agee's spectacular catches, Ron Swoboda's unbelievable diving grab, the hitting of Donn Clendenon and the pitching of Gary Gentry, Nolan Ryan and Tom Seaver.

Now it was Game 5—and a chance to do what everyone thought was impossible. And I had the starting assignment. But the great stuff from Game 2 temporarily deserted me.

After allowing three second-inning runs, I marched into the dugout angrily, stating, "They're not getting any more. Let's go beat 'em!"

And, of course, we did.

Thanks to several big hits, I was given a 5–3 lead heading into the ninth. As Davey Johnson came up with two outs and a runner on first, I was as nervous as ever. I didn't know where the ball was going anymore. I'm simply trying to throw strikes.

When Johnson hit a fly ball to deep left field and Cleon Jones raised his glove for the catch, it was a moment I'll never forget. Catcher Jerry Grote and I embraced near the mound. Fans stormed the field in unrestrained excitement. It was the culmination of our wildest hopes and dreams.

Four years later, we nearly completed another miracle using the same tactics that got us the World Series in '69: great pitching, fine defense and timely hitting. Overcoming injuries and using Tug McGraw's "Ya Gotta Believe" as our rallying cry, we came all the way back from last place in the NL East on August 30 to win the division, then beat the Cincinnati Reds in the National League Championship Series and took the Oakland Athletics' dynasty to the limit before losing the World Series in seven games.

Following the 1978 season, I asked for and was granted a trade to my hometown Minnesota Twins. I would pitch for two other clubs over the next seven years before finishing a nineteen-year career.

But nothing can match the experience with the Mets. I was so proud to be a part of two championship teams and, on a personal note, to reach the landmark achievement of twenty victories in 1976.

It was an honor to be taught and managed by respected men like Hodges and Yogi Berra, to play for a wonderful and caring owner like Mrs. Joan Payson, to be grouped with wonderful teammates and, above all, to pitch before loyal fans who supported me so much then and still support me to this day.

Mets fans always embrace this team—throughout the ups and downs of the last five-plus decades. Those memories, some of which I experienced firsthand, are included in this group of lists Brian has compiled.

I hope you enjoy reliving these players and moments in Mets history as much as I enjoyed pitching for the Mets over eleven seasons.

—Jerry Koosman
Mets Hall of Fame Class of 1989

PART I

BEGINNINGS

OPENING DAYS

10. 1989

If success in regular season premieres lent a reward, the New York Mets would reign as the hands-down holders of that trophy. Boasting thirty-six Opening Day victories as of 2017—and a winning percentage of .642—no franchise establishes a better first impression.

Neither the biting afternoon cold at Shea Stadium nor the St. Louis Cardinals did anything to change the air of optimism.

Howard Johnson, laying down the foundation for his second year of thirty home runs and thirty stolen bases, went 3-for-4 with three runs batted in and a long ball to right field—punctuating the 8–4 victory. Shortstop Kevin Elster and outfielder Darryl Strawberry each equaled "HoJo" in the hit column. Darryl doubled twice and stole two bases.

Cardinals' starter Joe Magrane, stung for nine hits and seven runs, was put out of his misery and sent to the safety of the clubhouse after 3.2 innings.

Dwight Gooden, meanwhile, making his fourth Opening Day start since 1985, enjoyed the assurance such support brings. Gooden allowed three earned runs and struck out eight as the Mets cruised to their eighteenth win in the last twenty openers.

9. 1970

The most fascinating aspect about the Mets' out-of-the-gate success? They lost their first eight. That included 1969—a season ending immeasurably better than it began.

As the Mets were basking in the glow of a remarkable World Championship from the previous October, they still were trying to figure out how to start 1-0. A far less majestic goal would be achieved at Forbes Field, the home of the Pittsburgh Pirates and months from demolition.

More magic from '69 would resurface—bookended by two noted hitting heroes.

Cleon Jones suppled the keynote, doubling off Steve Blass in the first to score Tommy Agee. Jones would complete the trip around the bases on Art Shamsky's single to right field.

Blass settled down and relinquished one additional run, while his Bucs teammates scratched out three on Tom Seaver—who departed after eight innings.

The 3–3 tie lasted into the eleventh, when the Mets were beneficiaries of shoddy Pittsburgh defense—as catcher Jerry May's error allowed Ron Swoboda to reach and put runners on first and second.

A sacrifice and an intentional walk let World Series MVP Donn Clendenon show he had another big hit to spare.

The former Pirate came off the bench and delivered a single to center, bringing in the two deciding runs. Tug McGraw worked around a Roberto Clemente leadoff walk to ensure that elusive game one victory.

8. 2001

Turner Field—a house of Met horrors where aspirations shatter from the tomahawk chop. The Mets, though, marched in sporting renewed confidence rather than the usual sense of dread.

For in this latest turn of a rather imbalanced divisional rivalry, New York—as defending National League Champions—held the upper hand.

Far too often in the late '90s and early 2000s, Atlanta's persistent ways would grind the Mets down into defeat.

Braves stubbornness continued here—as Mike Piazza's two-run home run greeting of Tom Glavine in the first inning was quickly answered with a one score in the bottom half against Al Leiter and another on Javier López's seventh-inning solo blast.

Robin Ventura's power stroke didn't appear until the eighth, yet it was right on time. With one on, he had the enviable duty of hitting John Rocker. Of course, the Braves responded to the Robin round-tripper with a pair of runs in their next try.

Except the Mets' self-assurance held true while Ventura stayed hot. Another two-run homer put New York ahead 6–4 in the tenth—and, at last, ahead to stay.

7. 1992

Occasionally an early statement win can serve as a prelude to the remainder of the season. But a 3–2 extra-inning Busch Stadium victory was no springboard. It would not be a portending of what lies ahead. It was just a lie.

David Cone's eight-inning, nine-strikeout, two-hit, two-run effort nearly went for naught. Cards closer Lee Smith inched toward a 2-1 Cone loss once Darryl Boston fanned with runners on first and third to create the top of the ninth's first out. But a grounder by slow-footed Mackey Sasser only resulted in a force out at second instead of a double play—and Howard Johnson was able to cross home plate for the equalizer.

On to the tenth, where ex-Cardinal Vince Coleman—exhibiting a rare moment of inspiration—led off with a bunt single. That heralded the Mets' newly minted free agency gain and winter headline-maker, with his extensive contract, to earn his wealthy paycheck.

For this occasion, at least, Bobby Bonilla delivered. The third baseman cranked a homer deep down the right-field line to cap a 3-for-5 night. Lee Smith was done. So were the Cardinals.

This night went the way of Bonilla and the Mets. But little else did over the ensuing six months.

A rare Opening Day to forget. On March 31, 2003, the Cubs drubbed the Mets, 15–2. *Jerry Coli/Dreamstime.*

6. 1998

The Mets are no strangers to marathons—many beset by prolonged scorelesness.

Of course, facing Philadelphia's Curt Schilling normally ruins prospects for a high-scoring afternoon. His allotment of power pitches struck out nine as New York mustered two hits in eight shutout innings.

Fortunately, the Mets' starter showed the capacity for being equally difficult to read.

Not as imposing, but almost as dominating—Bobby Jones went six, allowed four hits and two walks. Like Schilling, he kept the Phillies off a scoreboard that was becoming laden with goose eggs.

The scoreless deadlock carried through nine and became a staunch bullpen battle. Greg McMichael, Dennis Cook, John Franco, Mel Rojas and Turk Wendell successfully passed the baton for New York. Jerry Spradlin, Billy Brewer and Mark Leiter (watched by brother Al in the other dugout) were doing the same for Philly.

In games like these, where pitching staffs and benches wear thin, an unlikely hero emerges.

Enter Alberto Castillo. The backup catcher dug in to face Ricky Bottalico as a pinch-hitter for Wendell with the bases loaded and two down. Following fourteen innings and some four and a half scoreless hours, Castillo's walk-off single delighted—as much as it relieved—the home crowd.

5. 1975

Curt Schilling was to the 1990s Phillies as Steve Carlton was to the 1970s.

Sharing era and stature engendered frequent comparisons between the reticent "Lefty" and right-handed Tom Seaver. The Hall of Fame pair combined for 640 wins, over 7,700 strikeouts and seven Cy Youngs.

With ace status on their respective clubs well founded, these two locked horns on Opening Day five times—and three straight beginning in 1973.

Carlton-Seaver III saw each live up to their criteria—trading punchouts and faultless frames.

Only a Dave Cash third-inning RBI double off Seaver and a Dave Kingman fourth-inning solo homer against Carlton accounted for the entirety of the scoring heading into the ninth.

Neither starter would dare let a reliever settle this 1–1 tie. Seaver held up his end in the top half—stranding Greg Luzinski at second. Carlton was proffered an opportunity to match, but the Mets beat him to the punch.

Not wasting any time (or outs), Félix Millán led off with a single. John Milner then walked. And Joe Torre's base hit to left field scored Millán—chalking up another W in Seaver's corner.

4. 1988

It takes longer for hitters to get in regular season rhythm than it does for pitchers. Or so they say.

For the '88 Mets, their adjustment period lasted a little more than an inning.

With bats blazing, New York's six home runs set what would be—at the time—a club record for the most in a single game and the most by any team on Opening Day in a 10–6 victory over the Montreal Expos.

Darryl Strawberry and Kevin McReynolds, as they would be for the whole year, were the leading purveyors of power with two homers apiece and a combined 8-for-9 at the plate.

Of all the home runs, Strawberry's second captured the greatest attention—a titanic moonshot that could barely be contained by Olympic Stadium and might have cleared customs if not for the roof.

Kevin Elster (in the fourth inning) and Lenny Dykstra (in the sixth) levied the other long balls—Dykstra's blast coming with two runners on and the score knotted at four.

Dwight Gooden didn't pitch like his dominating self. Fortunately, he didn't need to. Even though Gooden gave up four runs and eleven hits over five innings and seventy-four pitches, the victory was his. Considering his situation at this time a year ago—suspended and in drug rehab—he couldn't possibly complain about it.

3. 1996

This isn't simply the most significant season-opening comeback. This ranks among the best comebacks ever made at any point in any Mets season.

Yet no rally is official without digging oneself a giant hole to climb out of. For New York, that abyss was six runs.

But 6–0 through three-and-a-half innings soon became 6–2 on the strength of a home run by Todd Hundley—the first of what would eventuate into a team-record forty-one. Bernard Gilkey, a wearer of Cardinal red as recently as the previous September, gave his new team a boost with a long ball that kicked off his most productive year.

St. Louis pointed toward a seventh-inning response, but Royce Clayton's attempt to score was foiled when rookie fielding prodigy Rey Ordonez miraculously threw him out from his knees in shallow left field.

Ordonez then got his first big-league hit in the bottom half, the beginning of four consecutive Met singles. This fashioned a four-run inning and a 7–6 advantage—which John Franco preserved with a 1-2-3 ninth.

2. 1983

Tom Seaver returned to familiar grounds with six shutout innings against the Phillies.
Jerry Coli/Dreamstime.

The dawning of each season brings about familiar names and new faces. Tom Seaver was both.

In the wake of a contentious breakup and a five-and-a-half-year Cincinnati hiatus, "The Franchise" returned to the team he made famous—and vice versa.

Making his record fifteenth Opening Day start (and eleventh as a Met), Seaver took on Steve Carlton and the Philadelphia Phillies. In other words, just like old times.

No louder was the sellout crowd than on two occasions: when Seaver walked in from the bullpen prior to first pitch and when he struck out leadoff batter Pete Rose.

A beautiful, sunny Shea afternoon agreed with the delightful presence of No. 41 back where he belonged, performing at the level his fans were comfortable witnessing.

One tiny detail proved elusive.

With Carlton matching zeros against his long-standing rival, Seaver departed after six entrenched in a scoreless tie—relegated to a no-decision despite allowing three hits and one walk. But the Mets belatedly pushed through for a pair of runs in the bottom of the seventh—the first on a Mike Howard single and the second on a Brian Giles sacrifice fly.

Doug Sisk's three effective innings in relief would polish off the shutout. His win, though, registered small typeface in deference to the day's headline.

Contrary to Thomas's Wolfe's famous book, you *can* go home again.

1. 1985

The fond expectancy that materializes with Opening Day was never higher.

Fresh from a ninety-win season, the Mets possessed a roster featuring the previous two Rookie of the Year recipients coupled with a veteran leader commanding first base. And now, through an offseason deal, they obtained baseball's premier catcher.

The validation of Gary Carter—plucked from the Montreal Expos—was hardly questioned. But for some who wondered how it would affect team chemistry, those thoughts dissolved once he ended his inaugural Mets chapter with an extra-inning, walk-off homer to beat the St. Louis Cardinals.

A fabled conclusion was preceded by a back-and-forth duel to predate an NL East pennant race that would take on a similar seesaw complexion for the duration of the season.

The plate discipline of New York hurt Joaquín Andújar as much as Flushing's cold and wind. St. Louis' starter was touched up for two hits, two walks and a pair of first-inning runs.

Dwight Gooden also found warming up problematic. He allowed the Cards to answer with single runs in the second and third. New York countered by scoring once in three straight innings and clung to the lead through Doc's departure during a two-run St. Louis seventh.

But Doug Sisk couldn't close the way he did for Seaver in '83. A single, a hit-by-pitch and a walk filled the bases. Jack Clark, who took Gooden deep earlier, also drew a free pass. Five apiece.

All it did, though, was set the stage for the brand-new Met to provide tenth-inning heroics against a former one.

Neil Allen hung a curveball. Gary Carter didn't miss. The long drive eluded the glove of Lonnie Smith and snuck over the left–center field fence.

"Excited. Ecstatic. Enthusiastic," said Carter. "I wanted to do well today. I wanted to impress. If I had fantasized about my first game, it couldn't have been any better than this."

It was more than a 6–5 victory. It confirmed the winning ways were here to stay and the best days were on deck.

EARLY METS

10. RICHIE ASHBURN

As was customary with expansion franchises, the talent pool at the Mets' disposal rose about knee deep. With amenities lean, New York's initial outfit was mostly a mishmash of castoffs and veterans past their prime.

Like Duke Snider, Gil Hodges, Warren Spahn and Yogi Berra, the Mets brought in Ashburn more for what he was than what he could become. Name recognition and Hall of Fame credentials were established in Philadelphia, but a permanent imprint on New York history was made instantaneously.

Leading off on Opening Day against Cardinals pitcher Larry Jackson at Sportsman's Park on April 11, 1962, Ashburn was the franchise's first official batter.

He flew out on his maiden Mets voyage and went 1-for-5 in an 11–4 defeat but found greater success as the year progressed—a contentment not shared by his teammates.

During what turned out to be his major league swan song, Ashburn hit .306 with sixty runs scored, was the Mets' lone All-Star representative and named its most valuable player.

Such a distinction on a 120-loss team isn't something to be held in high esteem, and the prize he received for winning MVP embodied his club's 1962 fortunes.

"I was awarded a twenty-four-foot boat equipped with a galley and sleeping facilities for six," said Ashburn, who became a longtime Phillies broadcaster after retirement. "After the season had ended, I docked the boat in Ocean City, New Jersey, and it sank."

9. JACK FISHER

If *Jeopardy!* ever dives so deep to include a "Pitchers allowing historical early 1960s homers" category, you're in luck. Because Fisher, the star-

The departure of the Brooklyn Dodgers and New York Giants after 1957 left a National League void in New York City. William "Bill" Shea had the power to change that. The esteemed lawyer headed the idea of the Continental League as a straightforward way to get a new professional club in the Big Apple. Major League Baseball conceded, awarding two expansion franchises to the NL—our beloved Metropolitans and the Houston Colt .45s—for the 1962 season. *William C. Greene, New York World-Telegram & Sun Collection/Library of Congress.*

crossed server of the 521st and last long ball of Ted Williams's career in 1960 and Roger Maris' single-season record-tying 60th in 1961, is the default, go-to answer.

Jack transferred his services to Queens for 1964, where his new club was also experiencing a change of scenery.

Fisher got Shea Stadium's forty-five-year tenancy in motion by starting against the Pittsburgh Pirates on April 17. And, as accustomed ancillary brushes with fate would have it, Shea's first home run ball—cracked by Willie Stargell—originated from his delivery.

Fisher sidestepped defeat that day but wasn't so fortunate for the better part of four seasons. Twice he led the National League in losses, typically a source of embarrassment for starters anywhere else.

But such an ignominious distinction (on a team that won at a 35 percent clip) was hard to avoid—regardless of a Met-best 3.94 earned run average (ERA) and ten complete games in 1965 and despite maintaining the capacity to log a truckload of innings. Fisher's labors were well founded on June 21, 1967, when he executed the wire-to-wire act in a two-hitter of the Phillies.

8. CARL WILLEY

Injuries are impossible to avoid. They can keep you out of action for a day, a year or forever.

Willey had five above-average seasons for the Milwaukee Braves before pining to be traded to another big league team. Selling him to the Mets in March 1963, it's hard to say the Braves actually granted his wish.

If pitching for cellar-dwellers ruined his attitude, his performance didn't show it. Willey started twenty-eight games in '63, won nine times on a 51-win club, led the staff with a 3.10 ERA and fanned 101.

"Somebody'd make an error or somebody [on the other team] would hit a home run," he said, discussing typical frailties those days. "We were kind of loose about it. We had to be; there's not much we could do about it."

Nothing to do except contribute your own offense—like when Carl cracked a grand slam on July 15 of his first season with New York.

Then, enjoying a solid 1964 spring training, came a career-altering flashpoint. A line drive by Detroit's Gates Brown broke his jaw. And the injury bug kept biting. His arm later developed tendinitis and eventually turned into a torn muscle. Willey pitched thirty painful innings in '64. And following twenty-eight more in '65, he called it quits—preventing him the chance of ending on his own terms.

7. ED KRANEPOOL

On September 22, 1962, forty professional games and seventeen life years under his belt, the James Monroe High School standout debuted for an organization proportionally closer to him in age than he was to some teammates.

On September 30, 1979, 1,853 major league games and seventeen seasons later, he doubled in his final big-league at-bat—with 1,418 hits remaining the standard in Mets history for more than three decades.

Linking the start and finish was a road marked by perseverance. Through heightened hometown expectations and demotions, the Bronx native showed the diligence which brought him immense popularity.

His initial season of meaningful on-field action came in 1964. Still a teenager, Ed hit .257, had ten homers and forty-five RBIs. The next year, batting .288, he was the lone Met chosen for the All-Star Game.

But a more significant jump came in '66, when he posted personal highs in home runs (sixteen) and walks (forty-one) while driving in fifty-seven.

Better times were ahead for the only team he'd ever know. The longest-tenured Mets player experienced the highs of division championships, league championships and World Series, then beheld a full-circle transformation—though steadily sustaining as a perennial .300 hitter off the bench—in three straight last-place finishes at the end of the 1970s.

6. ROGER CRAIG

If a pitcher during the 1960s was interested in improving his win-loss record, he'd best stay far away from the Mets.

Craig embodied the franchise's "lovable loser" trademark. But despite a 15-46 record in two years, the former Brooklyn Dodger right-hander from Durham, North Carolina, maintained a sense of levity.

"You've got to be a pretty good pitcher to lose that many," said Craig, the starter for New York's first regular season contest. "What manager is going to let you go out there that often?"

He made thirty-three starts during 1962. But he was more suited as a reliever, going 4-2 with a 0.87 ERA and three saves over 10.1 innings.

His positive demeanor underwent severe tests, though, in 1963. Craig matched a National League record of eighteen consecutive losses between May 4 and August 4—several quality outings of two or fewer runs allowed notwithstanding.

After a year that ended with his ERA lowered to 3.78, Craig found salvation with a trade to the Cardinals—granting him the opportunity to pitch with conviction. It paid off in 1964, as St. Louis won the World Series and he was the victor in Game 4 against the Yankees.

The birth of the Mets, run by owner Joan Payson and general manager George Weiss, brought out droves of fans eager to see National League baseball return—even if growing pains became historically painful. Their 40-120 mark remains the worst since the turn of the twentieth century. But to those of a certain age, the names "Marvelous" Marv Throneberry, "Hot" Rod Kanehl, and Clarence "Choo-Choo" Coleman remain indelible. *Author's collection.*

5. CHARLEY SMITH

He stayed employed in the majors longer than the average player but barely had time to unpack his boxes and arrange the furniture. Smith zigzagged across the United States with bat and glove in-tow, moving from Los Angeles to Philadelphia, to Chicago, to New York, to St. Louis, back to New York, and again returning to Chicago—all before the end of the 1960s.

His two-season layover in Queens—which initiated from a late April 1964 transaction from the White Sox—began with a familiar lack of stability. That's because his spot in the lineup changed by the week. Much like his playing locations, Smith toured from lead-off hitter to the no. 8 hole and everywhere in between.

It didn't really matter when his turn in the order came up. Smith's propensity to strike out (112 per year) was the tradeoff for his ability to hit 'em out.

Twenty exited the park in 1964, which turned out to be his best pro season. Sixteen more went yard in 1965. Although his subpar batting averages (.239 and .244) and humble on-base percentages (.275 and .273) left much to be desired, Smith's 1964 home run total was most among Mets, as was his RBI and total base figures for '65.

4. Al Jackson

If losing is contagious, these young Mets suffered an epidemic. And their tough, diminutive lefty was most prone to this widespread malady.

But "Little Al Jackson" stood tall, even as his club sunk to the deepest of baseball's depths.

Of the four shutouts Mets pitchers tossed in 1962, each belonged to Al. He completed twelve games. He led the team with an ERA of 4.40. And he lost twenty times.

One might have been convinced to think he and Roger Craig engaged in a personal tug-of-war to see which starter would engender the most sympathy.

But similar to Craig's approach, constantly coming up on the short end of the score did not bring about defeatism.

A favorite of Casey Stengel for his guile, Al decreased his 1963 ERA to 3.96, and 142 strikeouts were the peak of a four-year term in which he averaged 123. Jackson also won 13 games as other Met pitchers collectively won 38.

Al continued as the No. 1 starter through 1965, adding six more to his shutout tally. The ten for his Mets career still has him tied for sixth all-time.

3. JIM HICKMAN

A man for firsts and lasts, Hickman hit for the cycle against the St. Louis Cardinals at the Polo Grounds on August 7, 1963. Nobody in team history did it before, and (as of the end of the 2017 season) nine have done it since—although he is the only player to perform the feat in an orderly crescendo (singling, doubling, tripling and homering, successively).

Approximately two years and one month later—September 3, 1965, to be specific—he cut the ribbon on the Mets' three-home run club, also at the expense of the Redbirds.

Homers didn't always come so frequently, but they did occur often enough for Hickman to be the team leader in '63. And his seventeenth and final round-tripper for that season turned out to be the final one in the seventy-four-year history of the venerable Polo Grounds.

Hickman, though, wasn't reserved for special occasions—proven more so when he latched onto the Chicago Cubs roster and made the All-Star team in 1970. Despite a high strikeout ratio, he is the lone Met to register double-digit home run totals in each of the franchise's first four years—which made him a superlative source of reliable power during that era.

Mr. Met, baseball's first mascot, was introduced in 1964. *Zhukovsky/Dreamstime.*

2. FRANK THOMAS

Not a castoff and not an aged veteran, Thomas didn't fit into any of the distinctions that primarily comprised the original Mets.

Acquired from the Milwaukee Braves on November 21, 1961, the three-time All-Star with Pittsburgh clouted at least twenty-five homers in five different seasons—having to do much of the yard work in spacious Forbes Field.

The enticing short left-field porch of the Polo Grounds presented an easier assignment for a pull-happy thirty-three-year-old right-hander.

In a needle-in-the-haystack combing for positives from the historically inept team of 1962, Thomas was a rare gem. He struck a big hurt on baseballs before it would be associated in moniker with a future White Sox slugger of the same name, especially when he went three straight August games belting two home runs apiece.

The thirty-four home runs that year—among the bevy of offensive categories he led—almost created the unusual feat of achieving as many homers as his club's victory total. But it did establish a single-season franchise mark that lasted into the mid-1970s.

Although his clout eventually subsided, Frank topped the 1963 team in RBIs with 60—giving him a two-year total of 154 before getting sent to the contending Phillies in August 1964.

1. RON HUNT

New Yorkers are magnetically drawn to scrappy spitfires as much as polished, elegant superstars.

At the Mets' infancy, graybeards outnumbered promising youngsters. Hunt's entrance onto the Mets' roster gained almost immediate fan interest—representing the franchise's first sign of potential.

Hunt wore orange and blue in four seasons. His true colors over a twelve-year career were black and blue.

Plunked forty-one times as a Met, he advanced this so-called art to a whole new level after New York.

Nobody mastered the mantra of "taking one for the team" any better—topping the league in hit-by-pitches each year from 1968 to 1974 (including an unfathomable fifty in 1971 with Montreal).

Novelty aside, Hunt demonstrated he was adept at getting on base in the more conventional fashion.

He had 145 hits in 1963—28 of them doubles. Both of those were team highs, as was his 211 total bases. The second baseman nearly matched that hit mark in 1964, ultimately coming up 1 short. He did, however, eclipse the .300 batting average (.303, to be precise) and was the first Met to be named an All-Star starter—doing so, appropriately, with the game hosted at Shea.

"The Mets on the field treated me good," he said. "Off the field, the fans treated me really good."

Ron's no-nonsense manner garnered favor with the public and another All-Star nod in 1966. He concluded that season leading in batting average (.288), on-base percentage (.356) and hits (138).

DEBUTS

10. Mike Bordick and Bubba Trammell (July 29 and 30, 2000)

It's impossible to change a first impression. But Bordick and Trammell each made such great ones—on consecutive days, no less—that neither would ask for a redo.

Bordick's acquisition came in response to Rey Ordonez's injury—adding a bit more offense while sacrificing a little defense.

His introductory at-bat, leading off the bottom of the third against Cardinals' hurler Andy Benes, turned out as well as could be anticipated. One pitch, one home run. Bordick obliged the curtain call clamor and New York topped St. Louis, 4–3.

As ideal as Bordick's Met entrance transpired, it might not have been the best of the weekend.

Coming from the backward Tampa Bay Devil Rays to the forward-thinking Mets was a change of scenery worth celebrating. No better way to do so than with two aboard in the second inning and round-tripper at the ready.

The three runs that came from Trammell's lumber were the last of the four the Mets would score in Bobby Jones's 4–2 complete game victory.

Like Bordick, Bubba emerged from the dugout after his homer to acknowledge the Shea ovation.

9. Tom Herr (September 1, 1990)

He was the sand in your shoe. The bug in your eye. Herr served as classic Cardinal nuisance, helping spoil New York's divisional title aspirations in 1985 and 1987.

The Mets took him from the Phillies to contribute in another National League East race. Shea fans weren't necessarily placing down a welcome mat.

When he homered against the San Francisco Giants decked out in his new team's colors, helping (not hurting) the Mets, you'd swear we were transported into a bizarro world—not only because the love-hate pendulum had swayed, but because it was just his fifth home run in 449 at-bats in 1990.

Making a big defensive play at second base—like he did in the eighth—was more his style. Herr took a grounder and, with a perfect throw to the plate, successfully cut down the potential tying score. The Mets prevailed, but the honeymoon soon ended.

A victory put New York a half-game ahead of the Pirates for first place—a race Pittsburgh eventually won. Herr, a capable veteran brought in to add experience, regressed into an aged veteran by early '91 and, thus, a disgruntled bench rider.

8. MATT HARVEY (JULY 26, 2012)

Considering how Harvey began as a quick-rising star and self-appointed "Dark Knight" to what he is now—an oft-injured, under motivated, deteriorating pitcher—lends credence to the axiom that past performance is no indicator of future outcomes.

It's poignant, with everything that transpired afterward and his reclamation project ongoing, to harken back to the developmental stage of what looked like the onset of this generation's Seaver or Gooden.

Harvey received a soft open in Arizona. But there was nothing soft about the pitches proffered to the Diamondbacks. A fastball routinely clocked at or near ninety-eight miles per hour aided him in totaling eleven strikeouts—the most by any Met in his first start.

Harvey also became the only pitcher since the turn of the twentieth century to fan that many batters while allowing two hits in an initial big-league outing. And he produced two hits of his own for good measure.

As good as Harvey looked through 5.1 innings, pitch count and preservation were of paramount concern. So as Terry Collins approached the mound to hook his soon-to-be victorious youngster following 106 pitches, it was a surprise he didn't drape Harvey in bubble wrap.

Not a bad idea, in retrospect.

7. WILLIE MAYS (MAY 14, 1972)

He was the rarest breed in professional sports—a player who achieved immortal status *during* his career.

Though the pages of Mays' storybook career were yellowing at the edges by 1972, his star had yet to fade. And now the Giant icon was returning to the city where his star materialized.

In a trade endorsed by Mets matriarch Joan Payson, a New York Giants stakeholder when Mays began reaching his height, New York obtained the forty-one-year-old from a franchise that had since moved to San Francisco in exchange for pitcher Charlie Williams and $50,000.

It seemed more sentimental than practical. Mays had hit .184 in sixty-seven at-bats, drove in three runs and was without a homer. But for the greatest center fielder ever, who stirred at the notion that the team he helped for so long found him expendable, it was a measure of motivation. Especially when his first game as a Met came against the Giants on a damp Shea afternoon covered in raindrops and dripping with nostalgia.

It took until the fifth inning for Willie to remind the fans and his newfound opponents what he had done 646 times before. After walking and scoring in the first, he stepped in against Don Carrithers.

Willie Mays mainly entered Shea Stadium as a beloved and respected visitor. But by May 1972, the New York hero would come back to the city where it all began—doing so with a moment that conjured up memories of his glorious days at the Polo Grounds. *Jerry Coli/Dreamstime.*

Mays connected—setting forth a literal blast from the past for what turned out to be the difference in a 5–4 Mets victory. His trot around the bases was accompanied by a raucous cheer, indicative of the adoration he still carried in New York.

6. Zack Wheeler (June 18, 2013)

Amid dark days, the conceptions of Matt Harvey and Wheeler were bright beacons of hope.

For nearly two years, discussion of their talents and potential in the minor leagues provided much-needed distraction from the eyesores presently in the major leagues.

But not until a doubleheader at Turner Field were they on the same starting staff. And how appropriate that, on the evening of Wheeler's premiere episode, Harvey would serve as his lead-in.

Matt set the stage splendidly: six no-hit innings, thirteen strikeouts and a 4–3 victory. Quite an act to follow.

Wheeler, a Smyrna, Georgia native, was prone to the nerves such a condition presents. Not yet as polished as his peer, five of his first seven pitches sailed wide of the strike zone. Despite two early walks and five total, Wheeler continuously snuffed out Braves rallies.

Through continuous velocity and improving command, Wheeler struck out seven over six scoreless frames—looking as advertised and validating the hype heaped on him after he came to the organization in a July 2011 trade that sent Carlos Beltran to San Francisco.

The Mets of the current day scored late and prevailed, 6–1. But the future appeared even better.

5. Collin McHugh (August 23, 2012)

He can always claim equal footing with Juan Marichal. McHugh and the high-kicking Hall of Fame right-hander each share a rare distinction from their respective entrances into the majors.

One difference: Marichal won. McHugh, who did everything but win, wasn't granted such a welcoming gift from his depleted offense.

Early signs suggested the Colorado Rockies were locked in on the twenty-five-year-old. McHugh conceded a leadoff double to Charlie Blackmon, who advanced to third on a sacrifice bunt. Two straight strikeouts, though, ended the danger—and the Rockies wouldn't threaten for as long as Collin remained on the mound.

Sentimentality gave way to necessity in the bottom of the seventh, when Terry Collins pinch-hit Ronnie Cedeno in McHugh's spot. Cedeno singled, only to be left stranded and failed to score—an affliction every Met suffered.

McHugh had the powerless task of seeing how long his shutout effort would be upheld.

Try two batters. A triple and a single hung the 1–0 loss on Bobby Parnell. The Mets managed one extra-base hit (a Rubén Tejada double) all game. It was a day to forget for the New York offense, but an afternoon to remember for McHugh, who became one of five pitchers during the modern era (including Marichal) to have allowed no runs, two hits or fewer and at least nine strikeouts in their first major league start.

4. MIKE JACOBS (AUGUST 21–24, 2005)

Pinch-hitting in the bottom of the fifth. Your team behind 7–0. It might be considered a comforting, nothing-to-lose scenario—even for someone making his first big-league plate appearance. But for Jacobs, plenty more was at stake—a chance to prove he belonged. If a three-run home run isn't convincing enough, what is?

The forty-two thousand fans, previously uninterested from the lopsided score, took notice of this thirty-eighth-round draft pick. Mets personnel did, too.

Rewarded with the starting gig at first base when the Mets traveled to Arizona, Jacobs parlayed his cameo appearance into an opening week for the ages.

Yes, we're stretching the rules here on what constitutes a debut—because Jacobs's beginning in the major league arena was that remarkable.

Likely too young and too raw to know better, he continued at a torrid pace. On August 23, another homer. The next night, two more.

Over those successive games, Jacobs went 6-for-8 with six runs driven in and reached base nine times.

Jacobs completed the year slugging .710 and knocking eleven home runs in the remaining one hundred at-bats—all the while enhancing his trade value. As such, the Mets shipped him (and his built-up hype) as part of a package deal to acquire a proven commodity in Carlos Delgado.

3. Kaz Matsui (April 6, 2004)

When a reporter asked the former Japanese star to gauge his chances of hitting a home run in his introductory major league game, Matsui—using what little English he had—responded: "No chance."

Kaz might not have been a sage prognosticator, but he was exceptional at starting his years with a bang—and not wasting time doing so.

On the initial pitch—both of the 2004 season and of his MLB career—he sent Atlanta starter Russ Ortiz's offering 429 feet over the center-field fence at Turner Field. He became the only player since 1938 to hit his first major league home run leading off the season opener.

When the Mets finished their 7–2 victory, Matsui was 3-for-3 with two doubles and three RBIs, and he reached base on each of his five trips to the plate.

Not bad for someone who hit .192 and struck out nineteen times in spring training.

Opening days for Matsui then became something like Groundhog Day.

Fast forward to 2005. At Cincinnati, he took ex-Met Paul Wilson deep as the year's second hitter. In 2006, following a three weeks' absence because of a right knee injury, Matsui (batting eighth) got another home run—this one of the inside-the-park variety thanks to the spaciousness of San Diego's Petco Park.

2. Dick Rusteck (June 10, 1966)

To reach the big leagues is to achieve an athletic pinnacle many dream of. The stay could be as brief as a day or as long as two decades.

Rusteck lands on the short end of the sojourn scale. His "cup of coffee," to use baseball terminology, was a blend of eight appearances—each gulp giving off a gradually less satisfying aftertaste than the first. But the first was one to savor.

Staked to four early runs against Cincinnati starter Jim Maloney, Rusteck permitted one base runner over the first four innings—and never allowed a man into scoring position the entire night.

Only four struck out, but only four got hits. Toss in a first-inning walk to Pete Rose, and you have a pitching performance bested by a select few.

He is among a handful to turn his career entrance into a complete game shutout. What happened (or didn't happen) in the aftermath, though, speaks pointedly to the fleeting nature of baseball stardom.

Both Noah Syndergaard (*left*) and Steven Matz (*right*) had to grow up quickly in 2015. Each opened to rave reviews, with Matz posting a 2.27 ERA in six appearances. And each got the start in Games 3 and 4 of the World Series, respectively. *Courtesy of Jim Maggiore.*

Rusteck's next outing, four days later against the St. Louis Cardinals, resulted in a profound reversal of fortune. Before he could get through an inning-and-a-third, the Cards had tagged him for four runs on five hits. More struggles sent him back to the minors, and persistent arm trouble kept him there—leaving Rusteck with one shining moment under the big league sun.

1. STEVEN MATZ (JUNE 28, 2015)

The waiting, as Tom Petty lyrically put it, is the hardest part. Matz mulled his first major league game—before a contingent of family members from nearby Stony Brook—as the rain-delayed completion of the previous day's contest pushed back a scheduled 1:10 p.m. start.

For a pitcher who saw two whole years snatched from his early baseball career because of Tommy John surgery, three-and-a-half hours was easy.

But when the Ward Melville grad finally delivered his opening pitch—nearly sailing beyond the reach of catcher Johnny Monell—and his second offering—driven over the left-center field wall by Brandon Phillips—perhaps the delay amplified the customary jitters.

Matz got his act together, allowing the Cincinnati Reds only one more run and four hits over 7.2 innings.

However, for start one to be victory one, New York's offense needed to awaken from a week-long stagnation.

Luckily, Matz—who fortified his Pacific Coast–leading 2.19 ERA with a .304 batting average at Triple-A Las Vegas—wasn't out to help his own case. He *made* it. First by lacing a two-run double over the reach of center fielder Billy Hamilton.

"We needed a big hit," said Terry Collins. "I didn't care where it came from."

But more was coming. In the next at-bat, with a man on, Matz sent a fastball through the hole between the third baseman and shortstop—eventuating into a 3-2 Mets advantage.

A bottom-of-the-sixth, bases-loaded situation with the pitcher's spot due would generally present a strategic dilemma. But Collins' best option was already up.

Matz delivered again—a two-run single to center. His three hits tied a single-game franchise record for pitchers. And he became the first pitcher (and the twenty-sixth big leaguer of any kind in the last century) to open his career with a four-RBI performance.

ROOKIE SEASONS

10. Jay Payton (2000)

As the batting champion at .365 and Most Valuable Player of the 1994 New York–Penn League, it stood to reason the major leagues—and perhaps a place atop the Mets batting order—would soon be Payton's place.

But for the twenty-ninth overall pick in the '94 amateur draft out of Georgia Tech, his road to the show confronted unwelcome speed bumps. Payton went through three unkindest cuts to a diminishing elbow (twice for Tommy John surgery) as well as an operation on his shoulder. He missed the entirety of 1997, and the well-rounded ability that made him a coveted Mets prospect rapidly depreciated.

This collection of impediments didn't prevent Payton from trudging forward—ultimately earning short-term employment with the Mets in 1998 and '99 before getting a full-time outfield gig in 2000. Voted third in the Rookie of the Year balloting, Payton hit seventeen homers, drove in sixty-two, scored sixty-three, and hit .291 while compiling a .778 OPS (on-base plus slugging).

Considering the amount of wealth of experience already under his belt, it would be hard to uphold the rookie label. But Payton acted the part in that year's Division and League Championship Series—then returned to mid-season form by batting .333 with a home run and three RBIs in the World Series.

9. Steve Henderson (1977)

Joe Torre, the recently appointed Mets manager, toed the company line when speaking about the "Midnight Massacre" aftermath on the year-in-review film.

"The June 15th trade, which I've come to refer to as the 'Steve Henderson trade,'" Torre said, "is the beginning of what the Mets future is going to be like."

Henderson (and the other principals involved) will always be associated with the team's darkest hour. Even winning Rookie of the Year, which almost happened, wouldn't have alleviated the sting of Tom Seaver's parting.

Nonetheless, his game-tying ninth-inning home run, followed by an eleventh-inning walk-off shot against the Atlanta Braves—less than a week after joining the club—went a long way to making a splendid introduction.

More notable was a streak of twenty-nine consecutive games reaching base. Henderson's .297 batting average, twelve homers, sixteen doubles, six triples, sixty-seven runs scored and sixty-five driven in over ninety games are figures worthy of postseason hardware. But it was Andre Dawson named as the NL's top rookie by a single vote.

8. Noah Syndergaard (2015)

From the first batter he faced in his big-league debut on May 12 to the first batter he brushed back in his World Series Game 3 start, Syndergaard sent the same statement: standing sixty feet, six inches from his flowing locks and howitzer arm was a thankless undertaking.

Noah fittingly began his career with a strikeout and concluded 2015 by attaining the lone victory over the Kansas City Royals. An average of ten hitters every nine innings became victim to the wielding hammer of "Thor."

While opposing offenses were trying to catch up, fans— welcoming his one-hundred-mile-per-hour aptitude—were catching on to Citi Field's newest superhero. Each home start morphed into a costume party—accorded with blond wigs and regalia reminiscent of the crown prince of Asgard.

Syndergaard's maturation was put on trial in four playoff appearances—especially Game 5 of the NLDS in Los Angeles, in which he made his first relief appearance and threw a scintillating seventh inning to maintain a one-run lead. Three days later, he held the Cubs to one run on three hits while striking out nine over 5.2 innings to win Game 2 of the NLCS.

7. David Wright (2004)

After more than one hundred players, over three decades, the departure of Mike Hampton and the awarding of a 2001 compensational draft pick from said departure, an interminable quest reached finality. The Mets had their franchise third baseman.

Introduced to the Flushing faithful on July 21, 2004, David Wright had an 0-for-4 day against the Montreal Expos. His ensuing days would be far better. *Jerry Coli/Dreamstime.*

Certainly, the anointing of such esteem wasn't a foregone conclusion from his Queens unveiling on July 21.

The necessary tools—in play and in presentation—to be a hot corner stalwart and team leader were readily present. Albeit a minimal sample size containing just sixty-nine games and 263 at-bats, the Norfolk, Virginia native finished with a .293 batting average, fourteen home runs and forty RBIs while carrying himself in a manner unbecoming of a twenty-one-year-old.

Too often, a highly regarded prospect succumbs to the pressures of New York. Skills diminish before they truly flourish, and strong character weakens under the city's searing heat.

Thankfully, as we later discovered, there was nothing to worry about.

6. DARRYL STRAWBERRY (1983)

The next coming of Ted Williams. A Hall-of-Famer in waiting.

These were the not-so-subtle labels being fed into the Strawberry hype machine. From the moment the Mets made him the top overall selection in the 1980 amateur draft out of Los Angeles's Crenshaw High School, inevitable hysteria preparatory toward an untouchable prospect's arrival to the major leagues mounted.

On May 6, the outfielder who possessed seemingly limitless potential entered the major league showroom on a Mets team already ten games out of first place and re-establishing its residency in the NL East cellar.

Strawberry underwent a steep learning curve. Over his first four weeks, he hit .165 and was a strikeout victim once every 2.5 at-bats.

Then, beginning on June 7, Darryl shook off the jitters and started a stretch in which his OPS would climb to .936—a number better than that of league MVP Dale Murphy. In August, he belted nine of his twenty-six homers and drove in seventeen of his seventy-four RBIs.

The eventual Rookie of the Year really turned it on when the calendar turned to September, hitting successfully in twenty of twenty-four games and batting .376. So far, expectations were on-point.

5. JACOB DEGROM (2014)

Unlike Matt Harvey or the other prized pitching prospects publicly championed through the Mets pipeline, Jacob deGrom came through the back door. Since his Rookie of the Year performance in 2014, he's proved it was no fluke. *Courtesy of Jim Maggiore.*

The typical fanfare surrounding an otherwise ordinary encounter with the Yankees didn't focus much on who the Mets were sending to the mound.

In fact, deGrom probably arrived at Citi Field without security by his side.

But following his debut start—a hard-luck 1–0 loss on May 15—and as he raised both eyebrows and reputation over his next twenty-one, the anonymity disappeared for good.

A short period of ups and downs gave way to pleasant surprises. DeGrom found his groove by July 8. From then on, he was victorious in eight of nine decisions, fanning ninety-one and computing a 1.90 ERA.

The solidification of his Rookie of the Year Award occurred in September, when he refused to yield an earned run for twenty-eight consecutive innings. None of the great Mets rookie pitchers—not Seaver, Koosman, Matlack or Gooden—can claim an arrangement of zeros as impressive.

That streak ended on September 15, yet the evening at Citi Field began with another remarkable sequence.

The first eight Miami Marlins deGrom faced struck out, matching the modern-day major league record and besting the previous franchise mark of six (by Pete Falcone in 1980). He wound up with thirteen Ks over seven innings. Win no. 9, however, eluded him.

It wouldn't in his last start of 2014 against Atlanta—highlighted by deGrom's fourth double-digit strikeout performance.

4. TOM SEAVER (1967)

The swagger, the power, the control and the erudite approach quintessential to the kind of pitcher he would become was apparent from the outset.

It's hard to imagine Seaver, who won sixteen and had a 2.76 ERA in '67, being associated with any other organization. If not for the luck of the draw, he would have.

The Dodgers originally selected Seaver in the June 1965 amateur draft. Instead, he opted to remain at the University of Southern California. The next January, Seaver was pooled into a secondary draft consisting of unsigned players taken the previous June.

The Braves chose him and signed him. Except a deal was reached after USC's spring season began. MLB Commissioner William Eckert voided the contract. The NCAA ruled Seaver ineligible to pitch for the Trojans. After Seaver's father threated MLB with a lawsuit, Eckert comprised a special drawing for any team to vie for Tom's services—under the condition that they would pay him a bonus of at least $50,000.

Three teams had the foresight and the expendable payroll: the Phillies, the Indians and the Mets. Three pieces of paper—each representing the willing participants—were placed into a hat.

You can figure out the rest from here.

3. JON MATLACK (1972)

A player's initiation into the big leagues is helped—or hurt—by the supporting cast surrounding him.

For Matlack, the second Met to be designated as National League Rookie of the Year, he couldn't have had a better education and a smoother transition.

"The fact that my locker was between [the lockers of] Seaver and Koosman says everything," he said. "It was a great spot to be in and a great way to learn."

The knowledge obtained would be demonstrated sans hesitation. With four innings (and one hit allowed) in relief of Gary Gentry, Matlack notched his first win on April 23 at Wrigley Field.

After closing the door on the Cubs, Jon got the chance to open (and finish) five days later in Los Angeles. The Dodgers could manage just one run on six hits in the first of his eight complete games—a fine way to ensure job security.

It took until June before Matlack dealt with defeat in '72. He'd end up with fifteen victories, which was second to Seaver—as was his strikeout total of 169.

But in the categories of Wins Above Replacement (WAR) (6.0), shutouts (four) and ERA (2.32), he stood a cut above. The pupil had outshone the instructors.

2. Jerry Koosman (1968)

Great pitchers can be unearthed in the minors, in college or—in Koosman's case—on an army base. The drastic exchange from battle fatigues to stirrups, however, almost came to an abrupt end.

Narrowly surviving roster cuts in 1966 and 1967, Koosman advanced to the big leagues ahead of 1968. And after observing two starts, there was never any inclination of letting him loose again.

On the second game of the regular season, at Dodger Stadium, he displayed the poise of a veteran—hurling a four-hit shutout. If that wasn't impressive enough, he followed it up in his next turn—five days later in the home opener versus San Francisco. Another complete game, another shutout.

He'd chalk up five additional blankings, seventeen more victories—complemented by 178 strikeouts and a robust 2.08 ERA. Each of these stats exceeded what Tom Seaver did a year prior. Koosman also made the All-Star team and tossed a scoreless ninth to pick up the save and preserve the only 1–0 final score in the exhibition's history.

To Flushing's faithful, he was its favorite newcomer. And if not for a future Hall of Fame catcher from Cincinnati named Johnny Bench, he would have been the National League's choice, too.

1. Dwight Gooden (1984)

There is a direct correlation between the trading of Tom Seaver in June 1977 and the moment when Shea Stadium, for all intents and purposes, went dark.

Keith Hernandez and Darryl Strawberry brought attitude and power, respectively, when they arrived in 1983.

But it was Gooden who brought the electricity back.

Once a baseball mortuary, with fans few and victories fewer, Shea now housed must-see off-Broadway theater. The lead performer was a captivating pitching wunderkind—not just the most exciting teenager in the big leagues, but arguably the best pitcher in baseball.

An every-fifth-day prescription "Dr. K" doled to his elders constituted a whistling high-nineties fastball countered with a drop-off-the-table curveball that took on the reverent merit of "Lord Charles."

Helpless opposing hitters were dealt the grim choice of being overpowered or fooled.

Either way, Doc was overwhelming. His 276 strikeouts (11.9 every nine innings) remains a rookie record. Of the 879 batters he faced, 31.4 percent ended in K—a notation commonly visible in adorned signage over the left-field Shea rafters each time he took the mound.

A 2.60 ERA led the Mets and nearly led the entire NL. He went 17-9, had the highest WAR among pitchers, became the youngest All-Star and was runner-up for the Cy Young Award.

The Rookie of the Year was a forgone conclusion.

PART II

ON THE MOUND

SINGLE-GAME PITCHING PERFORMANCES

10. Dwight Gooden vs. Cubs (September 7, 1984)

Nineteen-year-old rookies aren't supposed to strike out twenty- and thirtysomethings with such regularity. Then again, no nineteen-year-old—or any other rookie pitcher—ever dominated the way Gooden did.

The phenomenon was at his most marvelous by early September as the Mets were desperately trying to stay within sight of NL East–leading Chicago. Unleashing a heavy dosage of his bewildering arsenal, Doc laid down the best outing in a glittering rookie campaign.

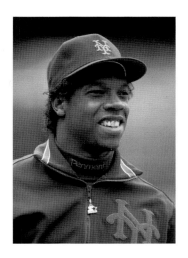

He had every reason to smile in 1984. Dwight Gooden established standards for future rookie pitchers to match. And at age nineteen, the youngest All-Star struck out the side in the fifth inning at the Midsummer Classic in San Francisco's Candlestick Park. *Jerry Coli/Dreamstime.*

Gooden justified his brief, but burgeoning reputation. Four of the first six batters he faced fell victim to the K. Meanwhile, Mets bats ensured the outcome would be settled early with a five-run bottom of the third. That made it 6–0—a sizable lead that would grow to ten.

Doc even contributed at the plate with two hits—twice as many as he allowed. Keith Moreland's fifth-inning infield single was the extent of the Cubs' befuddled offense.

Gooden fanned a batter apiece in the seventh, eighth and ninth—bringing the final strikeout count to eleven and giving him the NL rookie record. It also marked the thirteenth time (and third in a row) in which he registered at least ten—equaling records once held solely by Tom Seaver.

The Mets closed to within six-and-a-half games, yet would never catch Chicago. But that night would be a preview to Gooden's remarkable exhibition in 1985.

9. Matt Harvey vs. White Sox (May 7, 2013)

Only Harvey can match Gooden in glamor and clamor.

Matt in 2013 felt a lot like Doc in '84, as each home start became a happening. Harvey rarely disappointed (and rarely gave up any runs)—with a 1.89 Citi Field ERA.

The White Sox were the unwilling participants in his well-advertised spectacle.

It seemed the only thing that could stop Harvey was a bloody nose, which streamed down to his upper lip during the first inning. The Mets medical staff would stop the bleeding, and nothing would stop Harvey.

With ferocity, tenacity and command in peak condition, the unflappable Matt couldn't be touched. Each of the first twenty White Sox batters were methodically set down.

Then, with two outs in the seventh, Alex Rios's infield single broke up any hopes of a perfect game. That, however, didn't stop Harvey—who finished with thirteen punchouts—from maintaining his dominance.

The perfect game was done. But not a brilliant one. Harvey pressed on—striking out thirteen. And Rios would be the only base runner during his nine innings of work. But barren of run support, Harvey departed without a win.

The Mets would end the scoreless deadlock in the bottom of the tenth, and it would be Bobby Parnell gaining the victory. But everyone remembers who owned this night.

8. R.A. Dickey vs. Rays (June 13, 2012)

If Harvey took the fast track to instant stardom, Dickey took the indirect route.

On the short list of unlikeliest Cy Young Award winners is the late-blooming knuckleballer.

Just like the pitch he specialized in, Dickey didn't know where his career would end up. From Texas to Milwaukee to Minnesota and Seattle, R.A. was nothing more than a marginal starter.

Dickey gradually improved with the Mets in 2011, then shot to incredible heights in 2012 at the ripe age of thirty-seven. By early June, the baseball world was picking up on this feel-good story—even if batters weren't picking up his flutterball.

Tampa Bay certainly couldn't. Some twelve days after his teammate achieved a no-hitter, Dickey came oh-so-close.

B.J. Upton's weak first-inning grounder wasn't fielded cleanly by David Wright. But in the official scorer's discretion, it was a single. A protest by the Mets the next day confirmed it.

Dickey worked around the early base runner and worked over nearly every succeeding Rays hitter.

With one hit, no walks and twelve strikeouts in this complete game effort, Dickey added to a stunning string of success. In claiming NL Pitcher of the Month, he went 5-0 with a 0.93 ERA.

"I've never seen anything like this," manager Terry Collins said. "Never. I've seen some dominant pitching, but nothing like what he's going through right now."

7. AL LEITER VS. REDS (1999 WILD CARD ONE-GAME PLAYOFF)

Having stared elimination in the face for a week and surviving, the Mets entered this play-in contest—with a postseason berth at stake—well-versed in the meaning of do-or-die.

From Leiter's perspective, the one-game playoff at Riverfront Stadium against the Cincinnati Reds presented him with a chance to make amends from what had been a disappointing 12-12 season.

He'd been in this make-or-break spot before—on a grander stage—as the starter for the Florida Marlins in Game 7 of the 1997 World Series.

Any burden Leiter felt was lightened early when Edgardo Alfonzo lifted one over the center field fence for a two-run first-inning homer.

Leiter would take all the help he could get. But, in truth, he needed very little.

The Reds could only scrape together four base runners through eight, and their ninth-inning threat was merely to try and end the shutout. They couldn't even do that.

Giving up five hits and getting seven strikeouts, Leiter dotted the strike zone beautifully and his pitches rarely induced hard contact.

The last batted ball, by Dimitri Young, lined into Alfonso's mitt and put the finishing touch on a 5–0 victory.

Leiter broke even. And the Mets broke through for their first postseason berth in eleven years. Behind the finest night of their lefty's career, New York dispatched Cincinnati and departed for Arizona to embark on more October adventures.

6. DAVID CONE VS. PHILLIES (OCTOBER 6, 1991)

The final day of a forgettable season for both the Mets and Phils would constitute as a reasonable excuse to play out the string and pack for the winter.

That was an idea never relayed to Cone, the defending National League strikeout leader and on the verge of retaining the crown for another year. He not only remained the NL's king of Ks, but inserted a new entry into the record books with his afternoon at Veterans Stadium.

Cone fanned the side in the first, second and fourth innings. After six, Cone's strikeout accumulation tallied up to fifteen, with just one walk and a pair of hits allowed. By the end of eight, the count had reached seventeen.

The Mets were comfortably ahead, 7–0, so Cone didn't have to worry about being taken out. He could truly empty the tank for the ninth, as only two more strikeouts were needed to tie the team and NL single-game records.

Leadoff batter Kim Batiste went down swinging. And so did the next, Mickey Morandini, for number nineteen.

Twenty was there to be had, but a ground-rule double and a game-ending groundout kept Cone from equaling the all-time MLB high.

5. BOBBY JONES VS. GIANTS (2000 NLDS GAME 4)

Rarer than the fact that Jones tossed a postseason one-hitter against the team with baseball's best record was the unlikely notion of giving him a start in the first place.

He had been a Met since 1993 and journeyed along the organization's gradual improvement. But he was squeezed out of the 1999 playoff roster. And an 11-6 regular season record in 200 was marred by a 5.06 ERA.

Yet it would be Jones tasked to help take the Mets to the NLCS. Who could have seen such an historic deed coming? His wife.

Bobby Valentine informed Kristi Jones her husband would be starting Game 4 against San Francisco. She remarked: "well, he's going to pitch the game of his life."

Simple analysis, but superbly prophetic.

The powerful Giants—which tallied over nine hits per game and flaunted a lineup of pumped-up Barry Bonds and ex-Met Jeff Kent—were rendered powerless.

Jones, granted an early 2-0 lead, didn't combat fire with fire. Instead, the intermingling of mid-eighties fastballs and mid-sixties changeups turned a once-confident lineup unnerved—the exception being a Kent fifth-inning double off the glove of Robin Ventura. But no more.

Jones did not allow anyone to reach base from the sixth inning forward. The final out, courtesy of a Bonds fly ball to Jay Payton in center field, capped off what was (at the time) only the second one-hit shutout in postseason history and a 4–0 victory that sent the Mets to St. Louis.

4. JON MATLACK VS. REDS (1973 NLCS GAME 2)

Their backs weren't firmly against the wall. But the type of opponent can proliferate a certain sense of urgency.

With a lineup of Hall of Fame–worthy bats—Pete Rose, Joe Morgan, Tony Perez and Johnny Bench—this was as close as you could get to a 1970s version of "Murderer's Row." Thus, the need for young Matlack to retain the same poise he owned late in the regular season and construct a near-flawless outing was imperative.

He watched Tom Seaver do it, only to be done in by a pair of solo homers—one to Rose and a walk-off to Bench—giving Cincinnati the opener.

"I had to be at least as good as Tom was the day before," Jon recalled. "And that took every ounce of concentration."

Matlack's laser-focused approach ripped the gears from the heralded "Big Red Machine." He not only kept the potent Reds in the ballpark, he also barely let them put footprints on the base paths.

It eventuated into a two-hit, 4–0 victory, with the lone Reds safeties coming from unheralded Andy Kosco.

As for the distinguished middle of the order, the quartet of Rose, Morgan, Perez and Bench went a combined 0-for-16.

The Mets had their split in Cincinnati—a most-important outcome in a best-of-five series that would ultimately go in New York's favor.

3. TOM SEAVER VS. PADRES (APRIL 22, 1970)

A list of great Mets pitching performances without Seaver is like a museum of art without a Picasso.

Tom Seaver struck out 3,640 batters over his Hall of Fame career. The 10 he strung together on an April afternoon in 1970 were among his many remarkable feats. *Jerry Coli/Dreamstime.*

Seaver won 198 of his 311 games in the orange and blue. There is so much greatness to choose from. But there is no doubt which one finished with the most flourish.

The light-hitting Padres did little to invoke fear in many starting pitchers, especially one of the best ever. Seaver wasn't the slightest bit dissuaded by an Al Ferrara home run or a single by Dave Campbell—the sum total of the San Diego offense on this day.

And as dominant as Seaver was over the first 5.2 innings, while preserving a 2–1 advantage, the ceiling of his greatness had yet to be scratched. Cito Gaston's fly out in the top of the sixth was the second out of the frame. It would also be the last time a Padre would put the ball in play.

Thus began Seaver's overpowering procession into history. Ferrara strikes out looking. Nate Colbert goes down swinging. Campbell and Jerry Morales each go down looking. The same for Bob Barton to start the eighth. Pinch-hitters Ramon Webster and Ivan Murrel fan to end the eighth. Van Kelly, a swinging strike three. Gaston, down looking. And finally, Ferrara swinging.

The pitcher's equivalent of a mic drop.

Nineteen total Ks tied a major league record which has since been broken. The ten straight to end it, though, remains unmatched.

Said Bud Harrelson afterward, "I might as well have played without a glove."

2. Johan Santana vs. Cardinals (June 1, 2012)

Tom Seaver, Nolan Ryan, Dwight Gooden, David Cone. Each a recognized pitching name. Each showcased their talents in Queens. Each threw a no-hitter (or, in Ryan's case, seven). Each did it for a team *other* than the Mets.

Despite the wealth of talented arms to pass through Flushing, a fifty-year albatross lingered—as the franchise was one of two not to have a pitcher complete a game without allowing a hit.

Deliverance came in the form of a Cy Young winner, who eradicated the team's prolonged wait while also scripting his own comeback story.

Santana battled arm trouble for nearly his whole tenure in New York—having missed the entirety of 2011 recovering from shoulder surgery and undergoing numerous DL stints. But for nine magical innings against St. Louis, he rediscovered his once-reliable prowess and fortitude—even if it was at a personal cost.

To be fair, Santana's no-hitter wouldn't have been possible without some help—initially from the third base umpire and then from his outfielder.

Carlos Beltran, returning to Citi Field for the first time since departing the previous July, appeared to have pulled a sixth-inning hit down the third base line—called foul by Adrian Johnson. Be glad replay was then a concept and not a process.

One inning later, Yadier Molina—a haunting memory still fresh—hit one into left center field. Mike Baxter spectacularly retrieved it, careening into the fence and exiting with a shoulder contusion.

Santana ensured that Baxter's stuntman effort was not made in vain.

Despite five walks and a pitch count reaching a career-high 134 (much more than Terry Collins would have preferred), Santana hung tough—and got David Freese swinging for a finish 8,020 games in the making.

1. Tom Seaver vs. Cubs: The "Imperfect" Game (July 9, 1969)

If the pitcher's mound is an orchestra pit, here is Seaver's magnum opus.

Facing their prime combatant in the Mets' remarkable run that emerged over the coming months, the lead on-field miracle worker began striking every note with utmost brilliance. The beat was seamless. Each chord was flawless.

It was perfection—almost.

Two outs from immortality, the legendary Seaver—who struck out eleven in a lineup filled with three future Hall of Famers and seven All-Stars—was done in by the unlikeliest of candidates.

Jimmy Qualls, with eleven big league hits to date (and would accumulate thirty-one for his MLB career) got a clean single to left center field, ending dreams of a perfect game.

Should Qualls fail to reach base in the top of the ninth, he would become one of many before and after who go virtually anonymous through the annals of baseball.

Instead, his one-out single—preceded by twenty-five fellow Chicago Cubs retired in succession—makes him forever known in Mets history as the man who put the sole blemish on an otherwise immaculate night.

Seaver retired the next two in order. On the occasion of the final out, he had both hands on his hips—distraught with how close he came to history.

The sold-out Shea Stadium reacted much differently—a rousing ovation in honor of the masterpiece conducted by Maestro Seaver. Bravo.

HONORABLE MENTION

Ron Darling vs. Cardinals (October 1, 1985)

Three games behind the Cardinals and the chances for catch-up minimal, the Mets entered a series against first-place St. Louis with no margin for error. Darling answered the call: nine scoreless innings and four hits. His opponent, John Tudor, matched him. Neither got a decision, and Darryl Strawberry's colossal eleventh-inning homer off the Busch Stadium clock kept the Mets alive in the NL East race, but only for a couple days.

Al Jackson vs. Phillies (August 14, 1962)

It's hard enough for starting pitchers to go nine innings these days. But try lasting fifteen. That's what Jackson did against Philadelphia. But even this tireless effort, in which he gave up six hits and two earned runs, ended in defeat—a feeling to which Jackson became well-familiar. The Phillies prevailed, 3–1, and the Mets—to nobody's surprise—lost for the fifth straight time.

Tom Seaver vs. Padres (July 4, 1972)

Occupying the unwelcome role of Jimmy Qualls nearly three years to the day: modest outfielder Leron Lee. With the exception of four walks, it was a near identical situation. And Lee's single, the lone hit from San Diego, came two outs from history. Seaver's splendid Independence Day outing—the front end of a holiday doubleheader—was underscored by eleven strikeouts.

Mike Hampton vs. Cardinals (2000 NLCS Game 5)

The Mets had no interest in a return trip to St. Louis for a Game 6. Hampton made sure it wouldn't happen—going the distance with three hits, one walk, and eight strikeouts in a 7–0 pennant clincher. Greener pastures (like $121 million over eight years in Colorado) soon awaited him. Hampton can point to this night as the springboard to that record contract.

Jacob deGrom vs. Phillies (July 17, 2016)

A day efficient as it was impressive. Marking his first career entry in the now-obsolescent achievement of a complete game, deGrom yielded a mere one hit to Philadelphia. Lo and behold, that hit came from his opposing number—a one-out, third-inning bouncer up the middle by pitcher Zach Eflin. He went on to face two above the minimum, struck out seven and methodically baffled the Phils in an economic sum of 105 pitches.

SINGLE-SEASON PITCHING ROTATIONS

Thanks to an added emphasis on bullpens, the criteria for starting pitching prowess has undergone a radical transformation—especially over the last three decades. Wins and losses, once regarded as primary measures, are now a passé measurement. Complete games (CG) and shutouts (SHO) used to be a common occurrence. Today, you'd be lucky to find one in a month.

ERA and strikeouts, however, still hold substance, while WHIP (walks and hits per innings pitched) has prominently entered the baseball lexicon.

More often than not, the mound is where the Mets have enjoyed their greatest successes. Thus, determining the ten best starting staffs is about as narrow as an inside fastball.

10. 1990

Frank Viola (20-12, 2.67 ERA, 7 CGs)
Dwight Gooden (19-7, 3.83 ERA, 223 Ks)
David Cone (14-10, 3.23 ERA, 233 Ks)
Sid Fernandez (3.46 ERA, 181 Ks, 130 hits)
Ron Darling (4.50 ERA, 44 BBs)

9. 1976

Jerry Koosman (21-10, 2.69 ERA, 200 Ks)
Tom Seaver (14-11, 2.59 ERA, 235 Ks)
Jon Matlack (17-10, 2.95 ERA, 6 SHOs)
Mickey Lolich (3.22 ERA, 120 Ks)
Craig Swan (3.54 ERA, 44 BBs)

The Mets might have been floundering at the floor of the standings, but Craig Swan sat atop the league's ERA perch. His NL-low 2.43 came in 1978, coming with 207.1 innings pitched. A fourteen-win season the next year prompted new general manager Frank Cashen to reward Swan with the most lucrative contract paid to a Mets pitcher. A torn rotator cuff in July ended a promising 1980 and affected him for the duration of that deal. *Jerry Coli/Dreamstime.*

8. 2015

Jacob deGrom (14-8, 2.54 ERA, 0.979 WHIP)
Matt Harvey (13-8, 2.71 ERA, 1.02 WHIP)
Noah Syndergaard (3.24 ERA, 1.05 WHIP, 10 Ks/9 IP)
Steven Matz (4-0, 2.27 ERA in six starts)
Bartolo Colon (14-13, 24 BBs, 1.24 WHIP)

7. 1971

Tom Seaver (20-10, 1.76 ERA, 0.946 WHIP, 289 Ks)
Gary Gentry (12-11, 3.23 ERA, 3 SHOs)
Jerry Koosman (3.04 ERA, 1.27 WHIP)
Ray Sadecki (7-7, 2.92 ERA, 44 BBs)
Nolan Ryan (10-14, 3.97 ERA, 8.1 Ks/9 IP)

6. 1969

Tom Seaver (25-7, 2.21 ERA, 208 Ks)
Jerry Koosman (17-9, 2.28 ERA, 6 SHOs)
Gary Gentry (13-12, 3.43 ERA, 3 SHOs)
Don Cardwell (8-10, 3.01 ERA, 47 BBs)
Jim McAndrew (6-7, 3.47 ERA, 1.16 WHIP)

5. 1989

David Cone (14-8, 3.52 ERA, 190 Ks)
Sid Fernandez (14-5, 2.83 ERA, 198 Ks)
Ron Darling (14-14, 3.52 ERA, 153 Ks)
Bob Ojeda (13-11, 3.47 ERA, 2 SHOs)
Dwight Gooden (9-4, 2.89 ERA, 7.7 Ks/9 IP)
Frank Viola (5-5, 3.38 ERA, 73 Ks, 85.1 IP)

His prime was in the rear-view mirror when he joined the Mets in late 2004, fresh off a World Series triumph with the Red Sox. But even a diminished Pedro Martinez (seen with Jose Reyes to his left) shone more than most any other pitcher. The 2005 season turned out to be his only fully healthy year (of his four in New York), when he continued to overpower and outwit hitters with 208 strikeouts and a league-low 0.949 WHIP—while keeping the unmistakable effervescence that never abandoned him. *Mary A. Lupo/ Shutterstock.com.*

4. 1985

Dwight Gooden (24-4, 1.53 ERA, 268 Ks)
Ron Darling (16-6, 2.90 ERA, 167 Ks)
Sid Fernandez (9-9, 2.80 ERA, 180 Ks)
Ed Lynch (10-8, 3.44 ERA, 1.13 WHIP)
Rick Aguilera (10-7, 3.24 ERA, 37 BBs)

3. 1988

David Cone (20-3, 2.22 ERA, 213 Ks)
Dwight Gooden (18-9, 3.19 ERA, 175 Ks)
Ron Darling (17-9, 3.25 ERA, 1.16 WHIP)
Bob Ojeda (2.88 ERA, five SHOs, 1.004 WHIP)
Sid Fernandez (3.03 ERA, 189 Ks, 187.0 IP)

2. 1968

Tom Seaver (16-12, 2.20 ERA, 0.98 WHIP, 5 SHOs)
Jerry Koosman (19-12, 2.08 ERA, 7 SHOs)
Don Cardwell (2.95 ERA, 50 BBs, 1.14 WHIP)
Dick Selma (9-10, 2.75 ERA, 3 SHOs)
Nolan Ryan (3.09 ERA, 8.9 Ks/9 IP)

1. 1986

Bob Ojeda (18-5, 2.57 ERA, 1.09 WHIP)
Dwight Gooden (17-6, 2.84 ERA, 200 Ks)
Ron Darling (15-6, 2.81 ERA, 184 Ks)
Sid Fernandez (16-6, 3.52 ERA, 200 Ks)
Rick Aguilera (10-7, 3.88 ERA, 1.28 WHIP)

Left-handed pitchers aren't fond of Fenway Park and its nearby "Green Monster." Bob Ojeda, formerly of the Red Sox through 1985, let that be known. He felt much more at ease on the '86 Mets, pacing them in wins and ERA among starters. And he was unfazed in his return to Boston for Game 3 of the World Series— prevailing, 7–1, while allowing just one extra-base hit. *Jerry Coli/Dreamstime.*

SOUTHPAW STARTERS

10. JON NIESE

It's so hard to say goodbye when you can't leave.

When Niese's eight-season stint in orange and blue ended following the 2015 season, fans weren't upset that he would be pitching elsewhere. And according to Niese's comments shortly after departing for the Pirates, the feeling was mutual.

"I'm sure what I'll appreciate more than anything is the way [the Pirates] play defense," he told the Pittsburgh press. "I'm looking forward to that."

Beloved or not, the numbers on Niese aren't entirely unfavorable—especially knowing he pitched under dreary conditions for the franchise. He won sixty-one times (tied with Tom Glavine for eleventh on the Mets' all-time list), including twenty-four between the 2011 and 2012 seasons.

But in a society hell-bent on "what have you done for me lately," his latest was far from his greatest—even if his greatest wasn't very great.

Somehow, the Mets thought it would be prudent to reacquire Niese on August 1, 2016. They were proven wrong. Quickly.

Doing nothing to make fans forget his previously ungrateful exit, Niese surrendered eight hits, two homers and seven runs (all deservedly earned) in his first four return appearances. And there would be no one to blame but himself.

9. AL JACKSON

The lines of personal success and group achievement sometimes fail to intersect. When Jackson pitched his best, his teams seldom acquiesced.

Al averaged ten wins in New York, tossed forty-one complete games and achieved ten shutouts in the face of despairing circumstances. A 9-4 record and a 3.95 ERA wasn't enough to keep Al on the St. Louis Cardinals' postseason roster for 1967, the year they went on to capture the World Series.

The Mets brought Jackson back in 1968. This possibly sentimental gesture ended by the early part of '69. Al had paid his dues, but his arm—at thirty-three years old—was spent. He allowed thirteen earned runs in eleven innings and was released by June—near when the Mets meteoric rise was approaching lift-off.

Jackson missed out on being a member of a championship team, but he lent a hand in developing such talent.

Through longtime service as coach and consultant, his wisdom has ranged wide, touching many a noted pitcher—Tom Seaver, Jerry Koosman, Al Leiter and Ron Darling among them.

In his book, *The Complete Game*, Darling notes Jackson's guidance while as a minor leaguer in Tidewater. "I was young and single, living on the beach in Norfolk, Virginia. I was content," Ron wrote. "But Al kept on me. He'd say, 'What do you have to be content about? You haven't done anything. You haven't struggled.'"

Al knew whence he came.

8. JOHAN SANTANA

On February 8, 2008, the Mets created the biggest splash in the off-season trading pool.

Considering Santana's trophy case comprised two AL Cy Young Awards and his résumé consisted of four consecutive seasons of at least two hundred strikeouts, foregoing touted prospects like Carlos Gomez and Philip Humber—along with Deolis Guerra and Kevin Mulvey—would be a worthwhile plan if the dividends presented themselves in the short term.

But using a pitcher's past to determine the future—especially in earnings—is a tricky proposition.

It was a tall task for Santana, beginning his Mets term at age twenty-nine, to match what he accomplished in Minnesota and live up to his six-year, $137.5 million contract.

At twelve games above .500, 607 strikeouts in 717 innings, 3.18 ERA and nine complete games, it was apparent his best years were left in the Twin Cities. But many mounting factors worked against him.

Injuries hounded Johan even during his finest moments, like when he delivered a three-hit shutout in a must-win game on the next-to-last day of the 2008 regular season despite an undisclosed bum knee, or when in 2012—just a couple months after left shoulder surgery—he was able to

Arm troubles prevented Johan Santana from adding to his two Cy Young Awards, but he delivered on what had been a Mets hindrance for fifty years: a no-hitter. *Eviltomthai/Flickr.*

overcome a personal-high 134 pitches to attain the franchise's first no-hitter.

As glorious as that moment was, it wasn't long before arm failure brought his career screeching to an abrupt halt.

7. Frank Viola

Santana wasn't the first Twins ace to chart a Minnesota-to-Queens pattern.

Dwight Gooden's injury in the middle of the 1989 season necessitated the deal for Viola—the reigning AL Cy Young Award holder and less than two years removed from attaining World Series MVP.

For the Long Island native and St. John's alum, the move to New York proved easier than the transition to the National League.

Over twelve Mets starts in '89, Viola went 5-5 and had five outings in which he allowed at least four runs—a continuation of the struggles encountered the previous months with Minnesota.

But if the Big Apple soured, it sang a different tune when "Sweet Music" rebounded in 1990. As one of six Mets to eclipse twenty wins, Viola did so in 242.2 innings (tops in the NL) and by spicing in 182 strikeouts.

Taking into account the twenty-victory effort he posted for the 1988 Twins, Viola became one of eighteen pitchers to break that historical bi-league barrier.

He made the All-Star squad for a second straight time (third overall) in 1991 before losing ten of his last thirteen decisions—not exactly going out on a high note as he subsequently bolted for Boston via free agency.

6. Tom Glavine

Any recollection of Tom Seaver's last Mets start in 1983? How about the final pitching appearance of Dwight Gooden in 1994? Neither solicit strong memories.

But Glavine went out famously. And for all the wrong reasons.

With both a division title and the finality of a monumental September collapse at stake, he saved his most listless New York performance for the most crucial of moments. Seven runs allowed. One out recorded. An inauspicious ratio for sure.

The cynic in you wonders why this couldn't have happened during the late 1990s or early 2000s—when he won nearly 70 percent of his games against the Mets as a charter member of the Braves' famed rotation.

Glavine didn't have nearly the surrounding pitching cast like he enjoyed with Atlanta, yet still managed a 3.97 ERA and a 61-56 record in the course of five twilight seasons, beginning in 2003. His 56th win as a Met was also the 300th of his career. It came on August 5, 2007, at Wrigley Field—where a visiting crowd saluted the accomplishment of a pitcher destined for the Hall of Fame.

From sweet to bitter, his departure off the Shea Stadium mound on September 30 incurred a chorus of boos—the scapegoat for fans frustrated with a season gone adrift. Glavine got away too—back to Atlanta via free agency before retiring the next year.

5. SID FERNANDEZ

"El Sid" was pitching's optical illusion. A deceptive downward motion combined with a rising fastball gave the impression he was throwing uphill.

When examining the stat sheet, you discover the difficulty batters had in picking him up.

A rate of 6.85 hits every nine innings over fifteen seasons (with four different clubs) trends on remarkable. Only three other pitchers who pitched more than 1,500 innings gave up fewer hits: Nolan Ryan, Sandy Koufax and Clayton Kershaw.

His batting average against was regularly at the top of the major league charts from 1985 through 1992—the years he spent in New York. During that span, he struck out 8.5 batters per nine.

This normally would make Sid an ace for every other starting staff, including the Mets. But certain elements proved detrimental.

His weight and stamina, two factors that go hand-in-hand, were below par. Those can also be linked to location issues, especially in middle innings, which collectively prevented him from going deeper into games.

Fernandez required just 2.1 innings for his most important appearance. It came during the deciding contest of the 1986 World Series, in relief of Ron Darling.

Sid prevented the Red Sox from adding to their 3–0 lead with no hits and four strikeouts—energizing the Shea crowd and rejuvenating a Mets offense that eventually came to life. Ray Knight may have been series MVP, but Sid was Game 7's most valuable performer.

Sid Fernandez, once a product of the Los Angeles Dodgers farm system, set career highs in wins (sixteen) and strikeouts (two hundred) in 1986. His 1,449 strikeouts are fourth-most in franchise history. *Jeff Marquis/Flickr.*

4. Bob Ojeda

The headline names of the 1986 Mets roll off the tongue. Although not as noteworthy as Carter, Hernandez, Gooden or Strawberry, the offseason pick-up from Boston turned out every bit as substantial.

On a staff that had the major's best ERA, Ojeda's 2.57 led the way. Same goes for his eighteen victories. But the wins that mattered were the two he gave the Mets when they needed them most. Through resourcefulness that limited the Astros to one run (despite ten hits) over nine innings in Game 2 of the NLCS, Ojeda froze the Houston momentum generated from Mike Scott's Game 1 dominance.

Then, down two games against Boston, the Mets called on Bobby O again to sour the Red Sox dreams of a sweep. New York's offense began noisily with a four-run first, and Ojeda made sure the Sox would stay silent—tossing seven innings of five-hit, one-run ball.

A sequence of devastating injuries in successive seasons—ranging from the relatively normal (ulnar nerve damage in his left elbow) to the absolutely absurd (a hedge clipper severing a finger on his pitching hand while gardening at home)—impeded any chance of building on 1986.

For his Mets career, which lasted five years and ended with a December 1990 trade to the Dodgers, Ojeda went 51-40 with a 3.12 ERA.

3. Jon Matlack

If a "kill the win" movement arose during the 1970s, Matlack should have conducted the march.

Eighty-two victories merit the seventh most on the Mets' all-time leaderboard. Countered with eighty-one defeats, the narrow-minded view of a near break-even mark is severely misleading.

From his Rookie of the Year showing in '72 to his adieu in '77, Matlack racked up 26 complete games. Tom Seaver, during that same span, went the distance on 28 occasions and won 108.

Jon was frequently reduced to second or third fiddle in a "big three" rotation of Seaver and Jerry Koosman. But he ascended to the head of the food chain late in 1973—a year that started out rocky before turning perilous.

On May 8, Matlack encountered a pitcher's worst fear. A liner off the bat of Atlanta's Marty Perez struck his forehead and fractured his skull. Eleven days later, he returned. If Jon appeared timid in the wake of his brush with career mortality, it never showed.

He went 5-1 from August 18 onward and 205 strikeouts placed him third among NL hurlers. Matlack's hot hand continued into October, as his smooth delivery kept the Reds and A's off-balance for the better part of 25.2 innings, allowing a scant four runs. The loss in Game 7 of the World Series was really his lone postseason misstep.

When the 1975 All-Star Game co-MVP departed for Texas, he was second to Seaver when counting the lowest ERA (3.03) among pitchers who recorded more than seven hundred innings. More than forty years later, it still is.

2. AL LEITER

He wore his emotions on his sleeve, to borrow a tired expression. He also wore them on his hat, pants, shoes and anywhere else sentiments can be stored.

That would make Leiter a terrible poker player, but the Toms River, New Jersey native fulfilled his obligations of pitching quite well.

The Mets took advantage of a Florida Marlins post–World Series fire sale, and it paid immediate dividends. Leiter had his lowest ERA (2.47) with New York in 1998 (when the league ERA was 4.23), yielded only eight home runs and would win seventeen games—one of five times he would lead the club in victories.

Those triumphs were harder to come by the next year. In 1999, Leiter had his worst season, but it contained his best performance—the five-hit complete game against the Cincinnati Reds to win the one-game Wild Card playoff.

His most high-profile showcase of determination came in defeat, however, when two ninth-inning runs by the Yankees broke a 2–2 tie and spoiled an attempt to prolong the 2000 World Series.

While Leiter's cumulative ERA of 3.42 over seven seasons doesn't measure up to the other great Mets starting pitchers, it is impressive when taking into account the offensive-slanted period in which he worked.

1. Jerry Koosman

Being overshadowed by the legend of "The Franchise" could prompt feelings of resentment for a pitcher who totaled 140 victories, nearly 1,800 strikeouts and an ERA of 3.09.

But Koosman, who spent parts of eleven seasons as Tom Seaver's left-hand man, didn't object to being in the background. The numbers he put up, and the time in which he did it, make him as underrated and overlooked as anyone who wore a Mets uniform. And his unbeaten postseason record—coupled with some of the most important wins the team ever had—takes a back seat to no one.

Kooz narrowly missed being the 1968 NL Rookie of the Year. A 19-12 record, 178 Ks and an ERA of 2.08 over 263.2 innings made him superior in many voters' minds.

The 1969 season was outstanding in many ways, aside from the obvious. Koosman nearly equaled his '68 efforts. He got named to the All-Star squad for the second year in a row, but bigger moments lay ahead.

In Game 2 of the Fall Classic, Koosman held the powerful Orioles lineup hitless into the seventh as the Mets would proceed to even the series. Baltimore got three runs off him in the third inning of Game 5 in their attempt to send it back to Memorial Stadium, but one hit is all they could manage the rest of the way as Koosman completed the Mets' impossible journey to the World Championship.

His compilation of World Series success continued in 1973. Knotted at two wins apiece, 6.1 innings (combined with Tug McGraw's 2.2 innings in relief) helped shut out the Oakland A's.

The elusive search for a twenty-win season came to an end when he achieved the magic number on September 16, 1976, in a complete game triumph over the St. Louis Cardinals.

Koosman would eventually get to twenty-one and would surpass the threshold again as a member of the Minnesota Twins in 1979—the year after he was traded away from the Mets at his behest, marking the departure of one of the last links to the initial chain of glory years.

RELIEF PITCHERS

10. Francisco Rodriguez

The rate of saves has undergone an upswing, but sixty-two stands out. That's the amount of instances in which Rodriguez slammed the door on Angel opponents in 2008.

As he hit the free agent market that winter, the pre–Madoff Mets tempted "K-Rod" with money he couldn't refuse.

At three years and $37 million, Rodriguez swapped coasts. He saved thirty-five of his forty-two opportunities. It was the fifth straight season of thirty or more saves, but when matched up with his output of the season prior, it dwarfs in comparison.

The 73 strikeouts, though, were comparable to '08. He had 113 more punchouts on the mound in the coming years—and a few too many in the bowels of Citi Field.

The demonstrative Rodriguez let his emotions get the best of him when he allegedly assaulted his girlfriend's father after a 2010 defeat—leading to an arrest and a suspension. The fact that he needed surgery on his right thumb soon after is not happenstance.

His curtailed season ended with a 2.20 ERA and twenty-five saves. The twenty-three additional saves through mid-July 2011 were enough for the Milwaukee Brewers to accept his outsized personality.

9. Skip Lockwood

You're more likely to find someone of his glasses-bearing guise at the head of a middle school math classroom rather than striking out batters at a rate of 8.7 per every nine innings.

Lockwood would eventually receive a degree from the Massachusetts Institute of Technology after his playing career ended, so maybe looks aren't entirely misleading. Still, his pitches proved illusionary for opposing batters during the latter part of the 1970s.

He saved nineteen games in 1976 (second best in the National League) and twenty more the following year—during a period when the closer role was emerging, but not yet well defined, and the Mets weren't leading many games.

Despite often playing from behind, it didn't keep Lockwood bound beyond the bullpen gates—appearing in a Met-record sixty-three games in 1977, covering 104 innings.

Such a heavy workload possibly contributed to 1978's lingering shoulder issues. Lockwood labored through 90.2 frames until he was sidelined for good in early September.

When his five years in New York ended after 1979, his ERA was 2.80 and his save total reached sixty-five.

8. Randy Myers

The future Cincinnati "nasty boy" appeared once for the Mets in 1985 and ten times in 1986 before becoming a consistent Davey Johnson choice onward.

The straight-shooter style Myers owned during 1988 and '89 was nowhere to be found over his first eight outings of 1987. His ERA on May 11, a bloated 13.50, soon dwindled.

From August 5 to September 25, Myers made twenty-two appearances, gave up three earned runs and finished with ninety-two Ks in seventy-five innings—giving cause to jettison Jesse Orosco to Los Angeles and move their younger lefty to the top of the bullpen pecking order.

Myers inherited Orosco's portion of late-inning responsibilities with righty Roger McDowell. But Myers stood out most prominently.

Some closers, without intent, take the circuitous path to secure victory. Myers, with a well-located barrage of fastballs, took the direct route—on his way to forty-nine saves over the next two seasons.

His 1988 strikeout rate was down, but so was his ERA (a most-impressive 1.72) and his WHIP (a minuscule 0.912).

When McDowell went to Philadelphia in June 1989, Myers's workload increased (a team-leading sixty-five games). He averaged more Ks and finished with a 2.35 ERA.

Management made another bullpen-related trade before 1990. This time, the deal involved him.

A Myers for John Franco swap, production-wise, was pretty much a wash. It agreed quickly with Myers, claiming NLCS MVP and the World Series with the Reds.

7. BILLY WAGNER

On a four-year deal inked in December 2005, the Mets forked over $10.5 million—the most ever paid to a reliever. As 2006 progressed, and as Metallica's "Enter Sandman" blared with each arrival onto Shea's mound, it proved to be a sound investment.

Wagner might have shared Mariano Rivera's walk-in theme, but he bested his inter-borough counterpart in saves—nailing down forty of the Mets' ninety-seven wins. And by continuing to unspool ninety-eight- to one-hundred-mile-per-hour heat from his 5-foot,11-inch frame, the rate of 11.7 strikeouts per nine innings was his highest since 1999 in Houston.

Each of the three NLDS wins over Los Angeles ended with Wagner on the hill, but lackluster outings in the NLCS against St. Louis persuaded Willie Randolph to use Aaron Heilman in the ninth inning of Game 7.

The beginnings of his last two full seasons paralleled '06, only to peter out because of ineffectiveness or arm trouble. In 2007, Wagner saved twenty-six of twenty-seven chances with a 1.28 ERA. From August 21 onward, his ERA was 6.91.

A strong first half in 2008 earned an All-Star nod, but a forearm strain in August required Tommy John surgery.

The lengthy rehab, and the interest of the Red Sox, precluded him from adding to 101 saves. Still, he remains one of five Mets to crack the century mark in that category.

6. JEURYS FAMILIA

Whoever said it was impossible to lose—or gain—a job due to injury never witnessed the shift from Jenrry Mejía, who hurt his elbow warming up on Opening Day 2015.

The insertion of Familia as closer went from temporary to permanent within months, both because the new guy emerged as one of baseball's best and the old one became entangled in failed performance-enhancing drug exams.

Familia also couldn't avoid off-field issues—as a fifteen-game suspension for domestic violence to begin in 2017 preceded the diagnosis of a blood clot in his throwing shoulder.

But when healthy, and out of trouble, he is as dominant as any Met who occupied this function. Familia secured an NL-leading fifty-one games in 2016 to complete a fantastic two-year stretch that saw him convert on ninety-four of one hundred regular season save chances and, at one point, fifty-two straight.

Jeurys Familia converted 94 of his 104 save opportunities from 2015 to 2016. *Arturo Pardavila III/ Wikimedia Commons.*

He saved five postseason contests in 2015—obscured by the three times victory slipped away with him on the mound—although each shouldn't lay at his feet.

Thoughts of World Series blown saves resurfaced when he let the San Francisco Giants amass the tie-breaking runs to win the 2016 Wild Card showdown.

5. Armando Benítez

Closers and football kickers are kindred spirits. Their performance—and, ultimately, their fate—gets measured over a few fleeting pressure-filled moments.

Benítez was not immune to high-leverage failures that drove fans to intense fury.

Where do we begin? Game 1 of the 2000 World Series and the two spectacular September meltdowns against the Braves in 2001 recur like bad migraines.

Then there are the lesser—yet biting—pains that persist and add to some sort of PTSD, which made every ensuing flirtation with disaster a call for Mets fans to renew their indigestion medication prescription.

Those aggravations create a near-total eclipse over his 160 saves in nearly five seasons. Twice he established a franchise record for single-season saves (forty-one in 2000 and forty-three in 2001).

When you're the shutdown pitcher in the same town in the midst of Mariano Rivera's dominance, there's instant inferiority. The 89 percent save rate Benítez established from 1999 through 2002 is the identical ratio at which Rivera saved games during that same span.

But, as unfair as it might be, it's the important regular season games and the postseason pressures where ultimate judgment is made and where a distinct line of demarcation is drawn.

4. Roger McDowell

For the 1986 season, he split door-shutting duties with Jesse Orosco on the mound. For each season in New York, split sides everywhere else.

Like his specialized deceptive sinkers, McDowell's dugout antics bordered on deceitful. The leading practitioner of the hot foot, among other pranks, designated him the recurrent class clown.

But when his part-time gig as a funnyman gave way to his full-time job as a reliever, he was all business.

Never more so than the five shutout innings brandished in Game 6 of the '86 NLCS, holding a 3–3 tie through the thirteenth. The effectiveness of one hit over seven frames against Houston diminished when he faced Boston, although credit for the Game 7 victory belongs to him.

The mass of regular season assignments prepared Roger well for those high-leverage scenarios—entering seventy-five times, being involved in twenty-three decisions and winning fourteen. The 128 innings logged nearly matched what he did in 1985 as a rookie (127.1).

From seventeen saves in '85, he upped his output to twenty-two the next season and a personal-best of twenty-five for 1987—even if being revealed as the "second spitter" on a memorable *Seinfeld* episode did something to tarnish a faux reputation.

3. Tug McGraw

A reservoir of abundant enthusiasm, Tug's zest was on display in New York and Philadelphia and for the duration of his fifty-nine years.

He had a reliever's ideal mental makeup. An optimistic free spirit with a great sense of humor and the good sense to keep a short-term memory—never letting what happened in the prior outing, good or bad, affect the next outing.

The quotable McGraw saved his best line for a team meeting in 1973—and "Ya Gotta Believe" served as the rallying cry for New York's sudden ascent to the NL East crown and paralleled his own personal revival.

Countering a dreadful spring and early summer, McGraw regained faith in himself by falling back on personal success—like overcoming early career struggles to go 9-3 with a 2.24 ERA for the '69 champs and turning in twin 1.70 ERA seasons in '71 and '72.

For the last 60.1 innings he pitched during the 1973 regular season, Tug made twenty-five appearances, saved fourteen and had a 1.64 ERA.

The turnaround carried over into the playoffs. He spelled Tom Seaver to eliminate the Reds in the NLCS, endured six innings to prevail in Game 2 of the World Series and combined with Jerry Koosman for a Game 5 shutout of Oakland.

As beloved as he is among Mets fans, he holds a special place with the Phillies—helping them to their first title in 1980, almost six years after New York traded him there.

2. Jesse Orosco

Contrasting the frustrations of Benitez and Familia is the embedded visage of Orosco, both in the immediate aftermath of a sixteen-inning epic to finish the Houston Astros in the 1986 NLCS—fanning Kevin Bass with the winning run aboard—and in the instant following the World Series triumph, a strikeout of Marty Barrett, a far-flung glove and on knees with fists raised.

Those moments for which he was at the center, separated by twelve days, remain frozen in the annals.

But it was a flash in his light-year of a baseball career—crossing five presidential administrations and four decades.

If we compare the average lifespan for a big-league player to that of an ordinary citizen, Orosco was something like 110 years old upon his 2003 retirement.

Through durability, consistency and the increased use of left-handed specialists, Jesse wore the threads of nine different teams and appeared in a record 1,252 games.

The plurality of those entrances—375 exactly—came with the Mets, beginning in his rookie season of 1979 through 1987, during which he overtook Tug McGraw as the club's all-time leader in saves, with 107.

A New Yorker through and through, John Franco was raised in Brooklyn, attended Lafayette High School and went to St. John's University in Queens. *Jerry Coli/Dreamstime.*

More individual recognition occurred by way of two All-Star selections, including 1983, when he won thirteen games, had a 1.47 ERA and was third in the Cy Young voting.

1. JOHN FRANCO

Almost every Met, if they hang around long enough, is associated with a specific era.

Franco is one of a few who continually stayed through multiple transitional periods—from the back end of the Davey Johnson tenure through the Bobby Valentine playoff delights and concluding with the lowlights of 2002–4.

He finished his career with 424 saves over twenty-two years but doesn't head this list because he adheres to the prototypical reliever mold. Never could he be mistaken for someone with overpowering stuff.

Instead, over fourteen seasons in New York, this native of Brooklyn and alum of St. John's University became a local boy making good through a method of changing speeds and utilizing pinpoint control—spicing in the occasional late-inning high-wire act within 695 appearances.

"You have to have some thick skin to play [in New York]," Franco said. "It's hard. Especially as a relief pitcher, you have to be able to turn the page quite a bit. Some guys could handle it, some couldn't."

Acquired from the Reds for Randy Myers prior to the 1990 season, Franco led the NL in saves that year with thirty-three. He topped the league again during the strike-shortened season of 1994 with thirty.

Serving longer as a closer than a setup man, his 276 saves—116 higher than Benitez—are the standard for future Mets relievers to aim for, and he remains the all-time MLB leader among left-handed pitchers.

PART III

AT THE PLATE

SINGLE-GAME HITTING PERFORMANCES

10. Joe Foy vs. Giants (July 19, 1970)

For the duration of the spring and part of the summer, the Mets wondered when their prized new third baseman would awaken.

The futile Foy experiment, formulated the previous winter with the Royals in an exchange for young Amos Otis, equated to a lab exercise gone wrong—as Otis sizzled in Kansas City and Foy fizzled in New York.

One-third of Joe's home run output and five of his thirty-seven Mets RBIs were encompassed in these ten innings at Candlestick Park.

A 5-for-5 day (which bumped his season batting average up eighteen points) featured a double and two home runs, the latter coming in extras to procure a 7–6 win and giving a nominal glance of what the Mets thought he would be.

On the heels of Ron Swoboda's homer, Foy tagged Skip Pitlock with a two-bagger. A pair of singles—one in the fourth that drove in Donn Clendenon and another in the seventh that brought home Clendenon and Ken Singleton—were sandwiched in between his two long balls and helped overcome the Giants' early advantage.

Better late than never, even if it was never duplicated again.

9. Alex Ochoa vs. Phillies (July 3, 1996)

In 2005, as a member of the Chunichi Dragons, he hit for the cycle—some nine-and-a-half years and a world from his first. It registered little, if no attention, in the United States. For Ochoa, it brought his circuitous and once-bright baseball life full circle.

Twenty-two games into his MLB career—a career that began with adorned promise—he briefly fulfilled the combined hitting and speed potential scouts had longed bragged about.

At Veterans Stadium, Ochoa—obtained in the Bobby Bonilla swap the previous July—went 5-for-5 with two doubles, a triple, a homer and three runs scored. His twelve total bases were one shy of the franchise record. He became the sixth Met to hit for the cycle—and did so in style.

Batting in the eighth, needing a home run, Ochoa completed the illustrious hitting sequence by going deep to left-center—breaking a 6–6 tie in the process. The sore left shoulder caused by an earlier collision with the right-field wall suddenly didn't feel so bad.

New York scored three more, the last of which came when Ochoa tallied an RBI double in the ninth.

8. DARRYL STRAWBERRY VS. CUBS (AUGUST 5, 1985)

Many outcomes for hitters and pitchers at Wrigley Field are swayed simply by which way the wind blows.

Strawberry dealt with a multitude of distractions. The airstream wasn't one of them.

Breeze direction relegated minor significance to the Mets' 7–2 win over Chicago, which thrust the Mets into first place. Darryl, on the other hand, was the deciding element—a gust of air behind his team's back, if you will—in carrying New York forward.

Two home runs—one of the three-run variety in the first inning and a solo shot in the third (both with two outs)—were the day's downfall for Cubs starter Derek Botelho.

After being intentionally walked in the fifth (something the Cubs probably should have tried more often), Ron Meredith—entering for seventh-inning relief—had his opportunity to crack the Strawberry code. But he'd be consigned to the same fate. This was the first three-homer game in Strawberry's promising career and the first of 1985 by a National Leaguer.

A ninth-inning single was the result of Strawberry's lone chance at attaining home run no. 4 (and a share of the major league record). Inconsequential in relation to what he did earlier, but it still guaranteed a perfect showing at the plate to go along with five RBIs and four runs scored.

7. DAVE KINGMAN VS. DODGERS (JUNE 4, 1976)

Many hitters swing for the fences. Dave Kingman swung for the moon. When he connected, "Kong" sent many baseballs into orbit. In 1982, bashing thirty-seven, he became the Mets' first National League single-season home run champion. *Jerry Coli/Dreamstime.*

Strawberry became the third Met to attain the round-tripper trifecta—a chain begun by Jim Hickman twenty years earlier and seconded by Kingman eleven years after that.

As Tom Seaver was shutting out LA to the tune of three hits, Kingman let three fly to the sky in the City of Angels—accounting for eight of his club's eleven runs.

A strikeout victim to end the previous night with the tying and winning runs on base, the temperamental slugger took his frustration to the clubhouse by tossing hangers, equipment and a hairdryer.

The next night, the only damage done was on the field—to the baseballs thrown by Dodger pitchers.

A pop-up and a strikeout were obscured by the outpouring of power, activated by a two-run fourth-inning homer that broke a scoreless tie. As the Mets offense around him continued to set the table, Kingman cleaned house.

Following a fifteen-game stretch of three RBIs and struggles with men in scoring position, he sized up Burt Hooton and Al Downing for three-run blasts in the fifth and seventh, respectively.

The eight RBIs set a club record previously held by Donn Clendenon since 1970.

6. JEROMY BURNITZ VS. EXPOS (AUGUST 5, 1993)

Rookies were more nuisance than pleasure in the mind of Dallas Green. The disenchantment he expressed for Burnitz in a little more than a year together dissipated when the June call-up delivered a four-hit, two-walk showing at Montreal's Olympic Stadium.

New York's manager pleaded for someone—anyone—to incite some semblance of a stimulus during—at thirty and a half games out—what amounted to a lifeless and hopeless '93 season.

Burnitz, who eventually turned into a late bloomer and an All-Star in Milwaukee, batted fifth and represented himself superbly. A first-inning run-producing single initiated a deluge of runs on both sides.

Of course, he had much to do with it—and his grand slam in the fifth broke open New York's advantage.

But when Met pitchers threw away their passing prosperity by letting a 9–1 lead evaporate in a matter of two innings, Burnitz (who also tacked on another single in the seventh) was prepared to salvage them—even if he had to wait until the top of the thirteenth.

His fourth hit brought in Ryan Thompson and Joe Orsulak to pad what was a one-run lead, making it a seven-RBI afternoon in his thirty-seventh big league game.

5. Kevin McReynolds vs. Cardinals (August 1, 1989)

A seven-loss spell usually is an agent for change. The Mets sank into this swoon, prompting Davey Johnson to severely reshuffle his lineup. But he didn't remove (or move) McReynolds, who welcomed the turn of the calendar following a modest .255 July average with two home runs and fourteen RBIs.

In an 11–0 New York romp of the Redbirds, 1988's NL MVP contender packed the bulk of the Met brawn—hitting for the cycle and accounting for six runs.

Doubling and scoring to open the top of the second got McReynolds and his team back in sync. A fourth-inning groundout was merely a momentary lull, because McReynolds marked homer off the cycle to-do list with a sixth-inning shot that increased the New York lead by three.

The easiest of his four tasks—the single—came in the eighth and produced another RBI. The toughest, for most, took place in his last at-bat one inning later. And as a trio of Met runners came in to score, it was as productive as a triple could be.

This night instigated McReynolds's best month of '89, in which he drove out nine, drove in twenty-four and compiled sixty-two total bases.

4. WILMER FLORES VS. CUBS (JULY 3, 2016)

The message was heard loud and clear.

As José Reyes's impending arrival to the Mets beckoned a change in third base starting duties, Flores delivered his own stark signal to anyone feeling he should take a back seat.

If fear of losing your job is a motivating factor, then Wilmer was inspired six-fold.

The grand marshal of New York's pre–July 4 hit parade initiated a thirteen-batter second-inning procession and brought about Jon Lester's demise by smacking a home run to center—which ended a personal 0-for-14 drought.

He returned with a single to left that plated Yoenis Cespedes—sending Chicago's Cy Young candidate to the showers after a painful 1.1 frames.

It so happened that no Cubs pitcher enjoyed this afternoon—or this series. As the Mets finished on the long end of a 14–3 drubbing with twenty-two hits (equaling a franchise home record), they outscored the eventual champs 32–11 in a four-game sweep to evoke memories of last year's NLCS.

Flores himself was also in a record-making mood. His other four at-bats ended with three singles and a fifth-inning homer, to match a Mets' single-game high for hits.

3. CARLOS DELGADO VS. YANKEES (JUNE 27, 2008)

For the second time, the teams from the Queens and the Bronx engaged in a same-day, two-stadium doubleheader.

Delgado didn't wait to put on a show for the partisan crowd at Shea. Instead, he saved his best swings for the lefty-friendly fences at old Yankee Stadium.

Three hits registered nine runs batted in—the most by a Met in a single game, breaking a record previously held by Dave Kingman. His pair of home runs moved him one spot up on the all-time home run list—a place also once owned by Kingman. A bad day to be "Kong."

Delgado's initial two trips to the plate ended empty. But with a host of Mets aboard for his final three turns at-bat, he capitalized on the ample RBI chances presented.

A fifth-inning double scored two and put the Mets in front to stay. Then, in the sixth with the bases loaded, a single flick of his wrists turned a relatively close contest into a blowout.

That made it 11–4. When it was 12–5 in the eighth, Delgado didn't ease up. Instead, he sought three more runs—locking in on a LaTroy Hawkins pitch and depositing it into the right-field stands.

2. Yoenis Cespedes vs. Rockies (August 21, 2015)

In the twenty-one days since Cespedes arrived by trade from Detroit, the Mets elevated their rank in the NL East—from two games back to three-and-a-half ahead.

The lineup was a stark contrast from its look earlier in the summer. Cespedes's presence eased the burden off hitters who were once trying to do too much. But while the offense's overall temperature rose, his remained lukewarm. A .274 average with two homers and eight RBIs in seventy-three at-bats doesn't jive with his standards.

At Coors Field, an inviting venue to bust loose, Cespedes went on full blast.

Liftoff occurred with a two-out double that led to a first-inning run—a tease for later. The Mets tagged Colorado starter Jon Gray with six in the second—capped by Cespedes's opposite field grand slam.

The Mile High City was the site for Yoenis Cespedes to reach rarefied Mets air. *Debby Wong/Shutterstock.com.*

He must have liked that trot around the bases because he did the same in his next two turns. By the top of the sixth, Cespedes already had a three-homer evening—the last put the Mets up 10–8 in a scoreboard-rupturing 23–run affair.

A single through the right side of the infield to lead off the eighth made him the third major leaguer since 1920 with at least three homers, five hits, seven RBIs and a stolen base. Cespedes eventually came around to score for the fifth time.

Carlos González's nifty ninth-inning catch in the right–center field gap prevented a cycle-making triple and also prevented Cespedes from being the second Met to achieve a rare six-hit game. Who's the first? Glad you asked…

1. EDGARDO ALFONZO VS. ASTROS (AUGUST 30, 1999)

Someone forgot to tell him the Astrodome is a pitcher's park, because Alfonzo transformed the cavernous Houston stadium into a launching pad.

He homered to left center field in the first, singled to right field in the second (part of a six-run frame), connected on a second home run two innings later with Rickey Henderson aboard, went deep for a third time off Astro reliever Sean Bergman to lead off the sixth and doubled down the right-field line in the ninth.

By the time the dust cleared on Alfonzo's offensive explosion, he set three single-game club records and tied another. He became the seventh Met to sock three homers and remains the only one to collect six hits, which matched the same amount accrued during a rare ten-game recession that prefaced this night.

"Every player goes through a slump," Alfonzo told the *New York Times* afterward. "I tried to find out what I was doing wrong. Every day, I try to be positive and to hit the ball really hard. The home runs, I don't think about. They just come."

The sixteen total bases put "Fonzie" in equally esteemed company. At the time, only seventeen others since the turn of the twentieth century reached that mark in a nine-inning contest.

Alfonzo's outbreak proved infectious. The Mets scored seventeen times—three members of the lineup had at least two hits, while four others drove in at least four runs. But all of those efforts paled in comparison to the one by their unassuming but invaluable second baseman.

HOME RUNS

10. DONN CLENDENON (1969 WORLD SERIES GAME 5)

They are self-encompassed momentum shifts when done appropriately.

Home runs, particularly in the clutch, can simultaneously set the opposition on a defeatist route and place the offensive team on a victorious one.

For Clendenon, his path was cleared—both to enact a rally that would help the Mets achieve a World Series victory and to avoid a trip back to Memorial Stadium.

Cleon Jones stood on first—awarded the base when Gil Hodges's claim that a Dave McNally pitch had struck him in the foot was upheld by home plate umpire Lou DiMuro.

The Mets were behind 3–0 in the bottom of the sixth. But the Orioles—as formidable as they were—might have been resigned to impending doom that awaited. Clendenon, who feasted on left-handed pitchers, conveyed such a destiny.

Sure enough, destiny wasn't going to be stopped now. Donn's line drive knocked off the auxiliary scoreboard as it cleared the left-field fence. It was his third home run, each against southpaws, and brought the Mets to within a run.

The comeback had begun—and would be completed—thanks to the imminent MVP.

9. DARRYL STRAWBERRY (1986 NLCS GAME 3)

For his '86 postseason ledger, the busts far outweighed the booms. But sometimes, three out of the park can outweigh eighteen strikeouts.

The Mets' No. 18 got himself and his team energized with a homer that elevated—and sustained—the proliferation of building energy in the bottom of the sixth.

When the half-inning began, New York trailed the Houston Astros 4–0, with the series lead in question.

But a trio of well-placed balls—a bouncer, a bloop and a blunder—presented great possibilities with Strawberry digging into the batter's box.

Astro manager Hal Lanier stuck with his southpaw, Bob Knepper, to face the left-handed batter with twenty-six home runs on the year, yet 3-for-22 lifetime against the Houston starter. That decision became a regrettable one the instant Darryl made contact on pitch one.

Strawberry guessed fastball. And guessed right. The 0-for-August home drought washed away in a flood of cheers.

In just another half-inning, the Astros had the lead back, but the model of using the long ball as an efficient way to score runs proved helpful for the Mets later on.

Darryl Strawberry has gone deep more often than any other Mets player. The organization's first homegrown bona fide slugger put 252 over the fences in seven seasons. *Jerry Coli/Dreamstime.*

8. Daniel Murphy (2015 NLDS Game 5)

New York discovered a newer, temporary version of Mr. October.

It took Murphy 138 games in 2015 to reach 14 home runs—a single-season personal-high at that time.

It's not that what eventuated was beyond his potential. It was beyond limits of anyone—power hitter or no.

With six home runs in as many games, Murphy ascended to an unexplored height in postseason excellence.

He was merely warming up—not yet completely in scorching hot territory—when he provided the Mets with the most pivotal of those homers.

By the top of the sixth in the matchup to decide the NLCS opponent of the Chicago Cubs, Murphy contributed to both runs—bringing in Curtis Granderson on a first-inning double and scoring on a fourth-inning Travis d'Arnaud sacrifice fly, which was set up when he caught the Los Angeles Dodgers' infield napping and stole third base.

LA starter Zack Greinke had not lost from the Dodger Stadium mound since May 16 and hadn't yielded three runs in a home start since April

18. Those were trends for Murphy to scoff at. He was too busy forging his own.

Taking a similar flight to his tie-breaking Game 1 homer, his right-field drive single-handedly thrust New York ahead 3–2—to be preserved by outstanding pitching from Jacob deGrom, Noah Syndergaard and Jeurys Familia.

7. Benny Agbayani (2000 NLDS Game 3)

The Mets have found Hawaii to be a pleasantly surprising talent source. Sid Fernandez, Ron Darling and Agbayani can point to Honolulu as their place of origin.

Unlike the two pitchers of the 1980s, Benny's climb to prominence was far more unexpected. His underdog status endeared him as a cult favorite—very accommodating with patrons. Sometimes, too much so.

The Giants had loaded the bases in the fourth inning of an August 12 game. Agbayani caught a short fly ball near the left-field foul line, then handed it over to a youngster in the stands. A nice gesture, but an untimely one. That was the second out.

Before Benny realized his faux pas, two San Francisco base runners crossed the plate to overcome the Mets lead. New York still won 4–3. All was forgiven, even if it was hard to forget.

Nearly two months later, those teams dueled with much more at stake. Like the series itself, they were knotted up on the scoreboard—two apiece—once Edgardo Alfonzo doubled in the equalizer in the last of the eighth.

Journeying into the thirteenth inning, Benny's generosity resurfaced—more favorably to Mets success.

He used his bat, not his hand, to send the ball—delivered by Giants reliever Aaron Fultz—into the crowded left–center field bleachers. Soon after Agbayani had lifted Fultz's pitch far enough to give the Mets a 2–1 series edge, he was hoisted up on his teammates' shoulders.

6. Edgardo Alfonzo (1999 NLDS Game 1)

He was the Diamondbacks' worst nightmare—from start to finish.

Alfonzo hit a personal-best twenty-seven homers in 1999 (ten more than in any previous season), the last coming twenty-six hours earlier in the winner-take-all Wild Card play-in against Cincinnati. His power surge flared again in the Mets' first postseason appearance since 1988 and Arizona's initial entrance into this hierarchy after just two years of MLB existence.

Randy Johnson—six feet, ten inches of intimidation and the eventual Cy Young recipient—had looked like a mere mortal under the microscope of the playoffs—having lost his previous five decisions.

When "Fonzie" greeted him with a second top-of-the-first blast in as many nights and John Olerud followed suit in the third, grumblings about the "Big Unit" coming up small resurfaced.

Only one significant hit was

Bartolo Colon led the Mets in victories and innings pitched each year from 2014 to 2016. But a batsman he was not. Each flailing trip to the plate was an event. Each hit, celebrated like New Year's. But May 7, 2016, brought the apex of Bart-mania—a home run at San Diego's Petco Park. The jubilant Mets dugout playfully retreated to the clubhouse as "silent treatment." Colon savored his trot around the bases—measured by a sundial at thirty-one seconds. At age forty-two, he was the oldest player to hit his first home run. *Debby Wong/Shutterstock.com.*

needed from Alfonzo to keep the Mets ahead of the Reds. But as the D-Backs rallied from a 4–1 deficit, a bit more effort was required.

New York wore down Johnson by the ninth. A pair of singles and a walk loaded the bases and threatened to break the tie. Alfonzo coming to the plate prompted Arizona manager Buck Showalter to come to his senses and bring in a right-hander. It marked the end for Johnson and the beginning of the end for reliever Bobby Chouinard.

Alfonzo made Arizona pay dearly. The deposit morphed into a grand slam by the left-field corner—the first such momentum-swinging occurrence in Mets playoff history and the disparity that created an 8–4 win.

5. AL WEIS (1969 WORLD SERIES GAME 5)

A season replete with inexplicable events still had room for perhaps the most astounding episode in the Fall Classic.

Weis, a platoon second baseman and a .215 hitter in 1969, awakened his morbid bat to the tune of a .500 batting average and the Game 2 go-ahead single.

Of his four hits, none was a home run—not earth-shattering news. Because Weis's eight-year career included just six. His '69 total matched his personal high: two—which came during consecutive July games at Wrigley Field.

Over two Met seasons, he had yet to launch one over the walls of Shea. But there's a first for everything. And Weis used letter-perfect timing.

Leading off the bottom of the seventh, he faced Dave McNally—clinging to a 3–2 lead following Donn Clendenon's blast. Weis dealt with McNally as a member of the White Sox—and took him deep. By his standards, he owned him.

Still, he was about as much of a long ball threat as the Mets were to win the World Series when this year started. So naturally, during a period when the impossible became commonplace, Weis homered to left field. The outrageous fortunes that took the Mets this far took another incredible step.

As the Mets turned the tie into a lead with two eighth-inning runs and Jerry Koosman closed the deal in the ninth, Weis brought this year of wonder to a fitting conclusion.

4. LENNY DYKSTRA (1986 NLCS GAME 3)

Clutch postseason performers aren't made so because they rise to the occasion. It's because the magnitude of the event doesn't affect them.

Dykstra, never one to come across as a shrinking violet, played every game with the ferocity of an October contest. So why would the 1986 postseason be any different?

The man they called "Nails" (as broadcaster Bob Murphy once said) provided his first and most significant playoff moment at the expense of Houston Astros reliever Dave Smith. Wally Backman stood at second base as the tying run. The Mets were behind 5–4, two outs from defeat and the relinquishing of home-field advantage and nemesis Mike Scott ready to go for Game 4.

When Dykstra (and his five-foot, ten-inch, 165-pound frame) made contact, thoughts of a 2–1 series deficit were about to be reversed. Out it went—landing in the right-field bullpen.

Davey Johnson had inserted Lenny into the game as a pinch-hitter in the seventh, intent on him and Backman igniting the offense with the same aggressive, slap-hitting, base-stealing style they had kindled since season's outset.

Dykstra—with eight home runs for 1986 and an average of seven for his twelve-year career—had other plans.

3. TODD PRATT (1999 NLDS GAME 4)

Heroism in baseball has no prejudice. Unlike football or basketball, you can't always lean on your best player for a late-game must-score situation.

Up two-games-to-one on Arizona, the Mets couldn't turn to Mike Piazza even if they wanted. Suffering through the occupational hazards that come with being a catcher, Piazza was too beat up to play past Game 2.

Little did anyone think his understudy would steal the show. And for those unfamiliar with the Mets, little did anyone know of this former Phillie, Cub, Mariner, pizza delivery guy and baseball camp instructor.

There are journeymen, and then there are vagabonds such as Todd Pratt.

When his drive to center field off Arizona reliever Matt Mantei in the bottom of the tenth barely cleared the fence and Steve Finley's outstretched arm, he instantly transformed into the rarified air of New York postseason folklore. It ended Game 4, ended the series and sent the Mets to the NLCS against Atlanta.

Pratt became living testimony that in this sport, obscurity can become legendary with one swing.

2. RAY KNIGHT (1986 WORLD SERIES GAME 7)

With eighty-six more hits, a batting average improvement of eighty points and bolstering his on-base percentage by nearly one hundred, Knight served a bigger role than the platoon player he'd figured he would be that April.

Appropriately, the eleven-year veteran was the NL Comeback Player of the Year. But there was more to add.

Game 6's from-the-depths-of-defeat rally included his two-out, two-strike single off the fists to score Gary Carter and culminated with his exuberant dash home after Mookie Wilson's grounder under Bill Buckner's glove. If not for the late revival, Knight's seventh-inning error would have left him as a goat. Instead, he was able to right the wrong.

Even with destiny on his and the Mets' side, Game 7 didn't come so easily. New York had to rally from a 3–0 deficit. And once they evened the score, Knight put them ahead.

Calvin Schiraldi, scars still fresh from his failure to close the Mets out in the bottom of the tenth of Game 6 and unceremoniously serenaded by the crowd, hummed a 2–1 heater into Knight's wheelhouse.

The tie-breaking, seventh-inning homer to left center gave the Mets a permanent lead. An eighth-inning single put the finishing touches on a .391 series and the Most Valuable Player award.

Knight's finest moment as a Met was also pretty much his last. The World Series MVP did not get his wish of a multi-year deal and, thus, signed with Baltimore during the winter. Instead of receiving his championship ring in person, it arrived in the mail.

As unjust as the aftermath might have been for Knight, his '86 campaign, one of birth and rebirth, stands out among his thirteen major league seasons.

"[It was] the greatest year of my life," Knight said. "Nancy [Lopez] and I had our second child and I happened to be on one of the greatest teams of all time."

1. Mike Piazza vs. Braves (September 21, 2001)

When Piazza was traded to New York from the Florida Marlins in May 1998, the plan was for his addition to enhance the team's hopes of becoming a World Series contender. Not only did Piazza's presence in the lineup enact change, but he also became the face of the franchise and arguably the Big Apple's top player.

As the city was suffering from the ultimate tragedy, Piazza would aid the healing process.

The stature of the Mets and the Braves meeting at Shea Stadium went well beyond a battle between NL East rivals in the throes of a pennant race. It was the first game in New York City following the events of 9/11—a brief, three-hour opportunity for solace and a temporary distraction from the horror that took place just miles from the ballpark only ten days prior—a conduit to normalcy.

"Many of you give me praise for the two-run home run on the first game back on September 21 [2001] to push us ahead of the rival Braves," Piazza said in his 2016 Hall of Fame induction speech. "But the true praise belongs to police, firefighters, first responders, who knew they were going to die, but went forward anyway." *Jerry Coli/Dreamstime.*

The sold-out crowd, understandably subdued, wasn't given much reason to cheer for the majority of the evening, as Atlanta held a 2–1 advantage into the bottom of the eighth.

As Piazza stepped up to the plate with one out and a runner on, it was impossible not to conjure up the series of events that could transpire. He had delivered key dramatic late-game home runs on several occasions before. But if there was a time for a real storybook ending, it was central casting for Piazza to be the man to write this script.

Almost on cue, Piazza hammered the pitch from Steve Karsay to deep center. As the ball went over the fence, there was an outpouring of cheers and sheer emotion from fans who didn't know when was the right time to express such emotions over a simple baseball game.

Now *was* the right time.

The Mets took a 3–2 lead—a lead they kept through the top of the ninth. New York City, at least on this evening, had something to celebrate.

For all of Mike Piazza's 427 career home runs—220 as a Met—none can match the emotional impact of this one.

HONORABLE MENTION

Lenny Dykstra (1986 World Series Game 3)

Saddled with a two-game deficit and devoid of an extra-base hit during that pair of losses to Boston, the Mets shuttled to Fenway Park in desperate need of a spark. They didn't have to look for long—as their season-long catalyst provided it. Dykstra led off against Oil Can Boyd and gave his club an instantaneous 1–0 lead, which served as the impetus to a four-run top of the first and a 7–1 victory.

Darryl Strawberry (1986 World Series Game 7)

Sardonic chants of his name from Boston fans were in his ear and in his head. He bristled at his early removal from Game 6. Even as the Mets were on the precipice of a championship, Darryl still wasn't exactly a paradigm of happiness. But in his final at-bat, with the Mets clinging to a 6–5 edge in the bottom of the eighth, Straw had the last laugh. A typical towering drive landed in front of the right–center field scoreboard and ensured Jesse Orosco would pitch the ninth with at least a two-run lead.

Steve Henderson (June 14, 1980, vs. Giants)

The oasis in a desert of hardship. Under new ownership, the Mets tried to convince their demoralized fans—whoever remained to claim such hardened devotion—that "The Magic Is Back." A desperate marketing ploy enacted four years too early. But for one evening, when Henderson successfully went to the opposite field for his first homer of 1980 and put an exclamation point on a six-run ninth-inning rally that gave New York a 7–6 win over San Francisco, that slogan held true.

Carlos Beltran (August 22, 2006, vs. Cardinals)

If he had won the MVP, this would have been his MVP moment. The Cardinals probably thought they were safely ahead with a 7–1 lead in the fifth and a 7–6 lead with one out in the ninth. In both instances, they thought wrong. Beltran's two-run, walk-off homer continued to reassure fans that the Mets were not just a playoff team with their substantial division lead—they were the best team in the league.

Edgardo Alfonzo (1999 Wild Card One-Game Playoff)

Al Leiter's two-hit shutout of Cincinnati justifiably overshadowed any other Met player. But in this pressure-packed do-or-die affair that decided a spot in the National League Division Series, Alfonzo's two-run, first-inning bomb to straightaway center field eased any tension Leiter might have been feeling. It took the wind out from the sails of both the Reds and starting pitcher Steve Paris—paving the way for a 5–0 win.

SINGLE-SEASON OFFENSES

Whether you're on board with it or not, the analytic movement doesn't appear to be a passing trend. While on-base percentage (OBP) and other sabermetric-friendly terms like OPS have become important lineup-building evaluators, the conventional back-of-the-card statistics—home runs (HR), runs batted in (RBI), stolen bases (SB), doubles (2B) and batting average (BA) remain timeless.

There are several reasons for the modern uptick in offensive production. But even as we factor each season relative to their contemporary competition, the Mets still were most prodigious over the recent half of their history.

10. 1988

Darryl Strawberry (39 HRs, 101 RBIs, .911 OPS, 29 SBs)
Kevin McReynolds (27 HRs, 99 RBIs, 30 doubles, 159 hits)
Howard Johnson (24 HRs, 114 hits, 21 doubles, 23 SBs)
Lenny Dykstra (116 hits, 19 doubles, .270 BA)
Keith Hernandez (.276 BA, 55 RBIs, 96 hits in 95 games)

9. 1996

Todd Hundley (41 HRs, 112 RBIs, 140 hits, 32 doubles)
Lance Johnson (227 hits, 21 triples, .333 BA, 31 doubles)
Bernard Gilkey (30 HRs, 117 RBIs, 181 hits, .317 BA)
Butch Huskey (15 HRs, 60 RBIs, 115 hits)
Jose Vizcaino (.303 BA, 110 hits in 96 games)

A pair of members from 1996's potent lineup. Before he became a Dodger, Todd Hundley (*left*) slugged forty-one home runs to briefly establish a Mets' club record and temporarily eclipse the MLB single-season high for catcher. Setting the table often for Todd was Lance Johnson (*right*). The former White Sox speedster spent just one full season with the Mets, but it was his best: 227 hits and 21 triples each continue to stand as franchise records. He also started and led off the All-Star Game in Philadelphia, going 3-for-4 in an NL victory. *Jerry Coli/Dreamstime.*

8. 2008

David Wright (33 HRs, 124 RBIs, 189 hits, 42 doubles, .302 BA)
Carlos Delgado (38 HRs, 115 RBIs, 162 hits, 32 doubles)
Carlos Beltran (27 HRs, 112 RBIs, 172 hits, 40 doubles, 25 SBs)
Jose Reyes (204 hits, 19 triples, 56 SBs, .297 BA)
Fernando Tatis (.297 BA, 11 HRs, 47 RBIs in 92 games)

7. 1986

Keith Hernandez (.310 BA, .413 OBP, 171 hits, 83 RBIs, 34 doubles)
Gary Carter (24 HRs, 105 RBIs, 125 hits)
Darryl Strawberry (27 HRs, 93 RBIs, 27 doubles, 28 SBs)
Wally Backman (.320 BA, 124 hits, 18 doubles)
Ray Knight (.298 BA, 145 hits, 24 doubles)

Left: Savoring an on-field postgame World Series celebration with Gary Carter, second baseman Wally Backman hit .320 for the '86 Mets as the other half of a two-pronged top-of-the-order dynamite package with Lenny Dykstra. Backman's whatever-it-takes, no-holds-barred mindset led to a fair share of drag bunts and head-first dives. *Jerry Coli/Dreamstime.*

Below: At age thirty-four and with 369 home runs to date, Carlos Delgado brought veteran savvy and a powerful bat to Queens. For three years, he didn't disappoint in either department. Delgado slugged 100 over the walls from 2006 to 2008 and drove in 316. A hip injury in 2009 derailed his career. *Jerry Coli/Dreamstime.*

6. 1990

Darryl Strawberry (37 HRs, 108 RBIs, 150 hits, 18 doubles)
Dave Magadan (.328 BA, .417 OBP, 148 hits, 28 doubles)
Kevin McReynolds (24 HRs, 82 RBIs, 140 hits, 23 doubles)
Gregg Jefferies (40 doubles, 15 HRs, 68 RBIs, 171 hits)
Howard Johnson (23 HRs, 90 RBIs, 34 SBs, 144 hits)

5. 2007

David Wright (30 HRs, 107 RBIs, .325 BA, 42 doubles)
Carlo Beltran (33 HRs, 112 RBIs, 153 hits, 33 doubles)
Jose Reyes (78 SBs, 191 hits, 12 triples, 36 doubles)
Carlos Delgado (24 HRs, 87 RBIs, 30 doubles)
Moises Alou (.341 BA, 112 hits, 19 doubles in 87 games)

4. 1987

Howard Johnson (36 HRs, 99 RBIs, 32 SBs, 147 hits)
Darryl Strawberry (39 HRs, 104 RBIs, 36 SBs, 32 doubles)
Kevin McReynolds (29 HRs, 95 RBIs, 163 hits, 32 doubles)
Keith Hernandez (18 HRs, 89 RBIs, 170 hits, 28 doubles, .290 BA)
Tim Teufel (.308 BA, 14 HRs, 61 RBIs, 29 doubles in 97 games)

3. 2000

Mike Piazza (38 HRs, 113 RBIs, .324 BA, 1.012 OPS, 156 hits)
Edgardo Alfonzo (25 HRs, 94 RBIs, 40 doubles, .324 BA, .425 OBP)
Robin Ventura (24 HRs, 84 RBIs, 23 doubles)
Jay Payton (17 HRs, 62 RBIs, .291 BA, 23 doubles)
Todd Zeile (22 HRs, 79 RBIs, 146 hits, 36 doubles)

2. 1999

Mike Piazza (40 HRs, 124 RBIs, 25 doubles, .303 BA)
Edgardo Alfonzo (27 HRs, 108 RBIs, 191 hits, 41 doubles, .304 BA)
Robin Ventura (32 HRs, 120 RBIs, 38 doubles, .301 BA)
John Olerud (19 HRs, 96 RBIs, .427 OBP, 173 hits, 39 doubles)
Roger Cedeno (.313 BA, 66 SBs, 142 hits)

1. 2006

Carlos Beltran (41 HRs, 116 RBIs, 38 doubles, .388 OBP)
David Wright (26 HRs, 116 RBIs, 181 hits, 40 doubles, .311 BA)
Carlos Delgado (38 HRs, 114 RBIs, 30 doubles, .909 OPS)
Jose Reyes (194 hits, 17 triples, 64 SBs, .300 BA)
Paul Lo Duca (.318 BA, 163 hits, 39 doubles)
Jose Valentin (18 HRs, 62 RBIs, 24 doubles)

PART IV

ANGUISH

VILLAINS

10. TERRY PENDLETON/MIKE SCIOSCIA

These are the names that induce cold sweats. Any mention of them (or the rest on this list), and a Mets fan winces.

The 1987 and 1988 seasons were irrevocably damaged because of their respective shots through our hearts. Yet they are easy scapegoats. In truth, the Mets only have themselves to blame.

Pendleton's two-run homer off Roger McDowell in a crucial September 11 contest completed a three-run top of the ninth, in which the Cards were down to their last out before mounting a comeback. Retire Pendleton, and the Mets would be a half-game back in the division.

Instead, St. Louis pushed ahead and won in the tenth. New York's late charge for first place halted and never regained steam.

A year later, the Mets were the ones being chased. But it seemed a futile attempt for Los Angeles. The Dodgers were behind two-games-to-one in the NLCS and behind by two runs facing Dwight Gooden in the ninth inning of Game 4. Doc had not allowed a hit since the fourth.

After John Shelby walked, Gooden threw a fastball over the heart of the plate to Scioscia—three home runs in 408 at-bats during 1988 and an average of four homers in his eight big league seasons.

LA's backstop knocked it into the New York bullpen—the pivot point from which this game (which the Dodgers won in twelve innings) and this series (which the Dodgers won in seven) turned.

9. YADIER MOLINA

The haunting offcuts of '87 and '88 conflated to produce the painful end to 2006.

It was the Cardinals once more ruining dreams of advancement. And in the anticipated and expected progression to the World Series as the far superior team, another powerless catcher—in this instance Molina—slung the dagger.

With a man on and the score knotted in the top of the ninth of the deciding seventh game of the NLCS, Molina—far more noted for his defense than his six homers in '06—made Met reliever Aaron Heilman lament his pitch. It turned Shea into a morgue and became the deciding margin in a contest that decided the National League title, as St. Louis (and its eighty-two regular season wins) marched on to ultimate glory.

Molina is a notch above the other pair of one-shot-through-the-heart wonders by his repeated nature to nab brazen Met stolen base attempters who dare test his arm.

The Redbirds' longtime backstop's .321 batting average (at the conclusion of the 2017 season) versus the Mets remains the best among any franchise he's faced more than seventy-five times.

8. PETE ROSE

New York has hosted many great bouts. But the quarrel between Rose, one of baseball's fiercest aggressors, and Bud Harrelson, the undersized, yet feisty shortstop, is particularly memorable—even if it never measured up in duration and competitive fairness.

A battle between the Mets and Reds in Game 3 of the NLCS would become the undercard in the midst of a fifth inning–ending double play.

Harrelson, the provider of self-deprecating comments aimed at the punchless Cincinnati offense, was greeted at second base by a hard-sliding Rose, who was set to carry out vengeance on behalf of his teammates.

Bud objected. Rose shoved. Harrelson shoved back. The fight was on. The Mets would go on to an easy 9–2 victory. It almost never got there.

Soon after the madness subsided (and after Pedro Borbón gnawed at a Mets hat), Rose took his position in left field—an easy target. Most fans heaved boos in Rose's direction. Others threw objects.

It took pleading from Rusty Staub, Tom Seaver and Willie Mays to keep the carnage from escalating.

The fight had no bearing on the outcome. Rose, though, fed off such resentment. With jeers undiminished in Game 4, he set out to avert the Mets from clinching the pennant. A twelfth-inning homer against Harry Parker, to cap a 3-for-5 day, made that happen.

Of his record 4,256 hits, the Mets were witness to 396.

7. Daniel Murphy

Regret runs rampant when it comes to the 2015 NLCS MVP. With every hit—way too many at New York's expense—the lament of not being more proactive in attempting to re-sign Murphy grows louder.

Murphy rejected a qualifying offer worth $15.8 million in November 2015, confirming his venture into free agency.

The Mets could have retained the second baseman, who holds one of the highest batting averages in club history. But when they traded for Neil Walker—formerly a second baseman of the Pittsburgh Pirates—in early December, the writing was on the wall.

Soon enough, Murphy's writing would be on a Nationals contract—a three-year deal worth $37.5 million. The Mets could have easily paid that much to a player who did so well through lean years, despite defensive and base path lapses, and carried them to a World Series.

That would have been so much simpler than the figurative amount Murphy is making them pay now. Seven of his twenty-five homers in 2016 came against the Mets. So did twenty-one of his 104 RBIs. He played in all twenty-nine games versus New York and hit safely in each one. The Nats won twelve of those and took the division by eight.

Murphy took it easier on his old mates in 2017—*only* hitting .354 with fourteen RBIs.

6. Mike Scott

Mike Scott: the man who almost single-handedly stopped the 1986 Mets. *Jerry Coli/Dreamstime.*

Had Game 7 of the 1986 NLCS occurred, it's likely—if not inevitable—the Houston Astros would have displaced the Mets as World Series representative.

Scott, sweetening the revenge on the team that dismissed him, would have been the reason. The series MVP displayed pitching mastery contrary to what he showed in New York.

A 4.64 ERA and 3.7 strikeouts per nine innings from 1979 to 1982, Scott's struggle with dependability triggered his trade to Houston.

Receiving guidance from Roger Craig, he added a split-fingered fastball to his repertoire.

In 1986, he found it: 306 strikeouts, 2.22 ERA and a no-hitter to clinch the NL West.

Baseball's hottest pitcher still sizzled when encountering the favored Mets—an immovable object in the way of New York's irresistible force. Scott followed up his fourteen-K Game 1 virtuosity by holding New York to a mere two singles in Game 4—frustrating them to the point of speculation.

Several Mets felt the sharp, downward movement on his splitter was aided by a bit more than good dexterity. When a foul from a Scott offering ventured into the dugout, scuff marks on the ball gave more reason for grievance.

Whether it was sour grapes or a legitimate gripe, nobody was going to stop it. Only the Mets could by winning the next two and avoiding a third Scott start in a winner-take-all. In seizing Game 5 and persevering through sixteen painstaking Game 6 innings, they did.

5. Jimmy Rollins

Painfully prophetic—that's the simplest way to describe Rollins in 2007. Part and parcel to Phillie fortunes as a top-of-the-order hitter and infield forerunner, the star shortstop captained a late-season manifesto.

Philadelphia spent most of the year peering behind the Mets before nipping them at the wire, affirming the statement Rollins made in March—that the Phils were "the team to beat."

The swagger inflamed a rivalry not burning so hot, as the Mets cruised to the NL East title by twelve games in 2006, and it appeared to be idle spring training chatter when New York held a seven-and-a-half-game margin with seemingly too little time left for comebacks.

However, Rollins and the Phillies were already tipping the scales in their favor before September. Philadelphia won its last eight against the Mets—five of them decided by two runs or fewer.

Rollins' performance against New York in '07 included hitting .346 with six homers, fifteen RBIs and eight stolen bases. In carrying the Phils to the division title, he was named NL MVP.

It ain't bragging if you can back it up.

No posturing was necessary for 2008. A recurrent dream scenario for the Phils and a recurrent nightmare for the Mets, only this time the Phillies went on to the World Series title.

As Philadelphia continued to have its way with New York into the next decade, Rollins did too. The Mets gazed at 14 percent of his career home run total (33) and 13 percent of his RBIs (122).

4. ROGER CLEMENS

Among the hoopla preparatory to the 2000 World Series, the conflict between "The Rocket" and the Mets' top hitter stayed a salacious sidebar. It evolved from a Clemens pitch in July that struck Piazza on the helmet brim and left him concussed—to which Mike claimed there was intent.

When Game 2 began, with Clemens starting and Piazza batting third, the inevitable face-off was front and center. And when the top of the first ended, it was all anyone could talk about.

Clemens flung the meat part of Piazza's splintered bat in No. 31's direction as he casually jogged toward first on a foul—causing a bench-clearing and a standoff of the two combatants.

Roger claimed he confused the bat—an elongated, jagged piece of wood—for the ball—a round piece of rawhide with stitching. Spoken like a guy who testified to Congress that he never took steroids.

The Mets evened the score to some degree at Shea in June 2002 by knocking Clemens around, even if Shawn Estes missed on a retaliatory plunking.

Clemens was deprived of higher Met killer status in 1986. He no-hit New York through three innings in Game 6 of the World Series and maintained a 3–2 lead after seven. If his departure was due to a blister on his pitching hand or Boston manager John McNamara simply removing his young horse, the Mets are glad it happened.

They jumped on Calvin Schiraldi to tie it. Clemens was relegated to watching the victory—both for himself and his team—disappear while gazing through the visiting bullpen window.

All this, and he could've been a Met from the beginning. In 1981, they drafted Clemens in the twelfth round. But after lowballing the contract offer, he optioned to attend the University of Texas.

3. John Rocker

Those inflicting damage with on-field execution are trivial affronts when compared to personal attacks. Whoever came up with the phrase that ends with "words will never hurt me" never encountered an obnoxious Neanderthal like Rocker.

When he mocked and took swipes at Mets fans in 1999, the Braves southpaw reliever might have been playing the part as a pest—no one to really take seriously. Neither he nor some Mets fans showed much decorum.

But his comments on those that pack Shea Stadium and especially New Yorkers in general—featured in a December *Sports Illustrated* profile by Jeff Pearlman—left no stone unturned in a bigotry maelstrom.

"The biggest thing I don't like about New York are the foreigners," he said. "I'm not a very big fan of foreigners. You can walk an entire block in Times Square and not hear anybody speaking English." And this was a relatively mild sample of hate-mongering spew guaranteed to turn a white nationalist red-faced.

He and the Braves arrived in Queens in June 2000 with police presence equal to a riot. Based on what was anticipated, the evening was rather tame.

Karma ultimately triumphed. Rocker's career cascaded into a downward spiral once he was sent to Cleveland the next season—a 6.60 ERA in sixty innings pitched over three seasons and out of baseball by 2003.

It couldn't have happened to someone more deserving.

2. Chase Utley

A movie could use mischievous Utley as a classic "bad guy" character prototype.

Teamed with Rollins, Pat Burrell and Ryan Howard in Philadelphia, he bedeviled New York as the Phils heel-turned their NL East rival beginning in 2007 and continuing for the next seven seasons.

Up until August 2015, Utley was a .217 hitter for an aging team falling on hard times. So when he was dealt to the contending Dodgers in a post-deadline trade, the thirty-six-year-old washed-up former All-Star had basically been put out to pasture—out of the division, out of sight and out of mind.

But in a manner that would warm the heart of Freddy Krueger, Chase rose from career comatose to inflict more damage—and not in the emotional sense.

It happened in Game 2 of that year's NLDS. Shortstop Rubén Tejada was on the harmful end of Utley's ruthless late slide on a seventh-inning force play at second base. Tejada flipped over—carted off with a broken fibula. Injury was compounded by insult: replay ruled that Tejada never touched the bag (even though Utley didn't either).

Utley, still called safe, got by with his bush league tactic. The Dodgers used that as a springboard to victory, and their goon skirted suspension for the remainder of a series the Mets won.

And Utley stayed immune to rebuke. Continuing to halt the hands of time, he hit better and haunted greater.

Noah Syndergaard tried to plunk him in late May 2016—couldn't. Noah got tossed, and Utley later bombed a grand slam—rounding the bases in his usual stone-faced manner, probably masking an evil laugh underneath.

1. CHIPPER JONES

The Mets have never had a regular season Most Valuable Player. But they watched one develop in front of them.

New York came into a six-game September 1999 showdown with Jones's Braves confident and one back in the NL East. Ten days later, it came out dazed and eight behind.

Chipper eviscerated the Mets' chances at a division title with four homers and was responsible for driving in seven of Atlanta's thirteen runs in a Turner Field sweep.

This added to his single-season, single-handed demolition at New York's expense: a .400 batting average, a .510 on-base percentage, a 1.000 slugging percentage and seven home runs. Fred Wilpon and Nelson Doubleday were left to wonder if the Mets' deed was still in their names.

Afterward, Chipper was left to survey the damage. "Now all the Mets fans can go home and put their Yankees stuff on," he said as the Braves trounced New York in five out of six, announcing their rivals' supposed demise.

But the Mets didn't become Chipper's favorite prey because of a single series or a single season. In fact, this display of one man dominating one team stretches back to when he hit his first two homers in his first two games at Shea Stadium in 1995.

Pick your poison. Whether it be a pain in the butt, a blow to the leg or a proverbial punch to the gut, John Rocker (*top left*), Chase Utley (*top right*) and Chipper Jones (*right*) are the banes of Met existence. *Jerry Coli/Dreamstime.*

Suddenly, the DeLand, Florida native found a home away from home, even as the fans' reverberating chants of his given first name, Larry, were the best attempt at unnerving him—because no Met pitcher could.

So comfortable was he, Jones hit .313 with nineteen homers and fifty-five RBIs in eighty-eight games and named his firstborn daughter in honor of the visiting stadium that housed his greatest successes.

"I always held New York to a higher standard than other cities," Jones said. "I was jacked up to play there."

Whether it be in the Big Apple or Atlanta, Jones held the Mets in the palm of his hand. Against no other opponent did this 2018 Hall of Fame inductee generate more hits, home runs, runs batted in or a better OPS.

For the fans whose hearts he tore out time and time again, familiarity with his exploits bred contempt. Eventually, greater familiarity bred respect. As Chipper came to his ol' stomping grounds for the last time, Citi Field gave him a standing ovation in deference to the mother of all Met killers.

DISAPPOINTING TEAMS

10. 1974

Regardless of the missed chances that led to a seven-game loss to Oakland in the 1973 World Series, the way the Mets finished had to leave them feeling a nearly identical roster (if healthy) could feed off the momentum of the past season's pennant run.

The '74 opener—a 5–4 loss to Philadelphia on a two-run walk-off homer by Mike Schmidt—would be a harbinger of the struggles to follow. New York tunneled itself into deep division depths yet again: 24-39 and ten games behind by June 19.

Only this time, despite heating up around the start of September, the Mets would never get themselves out—ending up with seventy-one victories and a fifth-place finish.

The overall team letdown was best manifested in the frustration of the starting rotation. Tom Seaver endured pain up and down his back and was unable to abide by his lofty standards—going 11-11 with a 3.20 ERA.

Jon Matlack was the NL's third best in ERA (2.41) and topped the league in shutouts (seven), yet he would be devoid of tremendous run support and had to settle for a meager 13-15 record.

9. 1989

Nothing can exactly corroborate a hangover from 1988, but the Mets of '89 never presented the urgency of a team vowing to atone for a premature playoff exit. They were a study in bewilderment—victimized by their own faults as much as by the skills of others.

A consensus choice in spring training to take the NL East for the third time in four years, Davey Johnson's bunch logged a course fraught with fits and starts—unable to establish the consistent pattern experts predicted.

Further complicating matters was Dwight Gooden's nagging shoulder problem, which forced a prolonged disabled list stint beginning in July and ending in mid-September—when the Mets were pretty much out of contention.

By the time they got hot—taking nine of thirteen—the schedule had run its course. For the sixth straight year, New York finished no worse than second. But second place didn't mean what it means now.

Rather than celebrating a return to the postseason, fans were acknowledging the imminent departure of Keith Hernandez and Gary Carter, both of whom had expiring contracts and combined to play in just 125 games.

Their exit, along with the earlier trades of Lenny Dykstra and Mookie Wilson, marked a significant transition in an era noted for sustained success and lost opportunity.

8. 1991

From 1984 through 1990, the Mets boasted MLB's greatest regular season success—averaging ninety-five wins. Yet when the result is one World Series championship, one league pennant and two division titles, that feat rings hollow.

The front office had every right to believe Bud Harrelson would pick up where he left off when he led the Mets to a 71-49 record and within arm's reach of division champ Pittsburgh after taking the manager's post from Davey Johnson the previous May.

Those beliefs strengthened when the Mets resumed their first-place tussle with the Bucs through the All-Star break. On July 13, New York was 43-34—fresh off a ten-game win streak. The Pirates were two and a half ahead.

Whether or not internal strife caused poor performance or if poor performance caused internal strife, the Mets proceeded to nose dive so quickly that Shea fans should have been fitted for oxygen masks.

August saw the Mets lose games, plenty of them—twenty-one of twenty-nine. They lost Doc Gooden to a season-ending injury. And it confirmed their manager had lost control of the team.

At mid-season, Bud was on a playoff track. By late September, he was squarely on the firing line. Mike Cubbage piloted the final thud of New York's 22-43 freefall.

Never has a Mets team gone from smelling like a rose to stinking like last week's garbage with more resoluteness.

7. 1972

The Mets began the year under the dark cloud of tragedy.

Gil Hodges died suddenly of a heart attack on Easter Sunday. A players' strike—the first of its kind—delayed the start of the season. Nothing was in order.

Yet whatever pall cast over the team—now led by Yogi Berra—was not apparent by the early returns. Perhaps they were galvanized by their leader's tragic departure. Perhaps it was due to the addition of Rusty Staub—who hit .317 over the first forty-four games—and the presence of rookies John Milner and Jon Matlack.

Whatever the reason, all cylinders were clicking. By May 20, on the heels of a record-tying eleven-game win streak and the gain of Willie Mays, a six-and-a-half-game spread lay between the Mets and the defending champion Pittsburgh Pirates. And by June 3, New York was enjoying a fabulous mark of 31-12.

Then, swiftly, the runaway train broke down. Staub suffered a fractured hand in mid-June, setting off a rash of debilitating injuries. Cleon Jones, Bud Harrelson and Tommie Agee each hobbled onto the DL.

As would be customary, the offense disappeared, too. New York would end up being outscored by fifty runs and batted a National League low of .225.

The injury bug chomped up the Mets. The Pirates never took any pity on their misfortune. Instead, Pittsburgh claimed another NL East Division flag with the Mets a distant third place—83-73 and thirteen and a half behind.

6. 2002

The need to be on the front burner of the hot stove league can yield third-degree consequences. To a fault, the Mets have often mined the offseason market seeking treasure—and finding trash.

Mo Vaughn, an MVP in Boston some seven seasons ago, had recently recovered from a biceps tendon injury that forced him to miss all of 2001. The contract the Mets gave him—at three years and $42 million—was as oversized as his waistline. He managed twenty-six home runs but was dreadful in the field—committing eighteen errors in 139 games at first base.

The sharp decline of Roberto Alomar, thirty-four years old (like Vaughn) and already bound for the Hall of Fame, showed to be an even greater point of disenchantment. When compared to 2001 with the Indians, his batting average (.266) saw a seventy-point depreciation. Alomar's on-base percentage (.331) fell by nearly eighty points. If that wasn't enough, the defensive range that made him legendary in San Diego, Baltimore, Toronto and Cleveland vanished once he came to the Mets.

Treading water through July, New York finally sank and hit its nadir in August—a month in which the Mets could only scrape together six wins and were 0-13 at Shea. By dropping the opener of a September 3 double-header against Florida, they established a new National League record with fifteen consecutive home defeats.

After going 75-86, Bobby Valentine got the boot. Steve Phillips, though, was granted another season to run the Mets further into the ground.

5. 1987

Reaching the pinnacle isn't as hard as staying there.

If the Mets thought their methodical march through the National League—then frenzied race to a championship—in 1986 put a target on their backs, the bull's-eye behind them the year after winning the title became exponentially larger. The amplified competitive fire of adversaries notwithstanding, complacency and injury were equal enemies that could hinder a return to the top.

However, the Mets' rocky road to repeat began before the season ever got going. Dwight Gooden's drug problems became public. He tested positive for cocaine in spring training. A sixty-day suspension by MLB—and entrance in a rehabilitation clinic—kept him out of action for the first two months. That kicked off a decimation of the pitching staff, as the disabled list became a familiar detour for key arms.

A rotation once forged by Gooden, Darling, Ojeda and Fernandez was now sutured together by unknowns like Terry Leach, Jeff Innis, Gene Walter and John Mitchell. This revolving door of starters would reach a total of twelve by year's end.

Leach stunned with his 11-1 record and 3.22 ERA. But overall, an inability to maintain consistency on the mound led to the worst team ERA since 1982.

Behind ten-and-a-half games to St. Louis in early July, the Mets recovered thanks to Darryl Strawberry (when his bat spoke instead of his mouth) and emerging Howard Johnson—becoming the first set of teammates to top thirty homers and thirty stolen bases apiece.

New York pulled almost alongside the Cards (getting to one and a half back), but a back-breaking September 11 home loss stunted such progress. The Mets were barely a .500 team the rest of the way, ultimately ending with ninety-two wins and three fewer than St. Louis.

4. 2009

It's a shock no one got hurt at the ribbon-cutting ceremony.

Did anyone who constructed Citi Field—the brand-new Mets home—check to see if it was built on a former sacred burial ground? How many pins can be stuck into one voodoo doll?

These were suitable questions in the search for explanations for the immeasurable injuries and other countless hardships occurring inside and outside their house of pain.

Dropped pop-ups, hitting into unassisted triple plays, pitchers falling off the mound, fences so far that not even David Wright could reach them, Oliver Perez, J.J. Putz, a player-development head tearing off his shirt and challenging minor-leaguers to fight and the general manager challenging a reporter in the middle of the press conference announcing the firing of said player-development head.

Citi Field should have come with a big top.

Patient fans wait out a rain delay on a day at brand-new Citi Field as dreary as the Mets' 2009 season. *David Leindecker/Dreamstime.*

It's hard to forget curse-inducing *Sports Illustrated* made the Mets its preseason World Series champion. That should have been the first ominous sign—or perhaps when it was discovered Fred Wilpon had entrusted millions of dollars to jail-bound Bernie Madoff.

Fortunes sunk for the foreseeable future, the Mets did their fans a favor. Instead of burdening them with a third-straight September dismemberment, they struck the iceberg long before they could engender any of the playoff talk spoken of so often in March—allowing fans to take in the visuals that surrounded Citi Field as a delightful distraction from the real-time ninety-two-loss misery unfolding on the field.

3. 2007

Seven and seventeen. A haunting combination when put together.

A victory over Atlanta on September 12, their eighth win in ten tries, put New York at 83-62. The Phillies, the closest pursuer, were 76-69.

It wasn't the substantial gap enjoyed in '86, nor was it the cushy position of a sixteen-game advantage the previous year. But the Mets were in a favorable, almost untouchable, spot.

If there was an NL East catbird's seat, Willie Randolph's club was sitting in it—legs hiked up. Never in MLB history had a team squandered this big of a lead with this few games remaining. But just when the Mets thought they could skate away unscathed from the Phillies, the ice beneath them began to crack.

Philadelphia came to Flushing from September 14 to 16, needing to win three straight. They did. Up three and a half with fourteen to play, the Mets had no reason to worry.

Then the Mets dropped two out of three to the last-place Nationals at RFK Stadium, shrinking the edge to two and a half. Get worried.

Three wins at Florida were offset by three straight inexcusable home defeats to Washington in which the pitching (which posted a 5.27 September ERA) allowed thirty-two runs and the bullpen (worn by a heavy workload) continued to implode. The lead was down to one.

After falling to the Cardinals the next night, September 27, the Mets and the Phils were tied. DEFCON 1.

A division title proved the only possible entryway into the postseason as the two clubs held identical records as the final day of the regular season began.

Not when it ended.

Seven Florida Marlins scored runs before the Shea Stadium seats were warm. Minutes after the 8–1 loss, the Phillies topped the Nationals and confirmed Jimmy Rollins's preseason forecast.

History was made. And the Mets brutally wound up on the wrong end.

2. 2017

If the regular season is a cross-country trip, the Mets car blew up on the driveway.

Their star outfielder became the embodiment of walking wounded. A star pitcher refused to take an MRI and then paid the price for it, a has-been star pitcher skipped out of coming to a game due to a "headache," a sex toy was visible in a postgame clubhouse interview, a ten-game division hole emerged and Mr. Met—who reached exasperation—flipped off fans. And we were barely into June.

Students learning evolution at Columbia University didn't need to delve into a textbook, because a real-time study of Darwinian principles unfolded miles away. In this natural selection of survival for baseball fitness, the Mets devolved at a rapid rate. It's too exhausting to go over the players who got hurt.

Only reliever Jerry Blevins and Jacob deGrom spent the entire season with the team and deftly avoided the training staff's Kevorkian touch. DeGrom withstood serious ailments and set personal highs in starts (31), wins (15), innings (201.1) and strikeouts (239).

But as the Nationals ran away and hid with the NL East by mid-season and as several Mets veterans were reaching the tail end of their respective contracts, Sandy Alderson engaged in a summer of self-dispossession.

Everything must go—and everything did.

The mass Mets exodus included the departures of Lucas Duda (to Tampa), Neil Walker (to Milwaukee), Jay Bruce (to Cleveland) and Curtis Granderson (to the Los Angeles Dodgers).

A period of tremendous old-timer turnover, which gave way to the call-ups of prospects Ahmed Rosario and Dominic Smith, also marked the end of the line for their manager.

The seventh year, which finished with the Mets at 70-92, was the last for Terry Collins, but not before one more unwanted headline—that he ceded control of the clubhouse and relinquished the trust of management.

An unnamed member concisely and aptly described the sentiment of those who watched, played and oversaw the Mets through a nightmarish this-can't-end-soon-enough season: "We were all miserable."

1. 1992

"Hardball is Back!" reads the inside cover of the 1992 yearbook. But so were the hardships. The revamped Mets of (*clockwise from center*) manager Jeff Torborg, Bobby Bonilla, Eddie Murray and Brett Saberhagen looked the part, then came apart by summer. *Author's collection.*

You can find a shelf-load of books waxing poetic about 1969. There's almost as many glorifying 1986. Championship teams get eulogized to the heavens in print.

The '92 season told its own special story. Its lead-up was awash with optimism—a winter reload headed by new general manager Al Harazin, bound to quench the bad taste from 1991's corrosion.

Bobby Bonilla's entrance would weaken his old team (division rival Pittsburgh) while strengthening his new one. Former Cy Young winner Bret Saberhagen was added to an already-stocked rotation. Eddie Murray, a Hall-of-Famer to be, presented power and steadiness that would rub off on the clubhouse. Jeff Torborg, who managed the overachieving Chicago White Sox in 1990, would establish solid player relations and a good rapport with reporters.

What could possibly go wrong? Try everything.

Bonilla sunk to a .249 batting average. The Mets fans let him hear it, even if earplug-wearing Bobby tried not to. Saberhagen—like John Franco and Howard Johnson—spent much of the year physically wracked. He made only fifteen starts and won three. Murray maintained model consistency and drove in ninety-three runs but may have inspired others, including the manager, to invoke media paranoia.

Torborg, fighting a dumpster fire with a water gun, couldn't handle the press or the overpaid whiners infiltrating his locker room and metaphorically pushing him around (except in the case of Vince Coleman, when he literally did).

Sordid headlines (e.g., a preseason rape allegation) and a bushel of second-half losses piled like rotting garbage—a distinctive aroma of toxicity. The stench lingered through 1993, when things somehow worsened. But '92 was the precedent setter.

Apropos of win-loss records, it's not nearly as bad as the early to mid-1960s. But those Mets, with no expectations, were lovable. These Mets, failing mightily on multiple levels, were loathsome.

The '92 Mets still got their book for a year despite being so putrid and swaying so far from the norm. The title epitomized this group of bloated contracts, irritable grouches and waning value: *The Worst Team Money Can Buy*.

DEVASTATING LOSSES

10. September 28, 2008, vs. Marlins

Same sad song, different verse.

The Mets fought through the relics from 2007's September fold and returned to the final month of '08 with another division lead—only to relapse and tumble off the wagon.

Digging up fresh skeletons, New York went from three and a half up on the Phillies in the NL East on September 10 to two and a half behind eleven days (and seven losses) later.

Only the Wild Card could be obtained. Even that would take a bit of effort. They needed to win the regular season finale. And the opponent was the same they failed to defeat 363 days ago.

It would be hard not to partake in fatalistic thoughts as the Marlins rode in on pale horses to exorcise demons while unofficially turning out the lights on Shea Stadium. The forty-five-year-old Mets' lair prepared for official farewell—whether that be today or another day.

Carlos Beltran's two-run equalizing homer in the sixth hinted at one more October, but not if the area of this team that malfunctioned most in the closing weeks—relief pitching—crashed with finality near the finish line.

Billy Wagner's recent season-ending injury created too many bullpen holes to plug. Wes Helms's and Dan Uggla's consecutive home runs to open the eighth were confirmation of what would keep the Mets out of the playoff picture again.

Shortly after Ryan Church flew out to the warning track to confirm Milwaukee's spot in the postseason, the grim-faced crowd tried to marshal their emotions for a postgame tribute to Shea—an unwelcome mixture of funeral and celebration.

9. 2015 WORLD SERIES GAME 1

Right from Matt Harvey's first pitch, you knew—keeping a pessimistic mindset—this wouldn't go the Mets' way.

Yoenis Cespedes, in center field, took a bad read on Alcides Escobar's fly ball into the gap. He compounded things by fumbling a backhand catch attempt and kicked the ball away—allowing Escobar to circle the bases.

Escobar would also score the last run—fourteen innings and five hours later.

To get to that endpoint—a point, despite assuming the inevitable, we naturally and painfully waited out—the Mets tied, took the lead, gave it back and took it back before Alex Gordon's one-out ninth-inning home run to center off Jeurys Familia made it 4–4 and propelled this contest toward being the longest Game 1 in World Series history.

The Mets ducked defeat multiple times before buckling in the fourteenth. Escobar reached on a David Wright throwing error. Ben Zobrist singled. An intentional walk loaded the bases.

Bartolo Colon battled Eric Hosmer to a full count before the first baseman lifted one deep enough to score Escobar.

A prolonged 5–4 Kansas City victory would prove an initial indicator of more Royals' resiliency to follow.

8. SEPTEMBER 11, 1987, VS. CARDINALS

Self-induced wounds hadn't eradicated the Mets yet. Despite infighting, injuries and underachievement, they could seize first place from St. Louis.

Winners in eleven of fifteen and having sliced the Redbirds' lead over two months from ten and a half to one and a half, New York was finally playing up to its capability.

And by snatching two from the Cards in a three-game home set, the defending champions would return to a spot they had sat in so comfortably last year.

Everything for 8.2 innings of the Friday night series opener pointed towards it. Four early runs from the bats of Keith Hernandez, Darryl Strawberry and Mookie Wilson were backed up by six solid innings from Ron Darling, a hitless frame from Randy Myers and another from Roger McDowell.

Holding a three-run lead into the ninth, McDowell returned to the mound needing three outs to pull within a half game of first. He got two. Then, with Ozzie Smith on second, Willie McGee singled to cut the lead to 4–2.

Terry Pendleton, a low-ball hitter, now faced a low-ball pitcher. A match made in Mets hell.

Pendelton's drive beyond the center-field fence shrunk Shea to its knees.

St. Louis won in ten innings, 6–4. New York fell and couldn't get up. The haymaker delivered by Pendelton and the Cardinals staggered the Mets for the last two weeks—leaving this game, with its crushing homer, as the breaking point in a disheartening '87.

7. 1999 NLCS Game 6

Even in their last gasps of playoff life, the '99 Mets continued to fulfill their year-long trademark.

Often enjoyable. Sometimes excruciating. Never, ever dull.

It seemed fitting that every emotion linked to this team from inception to culmination came to the forefront in their dramatic season's denouement. Once down three games to none, the momentum generated from a late rally to win Game 4 coupled with taking a taut fifteen-inning Game 5 epic carried them to Atlanta preparing to make history.

When the Braves bombarded Al Leiter for five runs and sent him to the showers before recording an out, it appeared to be a wasted trip. But there were a few more hair-raising loops to go in their year-long roller-coaster ride.

New York, suppressed by Kevin Millwood into the sixth, awoke for three. Atlanta added two runs. The Mets pushed back in the seventh against John Smoltz. Doubles by Matt Franco and Rickey Henderson and a John Olerud single made it 7–5.

Mike Piazza, without an extra-base hit in the postseason and with too many ailments to keep track of, used what strength he had for an opposite field, game-tying home run.

The impossible notion of three days ago—becoming the first team ever to come from 0-3 in a best-of-seven and force a deciding contest—was becoming a reality.

That conviction was fortified, but never fulfilled.

Neither Melvin Mora's eighth-inning single nor Todd Pratt's tenth-inning sacrifice fly, both of which scored Benny Agbayani, could be upheld by New York's bullpen.

Kenny Rogers then chose the wrong moment to lose command. With the bases jammed, knotted at nine, and one out in the eleventh, his 3-1 pitch to Andruw Jones sailed wide.

The Mets earned respect, but the Braves earned their fifth pennant of the decade.

6. 2015 WORLD SERIES GAME 5

Terry Collins's blueprint to prevent a Monday locker clean-out—to extend the season by two more days and one more flight 1,200 miles westward—rested with his right-handed ace.

Using every power to rescue Gotham from despair, Matt Harvey assumed superhero status. He struck out nine and held the Royals without a run through eight, concurrently turning back the clock to an era when pitching changes were rare and the locks on bullpen gates rusted from underuse.

Up 2–0, Collins now had a decision to make. Let his horse get them to the finish line or opt for Jeurys Familia on a third straight night. Harvey lobbied his way back onto the hill, but with his leash supposedly short.

Then came a walk to Lorenzo Cain. Then came an RBI double from Eric Hosmer. Collins pulled the plug and brought in his closer.

Familia induced two soft ground balls. The first advanced Hosmer to third base. The next was fielded by David Wright at third. As he went to get the sure out at first, Hosmer began a mad dash to the plate.

Lucas Duda caught Wright's toss and fired home—the Mets fates riding with its flight.

Would a good throw have nailed Hosmer and sent both teams back to Kauffman Stadium? We'll never know. What is known is that the throw errantly sailed to the backstop.

The Royals, as became their method, flew through the door the Mets kept slightly ajar—scoring five twelfth-inning runs and holding a championship-clinching celebration on the Citi Field turf.

5. SEPTEMBER 30, 2007, VS. MARLINS

Tom Glavine picked a bad day to have a bad day. And the Mets picked a bad month for their worst month.

Willie Randolph's club needed a victory to keep hopes of an NL East crown alive and keep the manager from being thrown into the proverbial frying pan for overseeing a collapse of gargantuan proportion.

In a flash, the Florida Marlins compiled seven runs before the home team could bat and were playing the best spoilers the Philadelphia Phillies could ask for.

For the next eight and a half innings, as the Mets' bats stayed firmly planted in the hole their supposed ace dug them in, the players and their distraught fans were tortuously left to rue what they let slip away.

Simultaneous to the Marlins' 8–1 win, the Phillies were in the process of beating the Washington Nationals and snatching away New York's once-presumed bid to the postseason.

"It hurts," said David Wright, postmortem. "But at the same time, we did it to ourselves. It's not like it blindsided us. We gradually let this thing slip away. In all honesty, we didn't deserve to make the playoffs."

The Mets plummeted from their post atop the NL East in September 2007 and crash-landed in the regular season finale against Florida. Tom Glavine exits to a disconsolate Shea Stadium crowd after relinquishing six runs in less than an inning. *David Leindecker/Dreamstime.*

4. 1973 WORLD SERIES GAME 3

From last place at the end of August to within a victory of the World Championship is a mountain most never scale. To come that far is a feat in itself. To come that close after scaling such a distance makes it tough to bear.

Such is the reason why the extra-inning setback to the Oakland A's at Shea resonates with so much angst.

Tom Seaver fed off the NLCS Game 5 victory by fanning twelve—the most Ks by a Met in a World Series affair. But the two innings in which he allowed Oakland to score, the sixth and the eighth, were enough to create a 2–2 draw.

Jointly, the Mets offense couldn't generate much of anything versus Catfish Hunter after tagging him for a pair of scores in the bottom of the first. The contest journeyed past regulation—like it did for Game 2. Having labored through twenty-two innings behind the plate with a cross-country trip in between, catcher Jerry Grote's reflexes were being severely tested. That frailty surfaced when Harry Parker threw a two-strike pitch to free-swinging Ángel Mangual with a runner on first base.

"The ball was scuffed on one side and the ball had been sailing," Grote said. "Apparently, Harry had turned the ball around without realizing it and the ball went the other direction a little bit. And being a little bit on the tired side at this stage of the game, I just couldn't react quick enough to catch the ball."

What could have been the inning's second out turned into men on first and second. Bert Campaneris followed with what eventuated into the game-winning RBI single.

Grote's error proved a metaphor for the Mets' series narrative—the one that got away.

3. 2015 WORLD SERIES GAME 4

The Kansas City Royals of 2015 weren't about to let any presented opportunity go unfulfilled. Give them a base; they'll take a run.

By using Met missteps as their springboard, the three runs seized in the top of the eighth punctured New York's burgeoning hopes of a tied series.

Optimism blossomed behind starter Steven Matz and outfielder Michael Conforto—neither youngster experienced stage fright. Matz, eight big league starts behind him, departed in the sixth after allowing his seventh

The 7 Line Army, a group of fans named in recognition of the subway train that takes patrons to and from the park, was in full force for the 2015 World Series—only to witness two heartbreaking losses and the Kansas City Royals celebrating in Citi Field. *Courtesy of Jim Maggiore.*

hit and second earned run. But he left leading, thanks to Conforto's two solo homers.

A 3–2 advantage wasn't enough separation to rid themselves of the relentless Royals. The Mets discovered that closing out Kansas City was an arduous endeavor, and they were done in by an ill-timed case of Murphy's Law.

Successive free passes from Tyler Clippard in the top of the eighth resembled an overture for a Kansas City rally. Jeurys Familia, though, got Eric Hosmer to hit a weak grounder to the right side.

Daniel Murphy's proclivity for fielding gaffes reared its ugly head at an ill-timed instance. A potential double-play ball instead slipped under the second baseman's glove. Ben Zobrist zipped home from second with the tying score.

Familia proceeded to surrender RBI singles to Mike Moustakas, scoring Lorenzo Cain, and Salvador Perez, scoring Hosmer.

That's how swiftly a best-of-three prospect can turn into a three-to-one deficit.

2. 2006 NLCS Game 7

Endy Chavez's perfectly timed jump-and-stretch over the left-field wall in the sixth inning to rob Scott Rolen of a two-run homer and the presence of mind to double off Jim Edmonds (who assumed he'd be greeting Rolen at the plate) was relegated to astounding footnote rather than the symbol of a pennant-winning triumph.

Frequently, especially with the lengthened postseason, the best team doesn't win. In 2006, the Mets were better than the rest. Despite being deprived of veteran pitchers Pedro Martínez and Orlando Hernandez at a critical juncture, they were a notch above the St. Louis Cardinals.

However, Adam Wainwright's knee-bending curveball—a pitch unchallenged by Carlos Beltran as it traveled over the heart of the plate—sent the eighty-two-win Cards onto an eventual world championship and sent the Mets home without much to show for their ninety-seven-win efforts.

The void of this lost opportunity was vast in the immediate aftermath—made greater by the nine ensuing seasons that kept them from avenging this defeat. Vivid still is Aaron Heilman's fateful pitch to Yadier Molina—which ended up a two-run homer into the visiting bullpen to break a 1–1 top-of-the-ninth tie. It was the second time in three home games the Mets bullpen let an unsuspecting power threat provide the eventual winning home run in their last at-bat. The So Taguchi Game 2 blast against Billy Wagner, which precipitated a three-run frame, had a margin for error. Not Molina's.

New York had three outs to answer the St. Louis catcher's gut punch. Singles by Jose Valentin and Chavez and a two-out walk to Paul Lo Duca brought up Beltran, a renowned Cards killer and a bona fide playoff performer.

Turns out it was only a tease—false optimism furnished by evil baseball gods.

1. 1988 NLCS Game 4

It didn't have the abrupt, winner-take-all sense of finality. However, the domino effects this loss enacted spread faster and farther than any other defeat.

Had the Mets won and gone up three games to one on the inferior Los Angeles Dodgers, a team they had beaten handily during the regular season, they probably could have carried that momentum into the next day or at least been able to win in one of three chances. That would have meant a World Series for the second time in three years.

They might not have engaged in narrow-minded personnel moves—trading away long-term potential for short-term gains. And typical conjecture says the Mets wouldn't have begun a decline that started slow and then picked up steam—hurtling downward until reaching an audible 103-loss crash in 1993.

Instead of taking that commanding 3-1 series lead, the Mets lacked the killer instinct so ingrained in their framework during 1986. Fourth-inning back-to-back salvos by Darryl Strawberry and Kevin McReynolds, Gary Carter's sixth-inning RBI triple and Dwight Gooden's rhythm on the mound—not having allowed a hit since the first—put the Mets in position to place their foot on LA's throat.

Gooden started the top of the ninth, up 4–2, by letting leadoff hitter John Shelby get away. The walk brought up the tying run: Mike Scioscia—an unimposing contact-hitting catcher. Scioscia made contact—all the way beyond the right-field fence.

Thus began the sole-crushing defeat symptom that has become an unsavory staple of this franchise ever since.

For a franchise accustomed to snatching improbable October victories from certain defeat, suffering a reversal of fortune was a fate too difficult to bear. Kirk Gibson's twelfth-inning homer put the Dodgers ahead. A bases-loaded, one-out situation in the bottom half couldn't produce a run. Orel Hershiser came in to get the last out. Series tied.

After trading off victories in Games 5 and 6, Hershiser returned three days later to almost singlehandedly boot the Mets from the playoffs.

For eleven years, they never returned.

HONORABLE MENTION

1973 World Series Game 7

Two statistics augment the frustration stemming from almost reaching the pinnacle. New York actually outscored the Oakland A's 24–21 over the seven-game set. And a record-setting seventy-two men left on base is a stark representation of the Mets' squandered opportunities. The last two runners were stranded in a ninth inning that ended with a Wayne Garrett popout. Oakland won 5–2 behind homers from Bert Campaneris and MVP Reggie Jackson to best New York in the only statistic that matters.

2000 World Series Game 1

On the surface, the first Fall Classic between New York teams since 1956 ended relatively one-sided—with the Yankees prevailing in five games to take their third straight title. So far, yet so close—three of the four Mets losses were decided by a single run. Most painful of those might have been the series opener—a twelve-inning defeat marred by poor baserunning and a blown save. Armando Benitez took care of the ninth-inning blues, surrendering their one-run lead. Jose Vizcaino made his former team pay for their gaffes with a walk-off single in the twelfth.

2000 World Series Game 5

Up three-games-to-one and knocking on the door to a three-peat, Al Leiter strived to personally blockade the pinstripes from adding to their lavish trophy collection. Alas, Yankee resolve outlasted Al's grit. Successive two-out ninth-inning hits against the exhausted lefty scored two tie-breaking runs. As the Yankees celebrated their 26th championship on the Shea Stadium turf, it brought to life a Mets fans' haunting nightmare.

June 12, 2009, at Yankees

Luis Castillo showed why no pop fly is a sure out. Victory handshakes, to hail an 8–7 Mets win, practically began once Alex Rodriguez sent a Francisco Rodriguez pitch sky high. Castillo drifted toward the outfield grass from his second base position. Two Yankee runners aboard, Derek Jeter and Mark Teixeira, jogged—no need for full gait. Then, absurdly, the ball clanked off Castillo's mitt. Before the Mets realized what happened, both runs scored. Yankees 9, Mets 8. From this point on, faith in the most routine of plays remains feeble.

September 29, 2001, at Braves

Didn't we see this horror movie six days earlier? Armando Benitez's meltdown tour wandered to Atlanta and somehow developed more spectacularly than the previous disaster. After letting the Braves score three in the ninth during a September 23 encounter in Queens, Benitez couldn't retain a 5–1 lead in Turner Field. Brian Jordan, who hit the tying and winning homers in the previous implosion, delivered another killing blow—both for the Mets' chances of victory and hopes for catching the Braves in the NL East race.

BUSTS

10. SHAWN ABNER

The expectations and the players that fall woefully below them are incorporated into two distinct categories. There are those with well-heralded major league careers who come to their new team amid great fanfare and leave amid tremendous regret. Then there are the highly drafted prospects, such as Abner, who are slapped with a "can't miss" designation.

The Mets proved in 1984 why being afforded the privilege of the no. 1 overall pick doesn't have its end rewards. With plenty of time to decide, they took the eighteen-year-old outfielder out of Mechanicsburg, Pennsylvania.

Abner's progression through the minor league system was not as swift as other prized prospects. In fact, the Mets had seen enough by the end of 1986. He became part of the eight-player deal that sent Kevin Mitchell to San Diego in exchange for Kevin McReynolds.

He made it onto the Padres but was far from a significant contributor. From there, Abner went on to the Angels and White Sox before his career ended in 1992 with a .227 batting average, eleven homers and seventy-one RBIs.

9. BOBBY BONILLA

Who knew $29 million could make someone so upset?

Bonilla seemed to take this most-lucrative contract for granted. New GM Al Harazin, not exactly following in the footsteps of Frank Cashen, probably learned not to.

At his introductory press conference in December 1991, a happier (and richer) Bonilla crowed, "I know you all are gonna try, but you're not gonna be able to wipe the smile off my face." It was a red meat initiative for a ravenous New York media.

In truth, the Bronx native and his underwhelming band of overpaid associates were wholly responsible for giving Bobby a frown rather than upside-down. While the Mets collapsed to fifth place, Bonilla batted .249 with twenty-three doubles—a year after hitting .302 and collecting forty-four two-baggers for Pittsburgh.

Bonilla's mild on-field showing contrasted his volatile off-field temper. Of the many run-ins, he threatened Bob Klapich in response to his co-authored book detailing the travails of the '92 team.

The Mets traded the disgruntled Bonilla in 1995. But like a bad case of insanity, Steve Phillips brought him back four years later. Lo and behold, the results were no different. Bobby Bo and Bobby Valentine butted heads; he played his way onto the bench and played clubhouse poker with Rickey Henderson during Game 6 of the NLCS.

Released after '99, Bonilla left the Mets roster—but not the payroll. His exodus, and the deferred $1.19 million annual payment through 2035, has made each July 1 a pseudo-holiday.

8. Mo Vaughn/Roberto Alomar

Roberto Alomar aged quickly when he put on a Mets uniform and was gone within a year and a half. *Jerry Coli/Dreamstime.*

Steve Phillips' pre-2002 shopping spree needed to have a time machine on the buy list.

Only that would justify the amount given to a pair of diminished stars, attesting to the franchise's cockeyed obsession with short-term solutions.

When comparing the two thirty-four-year-old disappointments, Vaughn—the 1995 AL MVP with Boston who was acquired via trade from Anaheim—was the least awful. Coming off an injury that forced complete absence of the 2001 campaign, Mo moved at a pace that snails would consider glacial. Thus, his range and defensive ability at first base—bad before coming to New York—rated markedly worse.

Defense had never been a problem for Alomar, whose drop-off-the-table regression (in every phase) was most startling. The ten-time Gold Glove winner committed seventeen errors in a year and a half and the .306 career hitter in Toronto, Baltimore and elsewhere batted .365 in Queens.

Vaughn hit twenty-six home runs in '02 but had little value elsewhere. He played twenty-seven games in 2003 (for which he was paid $17 million) before a bad knee ended his season and his career. The ill-fated $8 million Alomar experiment terminated with a trade to the White Sox, and his Hall of Fame journey was effectively over.

7. Don Bosch

Submerged beneath a billow of wasted potential was the supposed savior in center field. GM Bing Devine trumpeted Bosch's entrance to the organization, via trade with Pittsburgh in December 1966, as the second coming of Willie Mays.

Film of minor league exploits were darn near impossible to find, so the New York press corps and even Mets manager Wes Westrum had to go by Devine's judgment instead of visual evidence. Whether Bosch really merited such lavish praise will never be determined, but he couldn't even manage to fulfill the role as a garden-variety major leaguer—much less a Hall of Famer.

Whether the cause was inane pressure or his own apprehension unconducive to a city focused on his every move, Bosch never looked the part. He stood at five feet, eight inches and barely overwhelmed the scales at 160 pounds.

"My God, they sent me a midget," Westrum remarked upon initially gazing at the twenty-four-year-old. And with gray hairs and ulcers, it might have been Benjamin Button.

Bosch could command no leadership fielding a position that demands it. As a switch-hitter, it didn't matter from which side he swung—he couldn't produce from either. In ninety-four games spanning two seasons, his batting average was .157, and those pipe-cleaner arms could only produce three home runs and nine RBIs.

The Mets gave up by October '68 and dealt him to the expansion Montreal Expos.

6. TONY FERNANDEZ

Proof that Shea Stadium can convert into a talent vacuum, behold Exhibit A. The four-time All-Star with the Blue Jays and Padres came to the Mets via an October 1992 trade with San Diego toting a reputation as a good leadoff man (with a lifetime .285 average), possessing plus speed and great range at shortstop.

It wouldn't take long before Met fans wondered why none of that repute traveled with him on his cross-country relocation.

He logged a mere forty-eight games as a shell of his former self. Fernandez hit .203 in April, dipping further to .191 for May. By June 11, the patience of the front office and manager Dallas Green ran thin. On June 11, the Mets transferred him back to Toronto. Instead of reciprocating evenly with a box of balls or weighted donuts, the Mets actually got a pitcher in return—and a modest one in Darrin Jackson.

Whatever skills were sucked out of Fernandez in New York reappeared when he rejoined the Jays—helping them to a second consecutive World Series title. He would latch on to another Fall Classic participant—the 1997 Cleveland Indians—and made two more trips to the All-Star Game.

5. KAZ MATSUI

If only every day could be like his first. Kaz was wonderful at opening acts—homering in each of his three season premieres with the Mets. It's the rest of his seasons that were troublesome.

As the Seattle Mariners struck gold in signing Ichiro Suzuki and the Yankees found an everyday outfielder in Hideki Matsui, the Mets—which previously had Tsuyoshi Shinjo—tried their hand at bringing another Japanese hitting superstar to the United States.

A .272 average and 125 hits weren't exactly the return on investment for a three-year, $20 million contract. Buyer's remorse set in further with his incapability at shortstop. Not only did he commit twenty-three errors, but his presence briefly stunted the growth of José Reyes—who struggled at second base.

Matsui and Reyes flipped for good in 2005. Kaz gloved better but batted egregiously worse. Playing twenty-seven fewer games, the RBI total dropped from forty-four to twenty-four and his hit accumulation pretty much halved.

Shortly after his starting position disappeared in June 2006, so did his roster spot. The Mets shipped Kaz off to the Colorado Rockies, which instantly demoted him to the minors.

4. "GENERATION K"

This is a cautionary tale for any franchise (including our own) that pins its hopes on a youthful crop of delicate arms.

The triumvirate of Bill Pulsipher, Jason Isringhausen and Paul Wilson arrived to the bigs in the mid-1990s with lofty ambitions and a catchy nickname.

But even the best-laid marketing plans can derail. If blame was to be laid on a specific reason why the high hopes this trio perpetuated came crashing down to earth, injuries—and what led to them—are the chief culprit.

Relatively speaking, Isringhausen is the success story. Opening to rave reviews in 1995—a 9-2 record with a 2.82 ERA—three operations on his right arm, tuberculosis and a broken wrist (suffered when he impaled fist into trashcan) led to some two years on the mend. Traded in 1999, he eventually reinvented himself as a closer and even had a second Mets act in 2011.

Both Pulsipher, the organization's Minor League Player of the Year in 1994, and Wilson, the no. 1 overall pick out of Florida State that same season, were victims of overuse during development and pretty much damaged products when they reached big league status.

In his only season with the Mets—1996—Wilson went 5-12 with a 5.38 ERA. He would eventually miss all of 1999, and by 2005 (a record of 40-58 with a 4.86 ERA), his career was over. A sore elbow ended Pulsipher's 1995 campaign three weeks early. The pain lingered into the next spring training, and torn ligaments required Tommy John surgery that wiped out the better part of two seasons. He never regained his control again.

The Mets anticipated these three each would perennially challenge the twenty-win plateau like Seaver, Koosman and Matlack did in the '70s. Instead, they combined to win twenty-nine for the totality of their MLB careers.

3. STEVE CHILCOTT

There isn't much separating him from Reggie Jackson.

Not in final career statistics—there's a canyon between them in that respect. But in regards to when they were taken by big league pursuers, it's nothing more than a draft pick.

The Mets made the notorious choice of selecting Chilcott as first overall pick in 1966, leaving the Kansas City A's the chance of grabbing the slugger from Arizona State—the soon-to-be "Mr. October" and executioner of New York's 1973 World Series dreams.

While Jackson became a star of the postseason (and every season, for that matter), it's hard to say what Chilcott could have been had injuries not gotten in the way. The catcher dislocated his shoulder in the Florida State League in 1967, initiating a calamitous pattern that hindered on-field performance.

After one season in Triple-A, he was released by the Mets in 1971. Chilcott also fizzled out in the Yankees farm system and holds the dubious distinction of being one of two top overall draft selections to have never played a major league game.

2. JASON BAY

They should have kept him when they had the chance. The Mets got Bay as part of an inconsequential trade with the Expos in March 2002, then quickly shipped him to San Diego.

Fast-forward seven years, and the 2004 Rookie of the Year is averaging thirty homers and nearly one hundred RBIs with regularity.

His 2009 season with Boston featured 36 dingers and 119 driven in, which made him well sought after on the free agent market. With open arms and wads of cash, New York reeled in Bay with a four-year deal worth $66 million.

Minus the "Green Monster" to benefit him, it was questioned whether Bay would

Perhaps a bigger, pitcher-friendly stadium caused his power numbers to recede. But Jason Bay didn't come remotely close to what he accomplished in Pittsburgh and Boston. *Slgckgc/Flickr.*

falter when faced with the swirling winds and deep fences Citi Field presented. The decline was swift and spectacularly steep.

With production widely disproportionate to his earnings, Bay hit thirty fewer homers, had seventy-two fewer RBIs and batted .259. Nobody could question his effort (unlike others on this list), as shown by his crashing into the Dodger Stadium fence in July (which left him with whiplash).

It was one of the rare moments he hit something hard.

Bay never really improved in 2011. And by 2012, his batting average fell to .165 and his rank fell to platoon player. For someone to be paid so much and do so little could be considered illegal in most states.

The Mets broke ties with Bay, as he meandered to the Mariners for 2013 before being released that August.

1. VINCE COLEMAN

Rare is the person who can agitate the same team before he's there and while he's with them. But Coleman possessed such a rare and unenviable quality.

From 1985 to 1990 in St. Louis, he averaged ninety-two steals and was successful on sixty-four of sixty-seven attempts against New York.

Losing the prodigal swing yet petulant temperament of Darryl Strawberry to the Los Angeles Dodgers, it was Frank Cashen's ingenious plan to replace Darryl's power with Vince's speed.

New seeds were sowed in the old Strawberry field. It wouldn't take long before weeds sprouted.

Pilfering money more aggressively than stealing bases, Coleman swiped ninety-nine over three years. A modest total compared to what he did with the Cardinals. He missed more than half of the allotted games—partly because of fragility, mostly due to stupidity.

The countless faults away from the playing field made him the poster child for the franchise's disastrous public relations era.

He cursed out coach Mike Cubbage, shoved manager Jeff Torborg (for which he was suspended), recklessly swung a golf club in the clubhouse and whacked Dwight Gooden (forcing the ace to miss a start) and became a target of a rape investigation.

Mets management tried to trade him after 1992—except nobody wanted to take on such an aggravation.

The toxicity he emanated continued to poison the surrounding atmosphere until he officially set his Mets career ablaze on July 24, 1993. Coleman thought it would be a novel idea to toss a firecracker out his car window. The explosion of said pyrotechnics injured three bystanders—including a two-year-old girl. Initially charged with a felony, Coleman pleaded guilty to a misdemeanor.

The team placed him on administrative leave, then dumped him—eating the $3 million that remained on his ill-advised contract. It was a price worth paying to see him gone.

When they talk about going out with a bang, this is not what they mean.

PART V

THE CLUBHOUSE

BEST TRADES

10. Ron Darling and Walt Terrell from the Rangers for Lee Mazzilli

Team priorities don't always mesh with sentimentality.

During a serious rebuilding phase, general manager Frank Cashen desired additional assets for his restoration project. His roster lacked much trade value, but the Brooklyn-born Mazzilli had enough. Risking backlash from fans who wanted to see him and women who wanted to marry him, Cashen exchanged the popular outfielder/heartthrob for a pair of minor league arms. This, by no means, was a blockbuster move. However, it initiated a chain of positive outcomes for the Mets.

With nineteen wins in forty-two starts and a moderate ERA, Terrell turned out adequately. Yet his shipment to Detroit in December 1984 brought a key piece for 1986 and beyond: Howard Johnson.

Darling was hardly insignificant. Coming up to the show in late 1983, the Yalie mastered a split-fingered fastball that helped him win ninety-nine games—fourth all-time—while claiming the only Gold Glove ever awarded to a Mets pitcher.

Then came a satisfying boomerang effect. Mazzilli, having languished with another woeful club in Pittsburgh, returned to his hometown team in August 1986. The best player during the leanest of seasons was back for the glorious World Series journey as a factor off the bench.

9. Félix Millán and George Stone from the Braves for Gary Gentry and Danny Frisella

The mistaken belief that certain players wouldn't amount to as much as once imagined is part bad luck, part bad foresight. Inversely, November 1, 1972, marked a time in which the Mets beheld a psychic-like look into the near future.

Gentry won thirteen games as a 1969 rookie, went the distance in the NL East clincher on September 24 and was the winning pitcher in Game 3 of the World Series. But his career was not taking a tremendous upward track.

The Mets deemed him and reliever Frisella, who regressed after an outstanding 1971 out of the bullpen, expendable enough to nab Millán, a three-time All-Star and former Gold Glover, and Stone, coming off a dreadful 5.51 ERA posting in 1972, from Atlanta.

New York's two newcomers fit beautifully into the Mets system, which relied heavily on pitching and defense. During a year in which starters were dropping like flies from injury, Millán played in 153 games and helped the Mets turn a National League–leading 179 double plays while hitting .290 and establishing a franchise record 185 hits as the no. 2 batter in the order.

Stone, often punished for having to pitch mainly in the launching pad of Atlanta, thrived in pitcher-friendly Shea Stadium—going 12-3 with a 2.80 ERA.

While he could never come close to repeating his 1973, Millán remained steady. He typified the term *everyday player* and set team records for hits (191) and doubles (37) in 1975.

In cruel twists of fate, both Gentry and Frisella developed chronic arm injuries while with the Braves. Gentry had retired by 1975, and Frisella was killed in an accident on New Year's Day, 1977.

8. DAVID CONE AND CHRIS JELIC FROM THE ROYALS FOR RICK ANDERSON, MAURO GOZZO AND ED HEARN

With such a strong rotation heading into 1988, there could be several educated guesses as to who would stand out most prominently. None of those guesses would have been David Cone.

Although he was a filler in the depleted staff of a year ago, the talent the Mets had coming back lent itself to bump the twenty-five-year-old right-hander to the bullpen. Another opportunity knocked when Rick Aguilera went down with a right elbow injury. Cone burst through as a big-league revelation. A shutout of the Atlanta Braves on May 3 confirmed he wasn't solely a spot starter.

A 20-3 record and a 2.22 ERA (to finish third in the Cy Young Award voting) validated the trade Frank Cashen executed with Kansas City in March 1987 several times over.

David Cone transformed from conventional part-time starter to sensational ace almost in a blink. His superb 1988 season was the first of six two-hundred-plus strikeout campaigns. The Mets benefited from the lopsided deal they made with the Royals in '87. And when they faltered by August 1992, the Toronto Blue Jays took advantage of the Mets' offloading. Cone helped the Jays win a World Series. He'd win many more, as well as throwing a perfect game, with the cross-town Yankees. *Jerry Coli/Dreamstime.*

The Royals and John Schuerholz, a future Hall of Famer who rarely found himself this outmaneuvered, saw an unproven arm with potential hindered by a serious knee operation.

The Mets gladly received a power pitcher who used changing release points and a devastating slider to win 61 percent of his decisions, fan 8.7 batters every nine innings and pace his team in strikeouts four out of seven years.

7. Bob Ojeda, Chris Bayer, Tom McCarthy and John Mitchell from the Red Sox for John Christensen, Wes Gardner, La Schelle Tarver and Calvin Schiraldi

It's hard to find faults in a 1985 Mets team that won ninety-eight games and went neck-and-neck with the Cardinals for the East Division title. But if there was one surefire way to take down the Cardinals—or any team—it would be with starting pitching depth.

Ojeda was thought to be a left-handed adjunct slotted in the middle or at the end of the rotation. Not long after 1986 began, he rose to the top. While

Gary Carter is perceived to be the "final piece" to the championship puzzle, the Mets would never have gained ten additional victories on their season-ending total if not for Ojeda's 18-5 record and 2.57 ERA.

The chief asset New York received helped it win in '86 and, in a way, so did one of the pieces it gave up.

Schiraldi was miles away from modest during his cups of coffee with the Mets in 1984 and '85—a gaudy 7.63 ERA in 43.2 innings. Due to stellar success and the injuries around him, he became Boston's closer by August 1986 and was on the cusp of closing out the World Series altogether.

That was, until Schiraldi returned to the timid pitcher the Mets knew he was capable of being. And to their great appreciation, it came to form with the championship at stake.

6. Noah Syndergaard, Wuilmer Becerra, John Buck and Travis d'Arnaud from the Blue Jays for R.A. Dickey, Mike Nickeas and Josh Thole

Easy to forget, but Dickey arguably had the best pitching season of the decade. At age thirty-seven and after failing as a conventional pitcher for several teams, the knuckleballer won twenty-one games in 2012 and became the Mets' fifth Cy Young Award recipient.

As warm as Dickey's story is, the cold reality of this business reared its head not more than a couple months later. Dickey could still be good, as knucklers don't deteriorate as quickly, but probably not Cy Young good. And the Mets were far from good.

Thus, they willingly relinquished the best piece of their recent past for a potential battery of the future. The Mets turned out to be right in guessing Dickey had reached peak value. It's certainly a testament to him that he remained a viable starter in the league, but his ERA since '12 has been higher than 4.00 and his single-year strikeout tallies never were as high as it was when he attained 230 during the hardware-gaining campaign.

It might be a bit presumptuous to make an evaluation on the two most important pieces the Mets received. Still, d'Arnaud probably looks like, at best, a starting catcher—not a franchise catcher. Syndergaard, meanwhile, has already established himself an ace (or no. 1a) and a regular Cy Young contender himself, just as long as he remembers that he's training to be a starting pitcher, not "World's Strongest Man."

5. YOENIS CESPEDES FROM THE TIGERS FOR LUIS CESSA AND MICHAEL FULMER

Sandy Alderson would not, and could not, stand with the status quo.

A pitching staff, maturing on the fly, was keeping the 2015 Mets above .500 and within arm's reach of the NL East–leading Washington Nationals—despite an offense short on power and shorter on depth.

Terry Collins likely had to hold back his lunch filling out the lineup card. John Mayberry Jr., Eric Campbell and Anthony Recker comprised a middle of the order capable of challenging for first place—if that place was Triple-A. This is a sampling of what the New York Mets were trotting out in late July. A box full of kittens would be more threatening.

Hired as general manager in 2010, Sandy Alderson's most significant moves include the deals made for Noah Syndergaard in 2012 and Yoenis Cespedes under the wire of the trade deadline in 2015. *Courtesy of Jim Maggiore.*

As the July 31 trade deadline loomed, Mets management bewailed over the failed attempt two days before—however it failed—to acquire Carlos Gomez from Milwaukee.

Jay Bruce became the focus next, but a path to that deal became impassable. Try again next year, Sandy. The target then became Cespedes—eighteen home runs, sixty-one RBIs and a .293 average with Detroit.

At somewhere way too close to 4:00 p.m. cutoff, Alderson shipped off Cessa and Fulmer for an instant offensive upgrade while avoiding a village full of pitchfork-wielders and torch-bearers at his Citi Field office by sundown.

But no Mets fan could have anticipated the ripple effect his addition would have. The lead driver in a three-month thrill ride to the NL pennant, Cespedes was the switch-flipper on a lineup that evolved from powerless to powerhouse. Fifty-seven games, seventeen home runs and forty-four RBIs later, the Mets were postseason-bound.

4. Donn Clendenon from the Expos for Jay Carden, David Colon, Kevin Collins, Steve Renko and Terry Dailey

As Cespedes was to 2015, Clendenon was to 1969. The analogous nature of these transactions isn't connected by statistics but by impact on the eventual result.

Already staggering baseball's foundation in mid-June, the time of the old trade deadline, the Mets still trailed the Chicago Cubs by eight games in the NL East. Pitching was plentiful, but the contact-driven offense averaged 3.8 runs.

It's not about getting the best player. It's about getting the right player. Clendenon was a seamless fit. And Donn, languishing with the expansion Expos after leaving the Pirates and even briefly retiring, had found the right team. He deposited twelve home runs, thirty-seven RBIs and a .777 OPS—numbers which, while impressive, don't scream out season-changing catalyst.

But beyond the periphery, Clendenon reinforced the Mets' lineup against left-handed pitching, deepened a relatively thin bench, was defensively solid at first base and added experience to a team that had never faced the pressures of a pennant race.

It led to the overthrow of the Chicago Cubs' NL East lead, a steamroll to the division title and a conquering of the National League pennant. Those happenings were prologue to what took place in the World Series—when he batted .357 and went deep in Games 2, 4 and 5 to garner Most Valuable Player award honors.

Donn Clendenon's 1969 began with the expansion Montreal Expos and ended with him as the World Series MVP with the Mets, thanks to the mid-June trade that gave muscle to the New York offense. *The Sporting News Archives/Wikimedia Commons.*

While the five players traded for him proved to be of small consequence, Clendenon enjoyed a better season in 1970: slugging .515, charting an OPS of .863 and driving in ninety-seven runs.

3. Gary Carter from the Expos for Hubie Brooks, Mike Fitzgerald, Herm Winningham and Floyd Youmans

From 1983 to 1984, a twenty-two-win improvement, they crawled out from their cellar dwelling and ventured up a few flights in the process. Then came the last significant stride toward the summit.

A good hitting catcher who can also play solid defense and nurture pitchers is akin to a diamond in the rough. Frank Cashen, and just about everyone else who watched, knew this was their glaring weakness. While serviceable, Fitzgerald provided next to no impact on offense.

When the Mets' GM got word that the Montreal Expos were dismantling, he stumbled across a gold mine. Carter—a two-time All-Star MVP, Gold Glover, middle-of-the-order bat and natural-born leader—checked every box.

Even if it took dispatching the popular Brooks, a 1978 first round pick who enjoyed a twenty-four-game hitting streak in May, it was a deal worth making. The Mets had upgraded from having a catching void to having the best catcher. And with it came anticipation for a season unlike any they had in more than a decade.

The perceived reputation about his fixation for the camera and unabashed enthusiasm took a back seat posthaste.

Carter immediately curried favor with the public and his new teammates. A walk-off homer on Opening Day is a good way to do that. But so is a career-high thirty-two home runs; one hundred RBIs; a knack for cajoling a young starting rotation of Gooden, Darling and Fernandez to newfound success; and a blistering September that spurred the Mets to ninety-eight victories and belief that the pinnacle wasn't far.

By next year, Gary got what he came for, and New York got what it wanted.

2. Mike Piazza from the Marlins for Geoff Goetz, Preston Wilson and Ed Yarnall

It was a connecting point, not a permanent landing spot. That middle ground turned out to be Miami, the home of the Florida Marlins and a temporary locale for Piazza after the Los Angeles Dodgers sent him eastward.

Contract squabbling with LA ownership caused a mega-swap with Florida on May 15, 1998. But teams itching to add were cognizant that the Marlins—offloading players at a liquidation sale rate—weren't keeping him.

An insatiable appetite consumed a public insistent that management resist reluctance on what could become a transformative figure in the organization—one capable of turning the Mets from plucky overachievers into mighty pennant challengers.

Eight days after settling in South Beach, Queens got its special Piazza delivery. His ingress initiated tremendous buzz, even by New York standards. Standing ovations were easy to come by in his May 23 debut—less so in the following weeks.

Boos radiating from Shea when he didn't perform up to savior-like standards were just bumps in the road. Piazza ended his three-month Big Apple stint by hitting .348 with twenty-three home runs and a $91 million contract in the offseason—prolonging an eight-year stay in New York that earned him the rare distinctions of a retired number and a Hall of Fame plaque.

1. KEITH HERNANDEZ FROM THE CARDINALS FOR NEIL ALLEN AND RICK OWNBEY

In Frank Cashen's efforts to restore respectability, he had already cultivated promising players who had reached—or were approaching—the major league level. But no amount of veteran leadership would come from the farm system.

That's when at the edge of the 1983 trading deadline—ironically, six years to the evening when the franchise parted with relevancy by trading Tom Seaver—Cashen pulled a coup that sent the Mets' rebuild on the accelerator. Hernandez and St. Louis manager Whitey Herzog, formerly a Mets director of player development, were at odds—allegedly due to Keith's rumored cocaine use. Like a heaven-sent carrier pigeon, the Cardinals' first baseman was plopped in New York's lap—and all it had to give up was a declining relief pitcher and another arm who would make seven more big league starts and win once.

The Cards were fleeced. The Mets, of course, were ecstatic to be getting a player of Hernandez's caliber. Unfortunately, the initial feeling wasn't mutual. Going from a team fresh off a World Series title to a team languishing in misery was not a venture in which Keith wanted to partake.

"The Mets deserved and received no respect," said Hernandez, who batted .306 over ninety-five games in '83. "And here I was, coming over from

Keith Hernandez stuck it to his former team on several occasions while with New York, including a key game-winning hit during the 1985 pennant race. *Jerry Coli/Dreamstime.*

the world champions to a team with four last-place finishes in six years, and the other two next-to-last. Banished. Shipped to the Siberia of baseball."

Cashen convinced Keith of the prospects that had arrived and were in the pipeline. The sell job worked. Hernandez was the spearhead that commanded respect from teammates. In turn, the Mets got respect from the rest of the league before reaching its upper echelon.

June 15, 1983, turned out to be the turning point in Mets history that affected every progressive move to follow.

WORST TRADES

10. Rick Reed to the Twins for Matt Lawton

Reed spent seven years hunting for consistency. With four organizations, he traversed countless miles between the majors and minors and was even a potential replacement player as the strike carried over into 1995.

His search for steadiness ceased in New York, beginning in 1997—a year in which he went 13-9 and posted the sixth-best NL ERA (2.89). Twice he was an All-Star—1998 and 2001.

But no more than a month after his second Midsummer Classic trip, he was off to Minnesota. In return, the Mets got Lawton, an outfielder that general manager Steve Phillips believed could aid their difficulty in scoring runs.

Although the Mets rallied from thirteen and a half games out on August 18 to within three to nearly catch the Braves for the NL East title, the offense never showed significant improvement. Lawton, a .305 hitter with the Twins a year before, batted .243 and was basically a non-factor. Also lacking was a starting pitcher who could come through in a big spot—like Reed showed in a must-win early October 1999 contest with postseason hopes waning.

While the Mets were hurt by this exchange, for their departed right-hander—a former journeyman who retired by 2003—the trade cut deeper. "Baseball kinda died for us, my wife and I," he said to the *New York Daily News* in 2010. "I was tore up."

9. Xavier Nady to the Pirates for Oliver Perez and Roberto Hernandez

It was the cab ride heard 'round Queens: the sideswipe that changed the course of the 2006 season.

The unfortunate passenger, Duaner Sanchez, suffered a separated shoulder as part of a late-night July 30 Miami taxi accident with a drunk driver.

Season-ending surgery was required for the yielder of sixteen runs in 55.1 innings.

As Sanchez would fail to regain the form that made him one of the NL's first-rate set-up men, the short-term consequence was that it divested the Mets of their bridge to closer Billy Wagner.

General manager Omar Minaya, before the incident, was focused on adding starting pitching. Now, he had to scramble for bullpen help.

The Mets thought they might have been getting the prospect Oliver Perez was drummed up to be. Instead, they received a pitcher who still couldn't cure his erraticism. *Wikimedia Commons.*

With leverage slim to none, Minaya was willing to hand over his starting left fielder to Pittsburgh. In return, the Pirates sent Hernandez—a veteran who spent 2005 with the Mets—back to his old team. Thrown in was Perez, a once-touted prospect struggling with location issues. The immediate turnout wasn't horrific, as Hernandez had a 3.48 ERA and Perez overcame early struggles to pitch decently in postseason assignments.

Perez's continued wildness, noted by his league-leading 105 walks in 2008, made the careless three-year, $36 million deal a financial burden.

Greater lament from this trade is born of how it occurred and what could have been done instead to help New York into the playoffs.

8. Kevin Mitchell, Stan Jefferson and Shawn Abner to the Padres for Kevin McReynolds, Gene Walter and Adam Ging

On a 1986 squad rich with hell-raisers, Kevin Mitchell was the resident badass. Far removed from the San Diego–based gangs he immersed himself in growing up, Mitchell—whom Davey Johnson slotted in six different positions during his rookie year—still had the look of someone who fought out of enjoyment and openly discussed his vehement past around the clubhouse.

"Some people here thought [he] was a time bomb ready to explode," a team official said in a 1993 *Sports Illustrated* article.

That was affirmed only in on-field execution—winning the NL MVP in 1989. Except that occurred in the uniform of the San Francisco Giants.

In between was a stop in his hometown forged by a Mets front office that overlooked the player's mental toughness and suitability to the pressures of performing in New York. A comparison of the two principles of this trade from 1987 to 1990 stacks up slightly more favorable for Mitchell against the Mets' left-field acquisition.

The new Kevin hit 102 homers and 110 doubles, drove in 361 runs, batted .276 and had an OPS of .807. The old Kevin hit 123 homers and 103 doubles, drove in 388, batted .278 and had an OPS of .882.

The new Kevin came in third in the 1988 MVP voting. The old Kevin came in first in '89. But the scales really get tipped on a less tangible aspect. Mitchell brought the attitude that Kevin could never replace, and that edge the Mets had in '86 was noticeably absent in the years after.

7. JEFF KENT AND JOSE VIZCAINO TO THE INDIANS FOR CARLOS BAERGA AND ALVARO ESPINOZA

Perhaps the Cleveland Indians knew their switch-hitting second baseman, .300 or better in each season from 1991 to 1995 and an RBI machine, was headed on a downward track. Perhaps Baerga was having an off year through four months of 1996.

Regardless, the Mets snatched the Tribe's depreciating goods, then saw him erode further. Whatever hitting ability he had remaining in Cleveland stayed there when he moved to New York. Baerga, out of shape and out of place, sagged beneath the dreaded Mendoza line—posting a .193 average for the remainder of '96 (and .053 from the right side), then managed to drive in a combined 105 runs over the next two years—the same amount he had for all of 1992. Baerga's slowed step also restricted his fielding range. So, he couldn't hit, couldn't run and couldn't glove. Other than that, no problem.

Espinoza, pretty much a throw-in to the deal, only had a Met cameo role.

Kent, who spent fewer than forty games in Cleveland, made a second team regret letting him go when he established himself as the most prolific home run–hitting second baseman of all time with the San Francisco Giants. He won the NL MVP in 2000, the same year Vizcaino burned the Mets with his walk-off hit in Game 1 of the World Series.

6. Scott Kazmir and Joselo Diaz to the Devil Rays for Victor Zambrano and Bartolome Fortunato

Final judgment on a trade can't be passed for at least a year—often more. This one, though, had bewilderment written all over it from the onset.

Returning to this unfortunately recurrent trope called desperation, the Mets front office saw the division title in 2004 like the parched see water fountains in the Sahara. New York, behind by three games to the Atlanta Braves in the NL East in late July, sat in a dreary spot as they groped for pitching assets at the deadline.

Pittsburgh and Tampa Bay were much too willing to comply. The Mets mortgaged a tremendous chunk of their future—the twenty-year-old left-handed Kazmir, a top-flight pitching prospect—for twenty-eight-year-old Zambrano, who had a 4.43 ERA and led the American League in two categories nobody wants to head: wild pitches and walks. But Mets pitching coach Rick Peterson claimed he was an easy fix.

The trade for Zambrano occurred the same day as Kris Benson from the Pittsburgh Pirates in a less costly exchange. Before each could settle in, their new club lost three straight to a Braves team obviously toying with the rest of the division race—obvious, except to the bait-taking Mets.

Hook, line and sinker—the Mets were down to fourth place and ninety-one losses. Their quick fade to black made the short-sided decision, highly criticized in the immediate aftermath, more questionable.

Zambrano's ERA actually improved to 3.86 for the rest of '04 but then ballooned—to 4.17 after '05 (with a 7-12 record) and 6.75 for five starts in '06, until an elbow injury effectively ended his career.

In fairness, Kazmir didn't surge into the stratosphere as some believed. But at least, until recently, he had a working arm—enough to garner three All-Star trips and a strikeout crown.

5. Rusty Staub and Bill Laxton to the Tigers for Mickey Lolich and Bobby Baldwin

Lolich was the World Series MVP in 1968 and contended for the AL Cy Young in 1972 and '73. Too bad he was traded for in 1975, because over the course of the two seasons leading up, Mickey saw unflattering increases: his loss total, his ERA and his weight.

The Mets were undeterred by a potential decline and, likewise, were buying the stock of Mike Vail as a starting right fielder—especially when he concluded his initial big-league stint with a .302 average and a twenty-three-game September hitting streak.

So they sent away Staub, the incumbent twenty-nine-year-old right fielder coming off a 105 RBI season, and a minor league pitcher to the Motor City for Lolich and a prospect.

The deal was regretted within weeks after it went through. Vail ravaged his knee during the winter while playing basketball, sat out most of the '76 campaign and never came close to returning to his optimal condition.

Lolich went 8-13 in his only season sporting a Met uniform, while Staub enjoyed his three most productive years as a professional before returning to New York in 1981.

4. Amos Otis and Bob Johnson to the Royals for Joe Foy

Naturally, the offseason is the period when most transactions are consummated. Proving true holiday spirit can be demonstrated to a fault, the Mets were prone to absurd generosity in December amid the afterglow following their 1969 title.

What turned out to be the first of several winters of discontent during the 1970s began with an exchange between New York and Kansas City. Unfortunately, what the Royals received was of far higher quality than what the Royals relinquished. The Mets were stuck with a lump of coal.

Foy possessed the look of a long-term third baseman: a strong throwing arm and a right-handed power threat who hit sixteen home runs for pennant-winning Boston in 1967 at age twenty-four.

"Can't miss" became "complete miss" within a few months of the '70 season. Foy participated in ninety-nine games, yet it's difficult to prove if he was fully engaged. Struggling with issues both personal and professional, the Bronx native could only muster a .237 batting average, six homers, thirty-seven RBIs and twelve doubles.

Considering the baggage brought on top of the production he lacked, Foy was one and done in New York.

Otis stayed in Kansas City much longer. By leading the league in doubles twice and winning a stolen base crown in 1971, he made the All-Star team in each of his first four years, becoming a Gold Glove earner and an MVP candidate on multiple occasions.

With Otis initiating an emergence from expansion and George Brett taking it from there, the Royals became annual contenders and probably mailed the Mets greeting cards in appreciation for their gift.

3. LENNY DYKSTRA, ROGER MCDOWELL AND TOM EDENS TO THE PHILLIES FOR JUAN SAMUEL

On a Sunday afternoon in Philadelphia, completing a weekend series together, the Mets and the Phillies engaged in swap meet bartering.

And it was the New Yorkers who got their pockets picked. The trade is as perplexing now as it was then.

Dykstra, while sharing center-field duties with Mookie Wilson, ranked among the team's top eight in WAR from 1986 to 1989. And at age twenty-six, it stood to reason that he'd only improve. McDowell, age twenty-eight, wasn't worth tossing to a division rival, either.

Samuel, an All-Star in 1987, regressed to a below-average talent in '88. He maintained his subpar status through June 18, 1989—when his locale went up the Jersey Turnpike.

The Mets might have thought they could revive Samuel to the level he reached two years ago. But it was a deal dead on arrival. An immediate furor arose among fans who embraced Dykstra's aggressiveness and McDowell's eccentricity, only to intensify when it became apparent Samuel was lost at the plate (hitting .228) and further adrift in center field—a position he couldn't adjust to while in Philly. It didn't help that Samuel hated being in New York in the first place. He was gone by December.

McDowell continued to boost the Phillies with the same sinkerball he slung to such significant effect with the Mets, but the sting of losing Dykstra lingered longest. The 1993 Phillies resembled the '86 Mets in hardscrabble identity—with "Nails" being the common denominator.

Much to the Mets' chagrin, Lenny Dykstra went from platoon outfielder in New York to an All-Star and MVP candidate for Philadelphia in 1993. *Jerry Coli/Dreamstime.*

2. TOM SEAVER TO THE REDS FOR PAT ZACHRY, DOUG FLYNN, STEVE HENDERSON AND DAN NORMAN

June 15, 1977—a date in Mets history that will live in infamy. That night, the stubbornness of a team's two most prominent figures, for better and for worse, reached its tipping point.

Seaver should have been a Met for life. The three Cy Young Awards, nearly two hundred victories and thousands of strikeouts were as imperative as the identity he stamped on the team since his arrival in 1967. He was the most marketable player in the most marketable city.

This was of little significance to tight-fisted team chairman M. Donald Grant. His perception of cost-benefit analysis radically went in the direction of choices that aided his wallet and not the fortunes of the team he was overseeing. And he publicly aired out his grievances with the star pitcher's demand to be paid to the level of his immense value.

It devolved into a schism that couldn't be mended. Forever called the "Midnight Massacre," Seaver was dealt to Cincinnati, and Grant was cemented as persona non grata.

Well, *this* is unusual. Seeing Tom Seaver in anything other than a Mets uniform is downright wrong. After trading Seaver to the Reds in 1977, you'd expect newer management would've learned to avoid such a PR blunder when the legend returned in 1983. Instead, the Mets left Seaver unprotected in the lead-up to a free agent compensation draft. The Chicago White Sox scooped up the thirty-nine-year-old in January 1984, and less than two years later—August 4, 1985—he notched his 300th win down the road at Yankee Stadium. *Jerry Coli/Dreamstime.*

The cumulative Wins Above Replacement for the players the Mets received over their careers in New York (10.1 combined) was only slightly above Seaver's best WAR season (9.5 in 1973). And it certainly couldn't measure his stature.

Naturally, the subtraction of Seaver served as an organizational anchor. The Mets sank to the bottom in attendance and in the standings for the foreseeable future. "The Franchise" was gone—literally and figuratively. As Seaver departed, all hope vanished, too.

1. NOLAN RYAN, DON ROSE, LEROY STANTON AND FRANCISCO ESTRADA TO THE ANGELS FOR JIM FREGOSI

Who would have predicted that the young fireball right-hander from Texas would gain enough control of his fastball to endure for almost three decades and become a benchmark of pitching durability?

If Gil Hodges and GM Bob Scheffing did, he would have done more of it in New York and none of it in Anaheim. The Mets manager and general manager spotted abundant potential but were not willing to wait any longer for the potential to turn into the consistent results they had been promised since 1966.

With a starting staff well-established behind Seaver and Koosman and with a glaring need for third base consistency (after the flailing and failing of Joe Foy), they made what turned out to be one of the most fateful oversights in the annals of baseball dealings.

On December 10, 1971, Ryan and three prospects went to the California Angels for Jim Fregosi, a six-time All-Star—at shortstop. The trade drew quiet criticism initially. Those criticisms were totally reinforced once the Mets experienced a double barrel of misfortune in the aftermath.

Fregosi broke his right thumb during the early portion of 1972. He played 101 games that year and 43 the next before being sold to the Texas Rangers. Over the next three seasons of Ryan's remarkable and extensive twenty-seven-year career, he threw three of his eventual record-setting seven no-hitters while *averaging* nearly 360 strikeouts.

INTERNAL FEUDS

10. Darryl Strawberry vs. Keith Hernandez

Long on talent, but short on wisdom—Strawberry was equal parts powerful and pout-able.

As clubhouse leader, the words spoken and actions taken by Hernandez were held in higher regard than those of any other Met. So when Keith's tepid support for Darryl's spring training contract dispute became known around Port St. Lucie, Straw stirred.

The consternation permeated as the team yearbook photo awaited. It's much like those picture days you experience in school—minus the influx of New York–area news reporters and TV cameras. At least Strawberry was there to inject his brand of preteen immaturity.

Bud Harrelson, then bench coach, instructed that No. 18 (Strawberry) be next to No. 17 (Hernandez). "I'd rather sit next to my real friends," Darryl responded.

Hernandez, addressing Strawberry, retorted, "Why don't you grow up, you baby?"

Darryl shot back, "Why do you have to be saying those things about me?" and then welted in Keith's direction.

After a swing-and-a-miss, both were instantly restrained amid close quarters. Darryl, locked in the arms of his teammates, shouted to Hernandez: "I've been tired of you for years," before threatening Gary Carter (who had also voiced mild displeasure) with "You're next."

No principal's office was needed. Keith and Darryl ironed out their differences in a closed-door session mediated by the team psychiatrist.

9. Jordany Valdespin vs. Terry Collins

On May 10, 2013, Valdespin bat-flipped, admired his work and strutted joyously around the bases with a bottom-of-the-ninth homer. But this was no walk-off. It made the score 7-2. Thus, he became a miscreant in one of the unwritten baseball laws—drawing the ire of the opposing Pirates and even his own team.

An old-school manager, Collins was irritated by Jordany's grandstanding. He sent him up the next night in another pinch-hitting situation—cognizant that the Pirates would fulfill another rule of the sport that's never been printed but has always been understood. A vengeful pitch went straight toward Valdespin. The twenty-five-year-old angrily walked to first and remained angry as he found no solace in the dugout.

When his deteriorating contributions warranted a demotion to Triple-A, Collins delivered the news face-to-face in the locker room. Some players take it well, some take it badly. Jordanny took it atrociously.

He demanded he be placed on the disabled list, claimed a phantom injury, spewed expletives and called his manager (check that—*former* manager) something rhyming with "dockmucker." But Valdespin sucked as well, with a .188 batting average, a .250 on-base percentage and a .316 OPS.

Jordany retreated to Las Vegas—presumably to improve his skills and wash his mouth out with soap—and determined that cheating would be a better solution than working hard. But he failed there, too. On August 5, Valdespin was banned for fifty games for performance-enhancing drugs.

8. Darryl Strawberry vs. Lee Mazzilli/Wally Backman

The Mets hoped Darryl would set hit records, not try to make a hit record. While his home runs, runs driven in and runs scored were more than adequate, so too were the runs of his mouth.

Strawberry served as a primary source and bore the largest target of oral ammunition. Never more than the verbal warfare exchanged midway through 1987—a time when the clubhouse resembled a makeshift minefield. With the Mets engaged in a three-game series with division-leading St. Louis—already six and a half games in the distance from the Cardinals—their most productive player was swapping bat and helmet for mic and headphones.

Strawberry spent two days in a recording studio pumping lyrics for "Chocolate Strawberry"—a chart-dropper that never struck a chord with audiences but definitely struck a nerve with teammates. When the star right fielder begged off for the final two Cardinals contests with an illness he claimed was a "low-grade fever," Mazzilli and Backman diagnosed his excuse as straining credulity.

"They rip me and they can't even hold my jock," Strawberry retorted before singling out Backman, who was eleven inches shorter. "I'll bust him in the face, that little redneck."

The Mets actually won the games sans No. 18 before losing five out of eight in the midst of the Darryl-induced firestorm to fall ten and a half back.

Straw's pointed slings and arrows had a negligible effect on Backman. "That doesn't bother me," Wally said. "I am a redneck."

7. DARRYL STRAWBERRY VS. DAVEY JOHNSON

Darryl Strawberry's mean streak ruffled more feathers within the organization than would be desired. *Jerry Coli/Dreamstime.*

Circumstances did not prevent Darryl from his well-publicized griping. Who could forget Kevin Mitchell's season-saving single in the tenth inning of Game 6 in the '86 World Series (aside from most of New England)? Mitchell was inserted into the no. 5 spot in the batting order, occupied initially by Strawberry.

Darryl, 0-for-2 with a pair of walks, was removed from this do-or-die affair in the ninth as part of a double-switch involving Mazzilli and new reliever Rick Aguilera—and didn't accept it well. After Strawberry publicly criticized that move, he took his frustration out on Al Nipper in the form of an eighth-inning Game 7 homer that gave New York much-needed insurance.

In the coming years, Strawberry—by missing workouts, showing up late for batting practice and other instances of tardiness—gave Davey Johnson more bouts of irritation. His teammates, in turn, gave him an alarm clock.

The faults of the right fielder, of which there were many, didn't stop Strawberry from airing out his grievances with Johnson to the press. Take this quote from an interview with *Esquire* magazine, in which he partially faults him for the Mets' lackluster September 1987: "Davey would talk about strategy," Darryl said. "And we wouldn't know what the hell he was talking about."

6. M. Donald Grant/Yogi Berra vs. Cleon Jones

Cleon's career, no doubt impactful to the franchise, did not transpire without controversy—or, at least, perceived controversy.

His lack of hustle in left field, perhaps because Jones was nursing a leg injury, prompted Gil Hodges to come out and unceremoniously remove his .346 hitter and recent All-Star starter in the middle of an inning. That episode, on July 30, 1969, only lingered in the fact that it helped spur the Mets' run to the division title. But the incident from May 1975 marked his permanent discharge.

Coming off a 1974 in which he played hurt, Jones underwent offseason surgery and extended spring training at the St. Petersburg, Florida facility. There, Jones engaged in, and was charged with, indecent exposure—discovered by police in a van with a woman who was not his wife.

The charges would be dropped. That, however, didn't prevent Grant—team chairman and plantation owner—to fine Cleon $2,000 and emasculate the former All-Star by making his chattel publicly apologize with his wife at his side. The shaming tactics didn't stop. Grant insisted Jones get less playing time upon his return. A sulking Cleon refused Manager Berra's demand to take left field for late-inning defense.

Such insubordination was validation enough for Grant to eventually release a player deserving of a less impetuous removal.

5. Matt Harvey vs. Management

The rewards that come with being a star pitcher in New York can tempt the most hardened person to frailty. Putting cart ahead of horse, Harvey has given the impression of yearning for fame without meeting its prerequisites.

That's not to say he hadn't reached elite status. His early trajectory—from his first start in Arizona to his start in the Citi Field–hosted 2013 All-Star Game—suggested sustained stardom was possible.

Then came arm troubles, Tommy John surgery, a year on the mend and a 2015 rebound culminating in the World Series. Harvey resolutely stuck it out to the end that year—a scenario up in the air for much of September.

Scott Boras, the uber-agent for whom Harvey is a client, urged the Mets to shut down "The Dark Knight" once he reached 180 innings.

Sandy Alderson felt that boundary wasn't so rigid. Whatever Harvey's thoughts were, he kept them hermetically sealed. Instead, he enacted his waffling superpower—dodging media questions and deflecting answers.

Noncommittal morphed into commitment, and he fulfilled the challenges he long said he could face. But Harvey's elevated standing within the organization has since lapsed—a course yet to be reversed.

What's worse than equivocating with the media? Avoiding it altogether. Matt was in no mood to discuss his lousy outing in Washington on May 24, 2016, causing more PR nightmares. The retreat from vintage Harvey became clear when he prematurely terminated '16 for thoracic outlet surgery. Yet the limelight kept reeling him in.

Jilted by his model girlfriend (to which we can all relate) in May 2017, Harvey drowned his sorrows in Manhattan and failed to show up to the next day's game—earning him a suspension for three.

If only that were the low point. Needing a pitching instructor as much as a psychiatrist, the opposition rocked Harvey to the tune of a 6.70 ERA, which set a dubious Mets franchise high.

Alderson and Harvey remain tied to the hip for 2018—with no more chances to spare.

4. GREGG JEFFERIES VS. EVERYONE

He was a victim of peaking too soon.

The back-to-back Minor League Player of the Year came onto the Mets roster in late August 1988—the team primed to pull away from the NL East field and win a second division crown in three seasons. Not only did they accomplish that, Jefferies had much to do with such a strong finishing kick to the wire.

He batted .321, hit six homers and eight doubles and registered seventeen RBIs over 109 at-bats. Within twelve games, he was the National League's Player of the Week.

Basically, Gregg made a difficult transition appear seamless. But it only got more difficult. The expectations, already high to begin with, were raised higher. The organization, propping him on a pedestal as a golden boy before he could learn to walk through an entire major league season, did him no favors.

That never sat well with his more experienced teammates, who saw a kid with peculiar training habits suddenly supplant beloved Wally Backman as

Gregg Jefferies's impulsive pronouncement as a franchise savior, his eccentricities and a brittle emotional shell made him few friends. He openly admitted afterward that his leaving New York was a relief. *Scott Anderson/ Dreamstime.*

the everyday second baseman. Jefferies' production tailed off in 1989—a .258 average and chronic defensive mistakes. He continued to press in the field and at the plate. Transparent frustration exposed emotional fragility.

Teammates denounced him as self-centered and immature. Fans didn't hold back, either. To combat his stresses, Jefferies penned a nine-paragraph letter—with passive-aggressive overtones and an indirect jab at those in the clubhouse—which was read on WFAN. In it, he asked his fellow Mets to be more supportive instead of "complaining and bickering and pointing fingers."

The note induced little sympathy. Jefferies bolted to Kansas City in 1992 and found refuge in St. Louis with two All-Star seasons.

3. BOBBY VALENTINE VS. STEVE PHILLIPS

Bobby V's quarrels could generate their own separate list—and it would be hard to narrow it down to ten.

That said, his most consistent target was the man who controlled his fate for six seasons. Valentine made it known he didn't think Phillips, a general manager thirteen years his junior, was qualified to be in such an executive position. The notion that winning cures any ill wills was crushed under the weight of their pronounced powder keg.

This tug-of-war for power went beyond the customary manager-GM disputes. It might have been at its most strained in late May/early June 1999. Phillips fired the entire coaching staff—which Valentine had handpicked before—in the middle of an eight-game losing streak. The hope for Phillips was that Valentine, in a show of solidarity for his deputies, would leave with them.

He didn't. Instead, the Mets went 70-38 for the remainder of the regular season. Phillips strongly considered firing Bobby in April 2000 after getting word that Valentine's speech to students at the University of Pennsylvania included veiled shots at management.

He didn't. The Mets went on to the pennant, and the two sides were able to iron out Valentine's contract extension. Phillips ultimately had the final power play, exercising it by dismissing Bobby following a dismal 2002 season. But Phillips didn't stay for long—getting the axe himself midway through 2003.

In the years since, a remorseful Phillips became an advocate of Valentine more than a combatant. "In the end, I felt like I had won because I stuck around longer than Bobby did," he said. "But I let my stuff get in the way of our relationship, and I think that fed into the perception people have of Bobby. It's too bad, because he's really not like that at all."

2. FRED WILPON VS. NELSON DOUBLEDAY

August 14, 2002, concluded divorce proceedings between the team's two principal owners. More significantly, it signaled a transformative alteration—obscured in a swell of money talks.

Doubleday & Company, the famed publishing enterprise, purchased the Mets from the de Roulet family twenty-two years prior for a handsome $21.1 million. Nelson held 99 percent ownership. Fred had the rest. That changed in 1986 with the sale of Doubleday & Company, giving each equal control of the franchise.

But as connected as they were by the Mets, they were separate in every other way possible. Per the *New York Times*, Doubleday was "a blustery scion of publishing wealth, and Wilpon a quieter, self-made real estate developer. They were rarely seen together on the field at Shea Stadium, sat in luxury suites far from each other."

With all the commonalities to a strained marriage, neither could agree on weighty decisions concerning their shared asset—like when it came to giving Mike Piazza a contract extension after 1998. (Doubleday approved; Wilpon—shocker—was reluctant.)

When each reached the end of their respective ropes shortly after the turn of the century, Doubleday was gifted something helpless Mets fans have dreamed of: disassociating themselves from Fred Wilpon. And in continuing with the lack of revelations, this break-up process—in which Wilpon sought to buy out Doubleday's half of the club—went about as smooth as sandpaper. Major League Baseball commissioner and Wilpon ally Bud Selig mediated a settlement held up by legal bickering.

Eventually, Doubleday had his freedom (and more than $100 million).

The rest of us have been left to suffer. Over time, the new full-time owner proved which side held the franchise together so well for so long. But this business has evolved into a family business. Jeff—Fredo to Fred's Don Vito—will get the keys to the team, even if he doesn't know how to drive.

Therefore, the fallout from an acrimonious relationship that started in 1980 could reverberate for decades.

1. M. DONALD GRANT VS. TOM SEAVER

Seaver's June 18, 1977 start at Olympic Stadium resembled so many others. It ended in a complete game three-hit shutout. Another stellar outing in a career filled with them.

But this wasn't the same. This wasn't usual. This was done in a Cincinnati Reds uniform. Any Met fans who were witness to it had to rub their eyes to make sure it was real. And it was all too real.

How could this happen? How does "The Franchise" leave *the franchise*? In the prime of his career, no less.

The short answer is new-age player meeting old-school authorization head-on. Joan Payson's passing after the 1975 season left caretaking to her daughter, Lorinda de Roulet. With little acumen of baseball, she let all decision-making be done by Grant—who knew even less.

He certainly had no interest in the advent of free agency (which came in earnest in 1976) and the potential windfall it could mean for Seaver— perceptive and unafraid to voice his opinion, not to mention the best pitcher in the NL. To Grant, players of Seaver's ilk were more arrogant than dignified. He was unwilling to understand the changing lifestyles of the modern athlete and went so far as to refer to Tom as an "ingrate."

The sides had agreed to minimal gains when it came to extending Seaver's contract. If that made Tom modestly pleased, he was less happy about the team's unwillingness to play the free agency game—especially when the owner of the cross-town rival embraced it so.

If you think Grant was alone in challenging the beloved face of the Mets, he had a powerful voice on his side. Dick Young, the legendary and cantankerous columnist for the *New York Daily News*, shared Grant's disdain for free agency and regularly wrote of scorn for Seaver.

Tom went into 1977 disgruntled, continuing to pitch with little support in the lineup, but he had secretly worked out a three-year extension with de

Roulet two days before the trade deadline.

Then, on June 15, Young dropped the atomic bomb. Sitting poolside in Atlanta, where the Mets were playing, Seaver learned of Young's latest column—alleging that Tom's wife, Nancy, was jealous of Nolan Ryan's wife, Ruth, because his former teammate was making more on the California Angels. Seaver bolted from his seat and made the call to public relations director Arthur Richman.

"Get me out of here," he yelled. "Get me out of here." Tom got his wish, putting punctuation on a feud of pervasive and damaging consequences for the Mets that took more than six years to repair.

MANAGERS

10. Dallas Green

What a fine mess he found himself in.

Thirteen years past discovering paradise with the World Champion Phillies, Green washed up on the shore of baseball's island of misfit toys in the midst of a horrid 1993 season.

When Green leaped into this cauldron, the arduous task of helping put a clamp on chronic high-priced malcontents was of greater priority. Winning games was already hard enough.

Briefly a Mets pitcher in 1966, Green displayed a 180-degree turn from the ousted Jeff Torborg.

Dallas did his part to weed out weaklings—firecracker-slinging Vince Coleman foremost among them. The jokes levied on the team died down by 1994, and the losses became less frequent by 1995, when the Mets—fortified by the farm system—boasted MLB's best second-half record.

But the old-school firebrand could only keep the fire lit for so long. It burned out by 1996. Green's message wasn't getting through, and he was agitated by his players' slow progression. Whatever additional growing the Mets needed going forward, it was going to be with someone else. And in August, that someone was Bobby Valentine.

9. Casey Stengel

"Can't anybody here play this game?" Stengel once allegedly proclaimed. With a 174-404 record and permanent residence in the National League cellar, the answer was a resounding "no."

Casey's place as a New York legend had been cemented when the Mets tapped the seventy-one-year-old to take the reins of a ragamuffin franchise from birth.

No amount of brilliant strategy, however, could have steered this wayward group away from the beaten path. What the Mets lacked in on-field success (and it was plenty), they made up for in charm. Stengel supplied much of the charisma, holding court with reporters he had conversed with for so long—exploiting his unique vernacular.

As for player relations, he was known to bedevil younger players but generally earned immense respect.

"He probably forgot more baseball than I'll ever know," Frank Thomas said. "I enjoyed playing for him. If you were doing good, he'd just let you play."

A broken hip, suffered at his seventy-fifth birthday celebration, forced the franchise's surrogate father and originator of "Amazin'" in the Mets lexicon to yield leadership.

Casey Stengel—seven World Series rings as Yankee manager—was the first Met to have his number retired and was inducted into the first class of the franchise's Hall of Fame in 1981. *Author's collection.*

The countless amount of losses during a helpless situation rate secondary to his being a source of tremendous fan support and a turnout that outdrew the cross-town team he led before.

8. JERRY MANUEL

If the late-night firing of Willie Randolph in June 2008 was done to send a jolt across the Mets clubhouse filled with players appearing to be going through the motions, it was fruitful—if not entirely popular.

New York went 55-38 under the former White Sox field general over the regular season's final three-and-a-half months, but even that couldn't prevent another September pratfall.

It would be as close Manuel, claimer of the 2000 AL Manager of the Year with Chicago, would get to the playoffs. The next two seasons were a disheartening mixture of injuries, rough losses and overvalued free agent signings.

The Mets' demise was not entirely of his doing, but Manuel's laid-back disposition did little to pump life into a deflated collection of underperformers. Upon 2010's conclusion, with the front office bemoaning a second straight losing record, it also marked the end of the line for Jerry.

Widespread change was necessary. So the team made sure that the doorway Manuel was pushed out of also had space for GM Omar Minaya.

7. BUD HARRELSON

The only man to be in uniform for both championships got the call from Frank Cashen to replace the dismissed Davey Johnson in May 1990 with the Mets at 20-22.

The team responded marvelously to Harrelson's entrance—winning twenty-one of his first twenty-nine at the helm and advancing from five and a half behind first-place Pittsburgh to within one.

Even though a back-and-forth pennant race went the Pirates' way by season's end, Harrelson had proven himself capable of big-league managing. By Mets measurements, he was the fastest to get to 50 wins (in 83 games) and 100 victories (in 174). Through July 17, 1991, he was 37 games over .500.

But as fast as he seemed to grasp the role, he promptly showed how he couldn't handle it. Disputes with players and pulling the plug on a recurring WFAN pregame interview segment underscored his team's rapid about-face.

Bud didn't want to face the music. He often refused to depart the dugout during home games—to make visits to the mound, for instance—out of fear he'd be viciously booed.

Rumors swirled that he'd be fired at season's end. Those rumors were wrong. He was fired *before* season's end.

Despite what perpetuated his downfall, Harrelson maintains the Mets' second-best managerial winning percentage.

6. YOGI BERRA

Berra's incredible legacy is forever bound to Yankee lore. His effect on the Queens team, while acceptably dwarfed by comparison, doesn't get the notice it merits.

After seven years on the coaching staff (including a brief four-game turn as a player/coach in 1965), Berra received a promotion—albeit amid tragedy.

Gil Hodges's sudden death prior to the 1972 season forced the Mets front office into swift decision-making as to who it would choose as its next field leader. And Berra was that choice.

Compared to his predecessor, Yogi ran a far looser ship over three and a half seasons. But it almost never got that far, when a disappointing back end of 1972 followed by a distressing first half of 1973 put his job in jeopardy.

Then the Mets got healthy and heated up. Berra's once-hot seat now cooled. Yogi eventually found himself a pennant-winner and one victory from managing a World Series champion, something that also eluded him with the Yankees in 1964.

The Oakland A's prevented Berra from adding to his decorated résumé—and some critics claim that going with Tom Seaver on short rest in Game 6 over George Stone (and thereby subsequently tapping Jon Matlack to go in Game 7 instead of a Seaver/Matlack combo) was a miscalculation.

Just because it didn't work doesn't make it a mistake. The more consequential matter, and the one that probably cost him his job, occurred in 1975—when Cleon Jones (still not healed from an injury) refused Yogi's order to take the field.

Chairman M. Donald Grant felt Berra had been undermined and was let go in the wake of an August doubleheader sweep to Montreal.

5. Terry Collins

Evaluating his seven years on the bench is like taking a Rorschach Test.

One observation can conclude that Collins overworked his relievers, made curious if not fatal decisions with his bullpens, fumbled with the lineup and forgot how to spell "Michael Conforto" when filling out the batting order. And rather than guiding the Mets to consecutive playoff appearances, he rode the coattails of Yoenis Cespedes, Jacob deGrom, Noah Syndergaard and others to those back-to-back trips into October. They won (and in 2015's case, got to the World Series) in spite of him.

Another can see the same body of work and construe that Collins was initially given a bad hand as part of a financially strained franchise, kept the club afloat through the rough waters and oversaw a pair of late-season runs that resulted in an NL pennant followed by a Wild Card while maintaining relative tranquility in the clubhouse—a quality he lacked during his previous two managerial gigs.

Sporting a Rasputin-like capacity to steer clear of the guillotine, Collins altered the abrasive reputation that led to locker room revolts and firings in Houston and Anaheim.

But in 2017, there were no more life preservers. Injuries did an extraordinary number on his roster. And the able bodies Collins was sending onto the field weren't performing well, either. Contrary to what might have been said anonymously in a *Newsday* report that smelled of a smear campaign to validate his ouster, Collins departed post-2017 with the respect of his players intact.

And contrary to what might have been presumed when he was hired in 2011, with the Mets helplessly waiting to turn the corner, Collins—the longest-tenured manager in team history—was no placeholder.

4. WILLIE RANDOLPH

Entering 2005 with a fresh approach, intent on erasing the dreadfulness of three straight seasons below mediocrity, Omar Minaya went about hiring someone with deep-seated knowledge in New York baseball.

Randolph, a Brooklyn native, spent more than a decade as the Yankees' second baseman. His curtain call as an active player—1992—was as a Met. From 1994 to 2005, he was a Yankee coach.

The Mets immediately improved under his guidance—a twelve-win jump in '05. Then came ninety-seven victories and the 2006 NL East title.

Narrowing down to bare bones measurements, Willie was forty-nine games over .500. But triumphs and failures are never equal. Two defeats stand out as his collective undoing.

Willie Randolph averaged eighty-nine wins in his first three seasons. But he ultimately couldn't survive the fallout from 2007's end-of-year collapse. A 34-35 start in 2008 was his ticket out. *Jerry Coli/Dreamstime.*

Game 7 of the 2006 NLCS to underdog St. Louis elicited disappointment. The 2007 regular-season finale—to culminate the Mets' historic fall from first place—provoked anger and frustration.

The captain of a ship rarely survives a capsizing of that magnitude. Yet Willie was left to dangle in the aftermath until Minaya gave him a vote of confidence weeks later. That small measure of assurance waned when the Mets got 2008 off to a rickety start.

Failing to show any mark of consistency and losing faith in his players, Randolph's fate was inevitable by early June. Getting the 3:15 a.m. Eastern Time pink slip in the middle of a West Coast swing, though, was unwarranted.

3. BOBBY VALENTINE

Few possess as much baseball acumen. And he'd be the first to tell you. Whether in disguise or out front, Bobby V was a mixture of intellect and ego that made him—and the teams he led—utterly entertaining.

As blunt as a kick to the groin, Valentine held no predisposition with whom he abraded: players, front office, fellow managers and the media. It served as an unconstructive trait when the Mets wavered—receding from the playoff picture in 1998 coupled by an almost-repeated fold in 1999—and a marginal narrative when the Mets thrived—reaching the '99 NLCS, then the 2000 World Series.

Although a headline-maker, his record made such candor tolerable. The former Stamford, Connecticut star athlete won eighty-eight or more games in each of his first four full seasons and was sixty-nine games above .500.

Before Terry Collins did the trick in 2015–16, Valentine was the only Mets skipper to reach the postseason in back-to-back years. But his best job of managing the most out of his personnel came in 1997. After taking over for the closing thirty-one games of 1996 in the wake of Dallas Green's discharge, Bobby improved a Mets team lacking a bona fide superstar by seventeen wins (seventy-one to eighty-eight) and had them in Wild Card contention up until the final week of the regular season.

Valentine's only losing year, marred by an August losing streak and rumors of clubhouse marijuana use, became his last. The Mets fired Bobby in 2002, after which he jettisoned to future successes in Japan—leaving behind many triumphs, a few more enemies and a legion of appreciative fans who wouldn't mind having him back.

2. DAVEY JOHNSON

Davey Johnson remains tops in Mets managerial victories. Before Terry Collins passed him in 2017, Johnson had also served as field general more often than anyone in club history. *Jerry Coli/Dreamstime.*

His Mets threads were sewn even before joining the organization in 1981. The final out of the 1969 World Series, resultant of Jerry Koosman's pitch and Cleon Jones's catch, came off Davey's bat—one of many Baltimore Orioles humbled in their five-game defeat.

But there was nothing humble about Davey. The unshakable confidence in himself and his players would be hard to neglect.

Such strong conviction is a reason why Frank Cashen, acquainted with Johnson's studious qualities when Cashen served as Orioles GM, hired the former second baseman who had risen up the minor league managerial chain alongside some of the same players he would see when he attained his first big-league gig.

Davey didn't tread timidly. Shrewd personnel moves—most notably inserting Dwight Gooden at the head of his rotation—along with a forward-thinking approach hastened the Mets from last place in '83 to second place in '84. This kick-started a six-and-a-half-year window in which Johnson's teams won at a .588 clip and reached the mountaintop in his third season.

As Jesse Orosco secured the 1986 World Series, Johnson was witness to this Mets championship—not as an opponent but instead as the leader of an energetic group that exhibited confidence to dominate the regular season and tenacity to fight through the postseason.

The franchise's winningest manager rose to the challenge of producing championship-caliber teams while having to harness somewhat disruptive—albeit talented—personalities.

1. GIL HODGES

The list of watershed points in franchise history is short. And if the hiring of Hodges isn't on there, then that list isn't complete.

Gil's insertion into the dugout slowly shed the perennial laughingstock persona that had echoed loudly since 1962, when Hodges was an original Met and winding up a successful playing career.

Once a cherished Brooklyn Dodgers first baseman by the faithful who frequented Ebbets Field during the 1940s and 1950s, he would augment his New York legend—becoming the guiding force behind another beloved Big Apple team. The leader of boys he transformed into men.

Beginning in '68, Hodges maximized the talent at his disposal—teaching, coaxing and platooning a lineup to its utmost chance of victory. He was a man of unbending convictions who took no sides. Because the truth, which Hodges was so staunchly committed to, has no sides.

There wasn't a single player—not Tom Seaver and not Cleon Jones, whom he famously chastised by removing him from a July 1969 game in the middle of an inning for a sensed lack of hustle—free of his authority.

Hodges's word was law. His players fell in line.

The reverence and high esteem that they held for their manager have been seen and heard long after his death of a sudden heart attack in April 1972. "To people connected to the Mets," writer Leonard Koppett noted, "feelings towards Hodges were just this side of worship."

The fruits of his labor grew slightly in his first year and beyond anyone's wildest aspiration in his second. Who's to say what more he would have done to add to a body of work—both on the field and in the dugout—that is way overdue for induction in the Baseball Hall of Fame.

What is certain—there would be no Miracle Mets if not for him.

PART VI

NOTEWORTHY GAMES

SUBWAY SERIES VICTORIES

10. May 23, 2010

A two–home run game by Jason Bay between 2004 and 2009—when he was slugging for Pittsburgh and Boston—wouldn't have registered any astonishment. Considering he entered his forty-fifth game as a Met with just one homer and went on to double his season total in the space of three innings, it was as surprising as it was pleasing.

Bay afforded Johan Santana early backing with a two-run shot off C.C. Sabathia in the second. After targeting the left-field stands, he took aim at Citi Field's right–center field bullpen in his next at-bat. Bullseye.

Santana took his lead and went into the eighth with only six hits and one run on his ledger. He entrusted the five-run advantage to the bullpen—a trust that fractured as the Yankees chipped away. Three of the first four batters in the top of the ninth reached base. Francisco Rodriguez came in, allowed a double and induced an RBI groundout which cut the Mets lead to 6–4.

Mark Teixeira's two-out infield single put runners at the corners for Alex Rodriguez. K-Rod versus A-Rod. It was power versus power—until Francisco pulled the string and got a swinging third strike on an eighty-one-mile-per-hour changeup.

9. June 28, 1998

Dropping two at home and losing in each of the last four meetings, feelings of resentment grew. It didn't help that the Yankees were already fourteen games better and embarking on arguably the greatest season ever.

No amount of talent, even recent addition Mike Piazza, was enough to feel confident. Sacrifice flies, an unassuming task that culminated the Amazin's 2–1 victory, were challenging.

Luis Lopez's one-out, bottom-of-the-ninth, bases-loaded drifter to right field, hauled in by Paul O'Neill, was deep enough to assuredly let Carlos

A current Mets manager with a former one. Bobby Valentine (*left*) and Joe Torre (*right*) take part in a pregame interview spot before Game 1 of the 2000 World Series. Torre, who briefly had Valentine as one of his players, was in a helpless situation when he led the talentless Mets from 1977 to 1981—and his 286-420 record indicates that. *Jerry Coli/Dreamstime.*

Baerga tag up and score. O'Neill's no-look throw into the infield was intercepted by Derek Jeter, who threw to Tino Martinez in an attempt to nail Brian McRae returning to first base.

But by that moment, Baerga had crossed the plate. That didn't stop first-base umpire Bruce Dreckman from calling McRae out once it appeared Martinez clumsily touched the bag with his bare hand in time (even though he didn't have total control).

It took a brief conference with home-plate umpire Frank Pulli and Bobby Valentine chiming in to confirm what seemed so obvious initially.

Runs were, indeed, that hard to come by. Hits, too, as neither Masato Yoshii nor Orlando Hernandez allowed any over four innings. Despite combining for nine walks, the duo overcame their erratic tendencies to total nineteen strikeouts. Yoshii, who yielded two hits in seven innings, fanned a career-high ten, while Hernandez lasted eight frames in his two-hit showing.

8. JUNE 16, 2002

Roberto Alomar and Mo Vaughn—names greeted with mockery. Each a failed Mets experiment concocted prior to '02.

Both were playing below par as their team took a June tumble. Six wins in seventeen games, coupled with a red-hot Atlanta Braves, put the Mets from being tied for first place on May 29 to seven and a half behind in the middle of June.

David Wells was about to extend the hometown unhappiness when he carried a 2–0 edge into the bottom of the eighth with Alomar, Mike Piazza and Vaughn due up.

The future Hall of Fame second baseman doubled. The future Hall of Fame catcher reached on an error by Jason Giambi.

The upcoming lefty-lefty duel, along with Wells's pitch count, compelled Yanks manager Joe Torre to leave his starter in—despite Vaughn's eight career home runs versus Wells.

Mo still had David's number—which became nine. His heft and uppercut swing were the impetus that pushed the 0-1 offering beyond any defender's reach and gave the Mets a 3–2 lead that they wouldn't relinquish.

Armando Benitez's Yankee demons never reared their ugly heads in a serene 1-2-3 top of the ninth.

7. JULY 9, 1999

Many have a better batting average against Roger Clemens. Several have more home runs versus "The Rocket" than Mike Piazza's four. But because their clashes occurred amid the expected attention that New York–New York tilts receive, the significance of each becomes more noticeable.

On June 6, Clemens couldn't survive three innings—a Piazza double and a homer part of the whipping. Roger made it a bit longer a little more than a month later until he encountered unkindness from Queens's catching king.

Piazza upgraded his two-run shot from June for a three-run, tie-breaking bomb in the bottom of the sixth.

Al Leiter, who let the slim lead slip away only an inning earlier, prevented the Yankees from gaining any traction.

His eight strong innings and the sixth win in seven starts was preserved by Armando Benitez. Although he made Leiter and the rest of the partisan crowd sweat it out in the ninth—if they weren't already sweating from a humid eighty-two-degree evening. A strikeout of Chili Davis as the tying run gave the Mets their twenty-second victory in thirty-two games.

6. July 3, 2011

Mariano Rivera—as close as you can get to an automatic closer. So on the extremely rare occasion he couldn't add to what would turn out to be a record-setting 652 saves, it was more pronounced.

Preserving a lead—even as small as a single run—through the arm of Rivera was akin to a deadbolt lock. Curtis Granderson's eighth-inning sacrifice fly, which put the Yankees up 2–1, limited the Mets' chances. When Mo had little trouble getting the first two outs in the bottom of the ninth, his twenty-third save in the last twenty-four save opportunities appeared imminent.

Then, Jason Bay walked on a 3-2 pitch. Lucas Duda singled. Ronnie Paulino singled. Bay scored. Rubén Tejada almost won it with a sharp grounder under shortstop Ramiro Pena's legs, but Brett Gardner's perfect throw home nailed Duda and kept the game tied—for the time being.

In the tenth, Bay—who had little to rejoice about this year (or any year he was in a Met uniform)—clapped his hands in celebration after a bases-loaded walk-off hit, made possible by another Pena error that prolonged the inning.

Feelings toward the Yankees are binary. There is no nuance. The love-hate debate becomes much stronger when the Bronx Bombers are dominating—like they were at the end of the twentieth century. Owner George Steinbrenner, at the helm of seven championships, enhanced the hatred further. Having the upper hand—in resources, fame and trophies—didn't stop unrelenting George from wanting to increase his preeminence by ruling the back pages of New York papers as well as the baseball universe. *Jerry Coli/Dreamstime.*

5. June 16, 1997

Before the lines separating the American and National Leagues were blurred, the only way the Mets could meet their rivals from the Bronx (aside from World Series competition) was in the Mayor's Trophy Game—an exhibition that raised money for the city's sandlot baseball programs.

The event ended in 1983, with the Yankees holding a 10–8 edge (with one tie). But who's counting?

Now, with interleague play interspersing the schedule, this was the first time Big Apple bragging rights would be settled for real and the first instance in forty years in which two New York teams faced off in the regular season.

The Yankees—defending champions—boasted Derek Jeter, Paul O'Neill, Cecil Fielder and Tino Martinez. The Mets' answer to the Bronx's Goliath? Dave Mlicki, a winner in two of his previous thirteen starts—not exactly the imposing presence you want going against the champs in their home park.

Mlicki defied such logic. Much of the pressure heaped on the twenty-nine-year-old righty lifted when the Mets jumped on Andy Pettite for three first-inning runs. One would have been enough.

Mlicki silenced bats as much as he quieted the fifty-six thousand in the stands—save for the delighted orange-and-blue clan. The nine hits he allowed were neatly spread out. The closest they came to scoring occurred in the ninth. But a called third strike on Derek Jeter with the bases loaded put an end to a 6–0 masterpiece.

4. May 28, 2013

Following in concert with the other twenty-eight major league clubs, the Mets honored the soon-to-be-retiring and sure-for-Cooperstown Rivera in his farewell season by having him toss out the series finale's honorary first pitch.

Rivera also threw the last pitch—but not in the ceremonial fashion he was so used to. His reentrance onto the Citi Field mound came with his Yankees up 1–0 entering the bottom of the ninth—a customary scenario during his brilliant nineteen-year career.

When he departed the hill, it was with his Yankees having lost 2–1 and without an out recorded. Three straight hits—by Daniel Murphy, David Wright and Lucas Duda—engineered the rally versus mortal Mo.

Matt Harvey and Hiroki Kuroda were the two who pitched like supermen. While "The Dark Knight" maintained the strong showing he presented in his first full season with ten strikeouts, he encountered similar tough luck. The one run allowed—which came via a Lyle Overbay two-out single in the sixth inning to score Brett Gardner—made him prime for the unfortunate loss.

Kuroda's seven shutout innings, followed by David Robertson's easy bottom of the eighth, eventually fell by the wayside in a rare spurt of Met offense.

3. MAY 19, 2006

David Wright didn't need a signature moment to certify his rise to stardom. But this night was as good as any.

First, though, he and his colleagues would need to reel the Yankees in. A microwave-like Mets offense quickly cut leads of 4–0, 5–3 and 6–5 against Randy Johnson—bailing out beleaguered starter Geremi González.

Tied at six entering the last of the ninth, Wright entered the picture with two outs. The outfield played a tad bit shallower to protect against a game-winning single that could score Paul Lo Duca from second base.

Wright lifted a deep drive to center, sending Johnny Damon racing toward the 410-mark. Wright hopped up and down—as if body language could influence ball flight. A leaping prayer was answered. The ball fell on the warning track—just beyond Damon's reach.

"To come through in the Subway Series, versus a team like the Yankees, it's special," Wright said following the biggest hit in his young career. "You can say as much as you want that it's just another game, but there was a lot more energy tonight."

2. 2000 WORLD SERIES GAME 3

Nothing would create more satisfaction than to take down their more celebrated cross-town rival on the grandest of baseball stages. But in this New York street fight, the Mets tussled with combatants well equipped for their autumnal ritual.

Narrow victories became ingrained in the Yankees' resourceful fabric during the late 1990s. It seemed they couldn't lose—in October, especially.

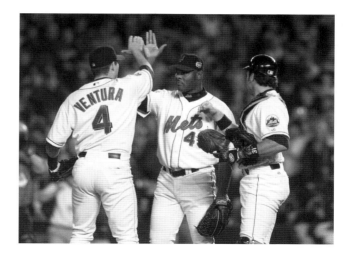

Robin Ventura (*left*) and Mike Piazza (*right*) show their appreciation for Armando Benitez closing out the 2000 World Series Game 3 victory. *Jerry Coli/ Dreamstime.*

Equally invincible was the Yanks' starting pitcher, as the teams arrived at Shea with the club from Queens down two games to none. Orlando Hernández put his 8-0 record in postseason competition on the line against a team that could ill-afford another loss.

Making good on their urgency, the Mets broke the ice with a Robin Ventura homer. Of course, the practical Yankees didn't let them enjoy the lead for long and countered with two runs. Todd Zeile hit a double to drive home Mike Piazza for a sixth-inning tie and was about to be in the picture again as the bottom of the eighth commenced with Hernández on the mound and more than 120 pitches deep.

Increasing his series average to .462, Zeile singled with one out in front of Benny Agbayani. A double in the gap would score the average base runner. Zeile, though, had a need for speed. As Benny laced a liner into the space between left and center field, Todd plodded 'round the bases—aiming to complete this 270-yard lead-footed dash.

But the only race to win was the relay home. He won. The Mets tacked on another run, won 4–2 and halted the Yankees' streak of fourteen straight Fall Classic victories.

Hopes of an extended series were restored. They would not be prolonged.

1. July 10, 1999

Contrary to what you've read, the cracks in Mariano Rivera's impenetrable armor are few and far between.

To say the Yankees were unbeatable once they held the lead heading into the ninth inning was no embellishment. Because for 125 straight games, they were.

The Superman-like aura Rivera radiated had much to do with it. But in a rare plot twist, Matt Franco served as his kryptonite. A barrage of six Yankee home runs should have been a knockout punch.

The Mets matched with an offense that remained within Shea's confines—two doubles and two sacrifice flies. But they had a haymaker ready. And it was a doozy. Mike Piazza's seventh-inning Titanic rawhide flight for three (runs)—which traveled 482 feet over the left–center field wall and included spontaneous bat flip—could have been traced by LaGuardia's air traffic control.

Whatever momentum that lead-changing swing generated turned out to be short-lived. As Jorge Posada cranked his second and the Yanks' last round-tripper in the eighth, an 8–7 deficit and the anticipation of inevitable defeat awaited.

But as Rivera granted a one-out walk and Bernie Williams misjudged a fly ball, the invincible force of the late-inning Yankees showed vulnerability. The two uncommon miscues allowed Ricky Henderson to get to third base and Alfonzo to reach second. John Olerud grounded out to first base, leaving the runners unable to move forward.

One hit could win it, and one out would lose it. Joe Torre wasn't going to let Mike Piazza do either. The Yankees walked him to set up a force at any base.

Franco, batting for Melvin Mora, did himself no favors by quickly falling behind 0-2. He then took a pitch that would be in most umpire's strike zone. Thankfully, Jeff Kellogg's zone was small enough.

Given a reprieve, Franco swung at the next pitch—placing a single in the hole between first and second. Paul O'Neill's throw reached the plate after both Henderson and Alfonzo had crossed.

The Mets celebrated their first series victory over the "Evil Empire" in a manner unsuitable to the buttoned-down Yankees. But it was hard to fault their exuberance. They had beaten the unbeatable.

REGULAR SEASON MARATHONS

10. October 2, 1965, vs. Phillies

One to be forever stashed in the vault—gone the way of modernization.

The starting pitchers tossed fifteen scoreless innings—*each*. New York's Rob Gardner and Philly's Chris Short were the pair that matched goose eggs for an outrageous distance.

Seven strikeouts, two walks and five hits against Gardner pale when compared to a headline-grabbing eighteen Ks credited to Short, who walked three, yielded nine hits and faced the minimum from the twelfth until his departure.

Out of the 109 plate appearances, few came in prime scoring chances. Each team could only get a runner to third base twice.

Driven into offensive exhaustion, a mandatory curfew—after eighteen innings and four and a half hours—put a halt to the fruitful efforts.

This was the nightcap of a doubleheader—and while the Phillies might have used up their runs when they scored six in the opener, the Mets' total ineptitude with the bats was a day- and night-long pattern.

To go twenty-seven innings in a single day and not score is impressive—in its own fascinating, putrid way.

The stats counted, but a brand-new game was played the next day, on top of the regular season finale that followed. Philadelphia won both by identical 3–1 scores, the latter lasting thirteen innings. Add it all up, and these weary teams faced off for forty-nine innings over two days.

Thankfully, the next game was scheduled for spring.

9. April 15, 1968, at Astros

A dueling string of zeros as far as the eye could see.

In the fourth season of the stadium known as the "Eighth Wonder of the World," patrons at the Astrodome watched in astonishment to see how long it would take for someone to score. The nineteen combined innings from starters Tom Seaver and Don Wilson were a very distant memory when the game reached the six-hour mark and the twenty-fourth inning of play—still, to this day, the longest-ever scoreless tie.

By then, with the foremost challenge being concentration and focus, an error—only the second of the contest—proved costly. With the bases loaded and one out in the bottom of the twenty-fourth, a potential double play turned into a game-ending misplay when shortstop Al Weis booted the grounder and Norm Miller scored. You read right—someone scored.

History was made in another respect. In response to GM Johnny Murphy's reaction to how the final play transpired, a rule was implemented where ground crews would drag the infield every seven innings regardless of game length.

8. June 8, 2013, vs. Marlins

New York's Shaun Marcum and Miami's Kevin Slowey didn't expect to be working. Paid as starters, they instead were tasked with putting an end to an unending struggle.

Marcum, who generated eight innings and gave up five hits, got the unfortunate losing pitcher tag, as he allowed a Marlin score in the top of the twentieth. The Mets offense should really harness the blame.

New York and Miami were among the worst in terms of team batting average—and proved it. Each had pushed one run across through nine. And after nineteen, nothing changed.

In the top of the twentieth, Adeiny Hechavarría took a Marcum cutter into left field for an overdue RBI single—which both frustrated and somewhat relieved an impatient and diminishing Citi Field crowd. Whatever difficulty there was in accepting a drawn-out defeat couldn't be compared to the horror of losing Matt Harvey, who exited prematurely with tightness in his right hip after another strong start that lowered his ERA to 2.10.

He would be fine, for now. New York's offense hurt much worse.

The Mets offense gave their fans a demonstration on the myriad ways to extricate yourself out of run-producing opportunities. They were 0-for-19 with men in scoring position (setting a dubious franchise mark), including clutch hit fails in eight of the final twelve frames.

7. July 19, 2015, at Cardinals

If ever victory could be torturous, it was done here at Busch Stadium. Sure, the Mets beat the Cardinals. But did they have to make it so hard to watch?

It took eighteen innings, thirty-nine stranded base runners and countless groans of discontent from Keith Hernandez—forgetting the mute button in the broadcast booth—to get to a 3–1 decision.

With pitching, especially Jon Niese's seven and two-thirds frames, keeping the opposing offenses in their sedentary ways, there became little reason to need a scoreboard for the first twelve innings. The Mets "exploded," if you will, for three hits and a run in the top of the thirteenth. And before you could utter "here's Jeurys Familia for the save," Kolten Wong's leadoff home run in the bottom half ended that hope.

The majority of the action to follow were of exercises in futility and malfunctions in simple execution, as each team was its own worst enemy. New York managed to manufacture two eighteenth-inning runs—through a Rubén Tejada sacrifice fly and a suicide squeeze by Eric Campbell with Curtis Granderson bearing down on home plate—that made the difference.

6. April 17, 2010, at Cardinals

To conquer an extra-inning affair, the objective is to outlast as much as outplay. In a game that witnessed position players pitching, relief pitchers pinch-hitting and starting pitchers playing the outfield, the Mets and Cards displayed far more ingenuity than offense. For thirty-six turns at the plate, neither club could circumnavigate the 360-foot route around the base paths.

At long last, in the top of the nineteenth, New York did what for nearly seven hours was declared impossible. It happened when Jeff Francoeur drove in José Reyes on a sacrifice fly. And it came against St. Louis utility man Joe Mather—who relieved Felipe López, an infielder.

Unfortunately, the Cardinals—which saw a bevy of golden scoring chances go unfulfilled—finally discovered the formula. Yadier Molina (hadn't he done enough to us already?) singled to right field in the bottom half to bring home Albert Pujols and latch a blown save on the ledger of Francisco Rodriguez.

The Redbirds extended it to inning no. 20, but with no one in the bullpen to turn to, they turned back to Mather. The Mets took advantage with two

Jose Reyes's sacrifice fly in the top of the twentieth inning, combined with Mike Pelfrey's save in the bottom half, instilled a sigh of relief to those waiting for the endless Mets-Cardinals affair in April 2010 to finally reach a resolution. *Scott Anderson/Dreamstime.*

singles and another sacrifice fly—this time off the bat of Reyes, scoring Ángel Pagán.

St. Louis ran its roster dry. New York had one fresh arm, Mike Pelfrey, to record the save. Twenty innings—and it wasn't even the longest game between them. That came some thirty-six years prior.

5. MAY 24, 1973, AT DODGERS

A journey to the West Coast—a twelve-game road swing—evolved into a trip headed straight for the unknown. As in, it was unknown if this game at Dodger Stadium would ever end.

New York used two crucial run-producing spates to beat Los Angeles 7–3. Unfortunately, for the impatient, they were separated by more than the length of an entire regulation game. Before the slumber, the Mets were stirred in helping Tom Seaver—who experienced his shortest outing thus far in '73—avoid a loss and his record dropping to 5-4.

Avoiding defeat for themselves and their ace, New York scrabbled for scores in the seventh and eighth to tie it at three, then skirted a culminating decision altogether for eleven innings.

Better late—very late—than never, Cleon Jones and Rusty Staub combined to find an escape route to the endless struggle. A Jones single and a Staub double were enough to break the long-standing deadlock.

Overcome with delayed gratification, the Mets then poured it on. Ken Boswell's RBI single was followed by Ed Kranepool's two-run double. And five hours, forty-two minutes past the first pitch, Jim McAndrew threw the last.

4. APRIL 28, 1985, VS. PIRATES

An early 4–0 Mets foothold, shaped by Darryl Strawberry's first-inning grand slam, buckled under three sixth-inning Pirate runs. New York couldn't get the offense out of neutral—as the Pirates relief staff combined to no-hit the Mets for ten innings.

From the seventh through the eleventh, the New York bullpen held its own—holding the Bucs to four hits. The defense also bailed out the bats—even earning some creativity points as the night trudged along.

For most of his twenty-three-year career, Rusty Staub—giving off a cumbersome appearance—couldn't be classified as a defensive liability.

However, at age forty-one and in his final season, Rusty was limited to pinch-hitting duties. But in the twelfth, with rosters thin and the hour late, Davey Johnson didn't have much of an option. His legs betraying him, Staub shuttled from right to left field eleven times to avoid having the ball hit his way.

Rick Rhoden, a great hitting pitcher, couldn't help but knock one toward him. Rusty ranged into foul territory down the right-field line and made a nice basket catch.

Then, one inning of decent offense made up for sixteen innings of none.

Clint Hurdle, who swapped position with Staub so often and who threw out a potential go-ahead run from left in the tenth, hit a ball hard enough to zip through the legs of first baseman Jason Thompson. The error scored Mookie Wilson, the last of the game's forty-three participants.

3. SEPTEMBER 11, 1974, VS. CARDINALS

Absent of time limit, baseball games can technically go on forever. The Mets and Cards put that theory to the test.

A crowd that began at 13,460—and slowly withered as the innings piled up—nearly could have had three for the price of one.

But it would have been a run-of-the-mill regular season contest had not Ken Reitz's two-out, two-run homer off Jerry Koosman in the ninth happened—the impetus that sent this matchup from ordinary to extra, extraordinary.

The Cardinals took ninety trips to the plate and left twenty runners stranded. The Mets outdid them by four and five, respectively—setting a team-high in the repentant "LOB" category. Together, the 175 official at-bats and the forty-five stranded remain single-game MLB records.

Fifty players made their way onto the scorecard—from Hall of Famer Lou Brock to former Met Ron Hunt to future Mets Joe Torre and obscure rookie Keith Hernandez.

St. Louis broke through in the twenty-fifth on a play created by speed and aided by fatigue. Bake McBride, caught leaning from first base, got off the hook from Hank Webb's errant pick-off attempt.

As John Milner retrieved it, McBride scooted to third base and headed for home. Milner's throw was good enough to nail McBride, but catcher Ron Hodges dropped the ball. McBride touched home safely for the Cardinals' fourth and winning run.

When the Mets were set down in the bottom of the twenty-fifth, the Shea clock read 3:13 a.m. It is the longest game in MLB history innings-wise played to a decision minus delay or suspension.

2. MAY 31, 1964, VS. GIANTS

The early Mets had far more bad days than good and weirder days than most. Chalk this one, without reservation, in the bizarre category.

Once upon a time, in a baseball era long ago—when fan interest wasn't superseded by cash flow—Sunday doubleheaders were routine, predetermined events and not just reserved for making up rainouts.

No schedule maker, though, could have envisioned the length to which Shea Stadium, in its second month, would be inhabited by the Mets and

Giants. The opener, won by San Francisco, lasted a swift two hours, twenty-nine minutes.

The back end of the twin bill persisted for an incredible seven hours and twenty-three minutes. Add it up, and take into account the breather between games, and you have a ten-plus-hour workday.

Still in its embryonic stage, the Mets had yet to truly figure out this little ol' thing called winning. Thus, Casey Stengel's squad was often relegated to seeking modest progress. Coming back from a 6–1 deficit against a team replete with names like Mays, McCovey and Cepeda qualifies as such.

However, once New York matched San Francisco at six apiece in the bottom of the seventh, it would take sixteen more innings—including a top of the fourteenth triple play—before they could settle for a moral victory in place of a real one.

Gaylord Perry earned the W by blanking the Mets for ten frames. But the man deserving of a time-and-a-half paycheck was Ed Kranepool, who played in all thirty-two innings—the day after he played the entirety of *another* doubleheader for Triple-A Buffalo before being called up to the majors.

1. JULY 4, 1985, AT BRAVES

More time and more innings enhance the capacity for more weird and unusual occurrences.

Nineteen innings between the Mets and Braves at Atlanta–Fulton County Stadium stretched out across a sodden eight hours and fifteen minutes. At no point, though, could it be considered uneventful. Many Mets games have been longer. None have been wilder or wackier.

There were a pair of rain delays (which combined to total more than two hours). There were multiple ejections (Davey Johnson and Darryl Strawberry among them). The Mets played under protest in response to said ejections. Keith Hernandez, who took a more conventional approach, hit for the cycle. There was a blown save in the top of the ninth and another blown save in the bottom of the thirteenth—with one more still to come.

But taking the prize for the most remarkable happening of the early morning was Atlanta relief pitcher Rick Camp—up at bat with no available pinch-hitter, no margin for error and no apparent hope.

To everyone's astonishment, he launched a game-tying, two-out, two-strike home run in the bottom of the eighteenth to confirm that this game had entered baseball's version of the "The Twilight Zone."

Collectively, the teams totaled forty-six hits. The twenty-eight on the Mets' ledger remains a team record. They combined for twenty-nine runs, with each New York position player producing an RBI.

Five of those runs occurred in the top of the nineteenth. The Braves, who had already mounted three comebacks, tried one more rejoinder—scoring twice and bringing Camp up incredibly again as the tying run. But Ron Darling struck him out at around 3:55 a.m.

The lengths taken to decide the 16–13 score might have been longer than the time it took to draft the Declaration of Independence.

Then the scheduled postgame fireworks were set off—a less-than-gentle wake-up call to those who were trying to be on a normal sleep pattern. But that overdue pyrotechnic show, no matter how elaborate, couldn't compare to the show that just occurred.

PART VII

CHAMPIONS

The following appear in chronological order.

REGULAR SEASON GAMES, 1969

MAY 28 VS. PADRES

It was a time of confrontation, experimentation and revolution. Americans were protesting the Vietnam War, preparing for a venture to the moon and finding themselves (modestly speaking) at Woodstock.

Baseball, too, was also undergoing its own upheaval. Four expansion teams meant four divisions—six teams in each. No longer was the regular season a direct avenue to the World Series.

Oh yeah—and the Mets were about to do the unimaginable.

There is no distinct moment of delineation when the perennial dregs of the National League transformed into the definitive inverse of the previous seven years. Like many mystical tales, you have to make your own assumptions.

Perhaps their encounter against the newly formed Padres, with the Mets at 18-23 and in fourth place, was when the inroads to their division title were crafted. Ten scoreless innings from Jerry Koosman, augmented with four hits allowed and fifteen strikeouts, assuaged any fretting about a recently diagnosed shoulder strain.

This continued with twenty-three consecutive scoreless innings and four wins in his next five starts. But he didn't win this game.

That's because the batting order, pre–Donn Clendenon, was reduced to a pair of hits and failed to take advantage of a seventh-inning error. They didn't miss on the next case of Padre generosity.

Cleon Jones, leading off the bottom of the eleventh, reached on a shortstop misplay, ambled to third on a Ron Swoboda single and trotted home when Bud Harrelson did the same.

The Mets prevailed 1–0 and did so through June 10—establishing a franchise record of eleven straight victories.

JUNE 4 VS. DODGERS

Manager Gil Hodges, unafraid to offer an honest evaluation of his team, asserted that the Mets could not be considered contenders until they reached .500. They did so, for the first time in team history, on May 21. Then gave it back—losing five in a row.

But in early June, in the midst of their long winning streak, Jerry Koosman and Tom Seaver—posting back-to-back gems—confirmed that losing records were a thing of the past. New York moved into second place in the NL East.

Jack DiLauro followed their two standout starts with an even better one. The left-handed Triple-A call-up christened his big-league career by baffling Los Angeles for nine innings—shutting them out on two hits and two walks.

But the same disobliging affliction that vexed Koosman on May 28 came to prevent DiLauro from personal victory. It took a Willie Davis error, made on a Wayne Garrett single, to break a fifteen-inning stalemate.

Divisional realignment assured the Mets of never having to be listed nine or ten lines down in the standings. However, after piling up victories at a rate Shea wasn't used to, talks of avoiding the cellar disappeared.

As voices for many a Mets fan's summers, Bob Murphy (*left*), Ralph Kiner (*right*) and Lindsey Nelson teamed up for the franchise's first seventeen seasons—before Nelson and his flashy sports jackets departed after 1978. Murphy remained a prominent broadcaster for the team through his retirement in 2003, and Kiner (one of the best power hitters of the 1950s) continued charming us until his death in 2014. All three are enshrined in the Baseball Hall of Fame. *Courtesy of New York Mets and NBC Television.*

JULY 8 VS. CUBS

Games at Shea Stadium had always been fun—never important.

But their engagement with the first-place Cubs—who were ahead by five and a half when the series began and trimmed to four and a half when it was done—had the unaccustomed, yet delightful, ring of postseason significance.

Chicago salvaged the final meeting, a comfortable 6–2 victory, prompting its glib manager Leo Durocher (when asked if "those were the real Cubs") to retort, "No, those were the real Mets."

Leo was all-too-quick to dismiss what took place the night before, when Tom Seaver stood two steps short of perfection, and the afternoon before that—when Chicago's commiserations and Mets magic officially converged.

Cubs starter Ferguson Jenkins cruised through eight innings but encountered a severe roadblock in the ninth. More specifically, it came courtesy of his raw and unprepared center fielder. The Mets put the 3–1 Chicago lead in peril with a fly ball that Don Young misjudged, granting Ken Boswell a double. One out later, Young sprawled for a running catch in left center on a tracer by Donn Clendenon, but the ball sprang from the webbing of his glove as he banged into the outfield fence.

Young found less support on his own team.

"My 3-year-old could have caught those balls," Durocher said postgame.

"He was just thinking about himself," griped third baseman Ron Santo. "He can keep going out of sight for all I care."

Cleon Jones extended the doubles chain, which matched Chicago at three apiece. Following an intentional walk and a groundout, and with Jenkins trying to solve his own dilemma, Ed Kranepool—who had seen all the bad years—placed a single in front of left fielder Billy Williams.

The Mets pulled it out 4–3, in a method that would become commonplace. To the Cubs and their leader, it was nothing more than an insignificant comeback.

AUGUST 19 VS. GIANTS

Nearly a month earlier, as Americans watched "one small step for man, one giant leap for mankind," the Mets were making one giant leap up the standings.

They might have been stepping foot on foreign terrain, perched in second place, but no headway was made on Chicago. Even after Gil Hodges's public removal of Cleon Jones in the middle of a July 30 drubbing, a moment that Jones felt "galvanized the team," the Mets weren't roused right away. New York dropped seven of ten, shortly after suffering a four-game skid. It was after a loss to Houston on August 13, which put them ten games out, that Gil lit into his team in a clubhouse lecture.

"He didn't holler much," Donn Clendenon later wrote. "[But] when he did it shook the whole team up." Met players responded to this edict—embarking on a rousing 37-11 finish to the regular season. Hodges's intensity sparked a turnaround. His ingenuity six days later against San Francisco led to a win.

Gil Hodges, the guiding force behind the Mets, managed with a steady demeanor and a firm hand. *Jerry Coli/Dreamstime.*

Gary Gentry and Juan Marichal tussled for ten unmarked frames. Willie McCovey came up in the top of the thirteenth, aiming to break the continuing impasse. Hodges, cognizant of McCovey's might, employed a four-outfielder alignment to prevent an extra-base hit. Sure enough, McCovey belted one to deep left. But Cleon Jones played it perfectly—robbing him of a would-be homer.

His Mobile, Alabama high school teammate Tommie Agee didn't find as much difficulty getting it over the wall. By doing so in the fourteenth, it made the Mets 1-0 walk-off winners—their fifth straight victory.

AUGUST 30 AT GIANTS

For eight seasons, the West Coast was the Mets' vale of tears.

But during their final California excursion of '69, they took six of ten—three straight against San Diego, one versus Los Angeles and a split at San Francisco. New York actually lost a small amount of ground to the somewhat recharged Cubs. It could have been more, if not for the bat and presence of mind of their veteran first baseman.

Tied at two, Willie McCovey, unlike eleven days earlier, found open field with a one-out ninth-inning double to left. Bob Burda, running from first, attempted to score. The relay and Jerry Grote's tag got Burda.

But Grote, thinking it was the third out, momentarily lost his head—rolling the ball toward the mound. Clendenon knew otherwise. He raced to retrieve the ball and nabbed McCovey as he tried to reach third base.

How often is it that the guy who makes the inning-saving defensive play leads off the next frame?

Well, it happened here, too. Clendenon cut through the sharp Bay Area winds to produce what turned out to be the game-winning homer. Giants' starter Gaylord Perry had gone the distance—and lost.

The margin between the Mets and Cubs was four games. A meeting between the prime NL East combatants was a little over a week away.

SEPTEMBER 8–9 VS. CUBS

To have faith in curses is to swear by Santa Claus or the Easter Bunny. In the sports realm, the implication of a jinx is merely concealing poor on-field performance or feeble off-the-field judgment.

Having gone longer than a century ringless, Chicago Cubs fans pinned their lack of a World Series title on everything from a billy goat to Steve Bartman.

As the 1969 pennant race tightened, with two and a half games parting the chief contenders, Shea Stadium was host to an average of more than fifty thousand fans—and one feline.

Dispensing with the preliminaries of this two-game showdown, the rivals renewed the beanball tussle that involved Tom Seaver, Ron Santo and Bill Hands back in May. Hands sparked the firestorm with a first pitch that whizzed riskily close to the head of Tommie Agee. Santo, who shared his manager's convictions that the Mets were nothing more than paper tigers, received the brunt of Jerry Koosman's retaliation—on his right elbow—leading off the second.

But Agee had a more efficient method of revenge. Unintimidated by the brush back and picking up the slack for injured Cleon Jones, the center fielder took Hands deep with a man on. The Cubs scratched together three singles and a sacrifice fly to even the score in the sixth—soon to be imbalanced when Agee slid and contacted the plate ahead of Randy Hundley's tag—to which the Chicago backstop leaped and pleaded in dismay.

New York carried momentum from a 3–2 victory into Tom Seaver's start the next night. The Mets put up crooked numbers in the first and third innings. Seaver got into cruise control by the top of the fourth, when a black cat appropriately strolled in front of the Cubs dugout before disappearing under the Shea stands.

Not much was made of it in the aftermath, and the Cubs scored their lone run during that inning, which turned out to be a 7–1 Mets win and Seaver's twenty-first victory of the season.

But as the Cubs went down into a September plunge of 8–17 and New York conversely went 23-7, the black cat became the telltale sign of the contenders' contrasting fates.

If Leo didn't believe it in July and didn't believe it before this series, he knew it now. *These* were the real Mets.

SEPTEMBER 10 VS. EXPOS

The conditions were ripe for the Mets to take care of business. They were as hot as could be. Montreal was not.

The same expansion club that took care of New York in its inaugural contest on Opening Day had dropped ninety-seven games since. The Mets used to know that feeling. No longer. They weren't about to engender any empathy in a Wednesday twin bill.

Montreal's Mike Wegener and New York's Jim McAndrew each hung around for eleven effective innings. They gave up two runs apiece, except Wegener fanned fifteen and the pair scored on him were the result of fielding errors.

The Expos looked to be taking the lead on a twelfth-inning single, but reliever Ron Taylor's heady play in retrieving a poor throw from Tommie Agee and tag of Remy Hermoso at the plate prevented the run.

The Mets then won it in the bottom half with Ken Boswell's single to center, scoring Cleon Jones. Nolan Ryan's complete-game effort in the second contest was the expressway to a sweep.

The Mets did their job and reveled as the Phillies did theirs, beating the Cubs. The right–center field scoreboard at Shea captured the seminal moment with a snapshot of the up-to-date standings and a headline above it: "Look Who's No. 1."

SEPTEMBER 12 AT PIRATES

For a relatively decentralized hero dynamic, the element that carried them this far—and to the end—was its pitching.

During a nine-game win streak, when the Mets went from three and a half games behind to three and a half ahead, New York hurlers allowed a total of eleven runs.

Jerry Koosman and Don Cardwell shut down the Pittsburgh Pirates during a doubleheader at Forbes Field and helped their causes at the plate when the Mets needed it. Neither Cleon Jones nor Art Shamsky were available—Jones because of injury and Shamsky due to the observance of a Jewish holiday.

With a depleted offense and less margin for error, Koosman went about humming through the Pittsburgh order. Save for a second-inning jam created by two walks, he faced the minimum through eight while allowing only three singles.

But it was his own single that made the difference. That came in the fifth and scored Bobby Pfeil. If a 1–0 final in which the starting pitcher drives in the lone run is unusual, then two (in the same day) is quite remarkable.

Jerry Koosman won eight of his last nine decisions, never yielding more than four runs in any start. *Jerry Coli/Dreamstime.*

Don Cardwell came to the rescue in the nightcap. A two-out, second-inning single from the thirty-three-year-old ex-Pirate brought in Bud Harrelson. And as the rest of the Met bats were held in check, Cardwell—like Koosman—was equally as steadfast to Pittsburgh hitters.

Don gave way to Tug McGraw in the ninth, who finished off a sweep that was as rare as it was cunning.

September 15 at Cardinals

Nothing was stopping them on their golden path to the NL East crown—not even the most overpowering individual pitching performance in baseball history. Steve Carlton humbled the Mets lineup, compiling a strikeout total of nineteen—then a single-game major league record.

Reality suggests that this signaled pure dominance—a game the Mets could only chalk up as a loss and tip their cap. But this was a year where reality took a vacation.

Ron Swoboda solved the Carlton mystery twice. A pair of two-strike, two-run homers—the latter coming in the top of the eighth to turn a 3–2 deficit into what eventuated into an improbable 4–3 victory at Busch Stadium.

"It was the best stuff I ever had," said Carlton, when he actually spoke to the media. "When I had nine strikeouts, I decided to go all the way. But it cost me the game because I started to challenge every batter."

Five days down the road, the Mets couldn't overcome another pitching buzz saw, as Pittsburgh's Bob Moose tossed what turned out to be the final no-hitter at Shea Stadium. But they maintained a four-and-a-half-game edge as the Cubs kept faltering.

September 24 vs. Cardinals

Cinderella was approaching the postseason ball.

The Mets, pennant race neophytes, never engaged in first-place tradeoffs with the Cubs once they caught them.

New York zoomed past so quickly that the club holding the top spot in the NL East for most of the year stumbled as it failed to match.

With the magic number near zero, starter Gary Gentry had two goals. Not only was he aiming to complete the Mets' quest for the impossible, but he sought to bring his overall win-loss record to .500 as well.

A perceived clash between the Mets' great pitching and the Atlanta Braves' great hitting converted into a slugfest. But New York, adding to a year's worth of surprises, showed more muscle—outscoring the Braves 27–15 in the inaugural NLCS and swept the best-of-five series. Nolan Ryan tempered Atlanta bats for seven innings in Game 3, a 7–4 victory at Shea that set up a date in Baltimore and had the public thinking about the unthinkable. *Jerry Coli/Dreamstime.*

With five first-inning runs, the offense—taking it to Steve Carlton—created a convoy that allowed the rookie to pitch more at ease.

Fittingly, Donn Clendenon—the key acquisition who ignited the Mets' summer charge—lifted a three-run homer. Then Ed Charles, in his farewell season, went deep. Ed clapped his hands as he rounded the bases, aware that he and most of his teammates were on the verge of a first postseason appearance.

Like the divisional chase itself, once the Mets got ahead, they weren't turning back. Gentry displayed no rookie tendencies, letting the Cards get only four hits while navigating along a shutout route.

With one out and one on in the top of the ninth, Joe Torre grounded into a division-clinching double play. The Mets and the field-storming fans went wild—not acting like they'd been there before, because they hadn't. It was 9:07 p.m. For Cinderella, midnight was far from near.

NL East Final Standings, 1969

	Wins	Losses	GB
Mets	100	62	
Chicago Cubs	92	70	8
Pittsburgh Pirates	88	74	12
St. Louis Cardinals	87	75	13
Philadelphia Phillies	63	99	37
Montreal Expos	52	110	48

REGULAR SEASON GAMES, 1973

APRIL 7 VS. PHILLIES

Youth started, experience finished. The National League's reigning top rookie, Jon Matlack, made the first outing of his sophomore year.

Not hinting self-righteousness for the hardware earned, he lumbered through a nine-inning self-induced obstacle course of five walks and a sixth-inning homer by Bill Robinson (unknowingly auditioning for his future role as hitting instructor, perhaps).

That canceled out the earlier home run by John Milner and the RBI single by Cleon Jones. The Mets aimed to break the 2–2 lock with a bottom-of-the-seventh threat, but it was only a tease.

Ed Kranepool, batting for Matlack, worked a leadoff walk on former teammate Dick Selma and was replaced by the speedier Ted Martínez, who advanced to second base on a Félix Millán one-out ground ball to the right side of the infield.

Needing a clutch hit to prevent extras, the onus fell on Willie Mays. He'd done and seen everything. So the production of a game-winning single was old hat.

For the Mets, it was worth celebrating. But the Mays-Martínez walk-off permutation would be viewed again in exactly three months and ten days.

JULY 17 AT BRAVES

"Who Should Mets Ax?" That was the headline of a *New York Post* poll that ran during the Mets' summer swoon—with Yogi Berra, GM Bob Scheffing and M. Donald Grant as choices.

Most put their support behind Berra, given a bad hand with the precipitousness of injuries. Nevertheless, Grant was rumored to be considering offering Yogi the pink slip with his team occupying the NL East cellar at 38-50.

A condition like this prompted buoyant Berra to generate his greatest pearl of wisdom: "It ain't over 'til it's over." Yogi was referring to the division race, but he could well have been talking about his own managerial fate. That phrase could be just as useful in describing the mid-July thriller in Atlanta.

Tug McGraw, before he (and everyone around him) would be a true believer, appeared to be throwing away any suspense. Not yet in the groove he would enter over the season's final months, Tug got a change of scenery in a starting role but grappled through six rocky innings.

The Braves, leading 7–1 entering the top of the ninth, threatened to drive the sinking Mets further under water. Carl Morton's route to a complete game then went under siege behind the clout of Rusty Staub and John Milner.

Following those homers, which brought it to 7–5 and the end for Morton, it was a walk and four singles (each with two outs) that overtook Atlanta.

On July 9, the Mets were 34-46, in sixth place in a six-team division. Team chairman M. Donald Grant held a locker room pep talk, emphasizing belief. Resident screwball Tug McGraw, who that day received similar advice from a friend, spontaneously blurted out the three-word mantra that became the rallying cry for the team's and the reliever's second-half renaissance. *Jerry Coli/Dreamstime.*

The last and most crucial of those came from the wizardry of Willie Mays's magic wand. Hit no. 3,271 brought home Jim Beauchamp for the tie and Ted Martínez for the win.

August 21 vs. Dodgers

Better late than never, the Mets solved Don Sutton belatedly—yet dramatically.

But without Ray Sadecki keeping pace with the Los Angeles ace, it probably wouldn't have been enough. Sadecki, making his seventh start of '73 since joining the rotation in early July, put up four straight zeros until an unexpected power source sought to put those efforts to ruin. Bill Russell, everything except a home run threat, defied logic with the bases empty.

The long ball was only a slight hiccup, as he retired thirteen of his final fifteen batters while keeping the Mets bullpen idle. One run, four hits, no walks in a complete game victory—a win that almost wasn't.

Sutton's stronghold over New York's offense relented by the bottom of the eighth. The Mets poked and prodded—with a John Milner walk, an Ed Kranepool single, a Jerry Grote sacrifice bunt and a Don Hahn sacrifice fly.

That method worked again as Sutton returned for the ninth. Wayne Garrett drew a bases on balls, and Rusty Staub received an intentional pass. Then the Mets dropped "The Hammer." Milner singled up the middle to score Garrett. Sutton had a complete game, too, but not in the way he wanted.

AUGUST 22 VS. DODGERS

Venerable LA manager Walter Alston might have thought he was viewing a replay of the previous day. For the second straight game, his Dodgers failed to close out the Mets in the late innings. And for the second straight game, the curtain-lowering was supplied by John Milner.

While the Mets comeback of some twenty-four hours prior began in the eighth, this one started with a smaller margin of error. Leading off against Dodger reliever Jim Brewer and behind 3–2 as the bottom of the ninth began, Cleon Jones—placed in a rare pinch-hitting role—delivered a single. A bunt by Tug McGraw and a fly ball from Wayne Garrett advanced Jones to third base.

But no more sacrifices could work here. Félix Millán, arguably the most reliable of all the Met starters in '73, came through. His single started a chain reaction because two ensuing safeties—first from Rusty Staub and second from Milner—made the Mets walk-off winners again.

McGraw, who contributed to the rally, received his first victory of the season after six defeats—perfectly working through the eighth and ninth innings with three strikeouts after the Dodgers emerged with the lead in the top of the seventh.

AUGUST 24 VS. GIANTS

For the inundation of woes that engulfed the Mets for most of '73, they were in the right place at the right time. Injuries and a subpar bullpen had them at 57-68. Bad enough for last, but the view from the NL East cellar

Not having healed from the ailment that sidelined him for a good chunk of 1972, Rusty Staub still led the '73 Mets in RBIs and belted three homers in the NLCS. Traded away after 1975, he returned to greater fan appeal in 1981 through the end of his playing career in 1985. *Jerry Coli/Dreamstime.*

to the penthouse wasn't too bad. They were a mere six and a half games behind leader St. Louis. The distance to catch up wasn't as daunting as the number of teams to surpass.

The Giants, meanwhile, might have wondered if there could be an in-season divisional realignment. San Francisco, at 70-55, was seven games back of Cincinnati in the NL West—a disparity in records, but nearly even in the amount of ground to make up.

It wasn't beyond the pale to see one—if not both—pitchers endure for the regulation game length, and Jerry Koosman and Juan Marichal took it a step (or an inning) further.

The Giants managed to place just five into scoring position against Koosman—and came away empty on each try.

Marichal of '73 was a deterioration from the '69 edition. But he could still show flashes of Hall of Fame form, and his rubber arm kept pace with New York's lefty through nine scoreless innings.

Finally, the thirty-five-year-old relented in the tenth. Ken Boswell singled, advanced to second on a Willie Mays bunt and came around to score the first and only run thanks to one of Félix Millán's team-best 185 hits.

SEPTEMBER 18 AT PIRATES

The hot potato pennant race was playing right into the Mets' hands. Improved health got them on the fast track during the season's stretch run, while their main NL East competition kept its respective legs in quicksand.

With nobody able to pull away, the Mets couldn't have picked a better time to shore up and heat up. And against the team leading this slothful chase, New York could make this tight divisional fight even more constricted.

Jon Matlack's one bad inning—the third—gave the impression it was one bad inning too many. The 4–1 lead the Pirates grabbed from that frame held up behind starter Bob Moose and reliever Roberto Hernández—about to ensure the Mets would lose both road contests of a five-game home-and-home series that would ultimately determine their aspiring postseason fate.

But like the season itself, the Mets came to life late. The third consecutive one-out hit came off the choked-up bat of Félix Millán. His triple made it 4–3. Four straight Mets reached base after that—with a Ron Hodges RBI single and a Don Hahn two-RBI hit canceling out Pittsburgh's lead and propelling New York ahead.

Bob Apodaca, though, almost gave it back. He walked Gene Clines. He walked Milt May. He then walked off the mound—supplanted by Buzz Capra.

A bunt and a grounder narrowed the gap, and two free passes hastened heart rates. But Manny Sanguillén flew out to Cleon Jones with two on, and the divisional jumble was as clear as mud. With less than two weeks to play, five teams were separated by five games. For the Mets, two and a half games and two teams stood between them and the Bucs.

SEPTEMBER 20 vs. PIRATES

If there's ever been a division, league or World Series champion that did so without a touch of good fortune, it's yet to be seen.

A rabbit's foot can be as beneficial as a hot bat, arm or glove. For the '73 Mets, such a charm came into being this night against a team they were just one and a half games behind.

It wasn't applied when Duffy Dyer doubled in the tying run with two outs in the ninth—nor did it reveal itself when Ron Hodges won the game with an RBI hit in the bottom of the thirteenth. Instead, destiny rose to the forefront in the top of the inning—confirming that, perhaps, remnants of 1969's magic was still lurking inside Shea Stadium's walls.

With two outs and Ritchie Zisk on first, Dave Augustine hit one destined for the Mets bullpen—except its trajectory sent it squarely off the top of the left–center field fence and back into play.

Cleon Jones snared it off the fortuitous bounce, turned and threw to cut-off man Wayne Garrett while Zisk—the potential go-ahead run—rounded third and headed home.

Garrett fired to Hodges, perched on the plate, who laid down the tag on a sliding Zisk with room to spare. Home plate umpire John McSherry, waiting to confirm, elevated his hand and closed it into a fist. Inning over.

The legend of the "Ball on the Wall" play was established. Roughly twenty-four hours later, the Mets completed a series sweep of the Bucs and finished their three-week climb from worst-to-first.

SEPTEMBER 23 VS. CARDINALS

The NL East had a full measure of good days and bad. But the last days and the best days belonged to the Mets. The months that led up to it, though, were rough.

Opening Day's roster weakened under the weight of countless ailments. Rusty Staub continued to deal with the hamate bone operation that curtailed his wonderful start to 1972. Jerry Grote, Bud Harrelson, John Milner and Cleon Jones each missed significant chunks of the schedule—causing daily lineup cobbling and a lack of stability.

They were knocked down—to the cellar—but not out. As those key pieces were coming back to full service, the rest of the middling divisional conglomerate was generous enough so that the Mets weren't left too far astray.

No hitter was more important to the Mets' push for the pennant than Cleon Jones. A .340 hitter for the 1969 World Champions, Jones shoved his early '73 malaise aside with six homers in the final ten regular season contests. *Jerry Coli/ Dreamstime.*

A recent clean bill of health and a fortuitous bounce during their blistering home stretch suddenly had New York eyeing the crown. A host of teams, though, were nipping at its tail—namely the Pittsburgh Pirates at a half-game out.

The late-season drama was forged, like four years earlier, behind great pitching and timely hitting. Tommie Agee, the third batter, went deep. Sadly, as a Cardinal, not a Met. Nostalgia quickly gave way to urgency. The Mets answered with help from contributors who weren't able to contribute before.

Jones produced a sacrifice fly in the third and a home run in the seventh. In between was a Staub fifth-inning RBI single and a Grote-induced sixth-inning rally punctuated by Wayne Garrett's two-run triple.

Harry Parker's four shutout innings in relief heralded a resurgent Tug McGraw—his twenty-third save, the Mets' season-best sixth straight victory and their first-place grip all on the line.

New York's knockout punch on a 5–2 win came when Mike Tyson flew to left. In what typified the vagaries of such a congested pennant race, their next series was against Montreal—fifth place and three and a half behind.

SEPTEMBER 25 VS. EXPOS

As New York's current heroes were aiming for playoff glory, a New York legend for all time was reaching the finish line of his wondrous voyage.

Willie Mays, forty-two years of age and several years past his prime, announced he would retire at season's end. Having not participated in a game since September 9, his original plan was to call it quits right then and there. But owner Joan Payson convinced him otherwise. As was richly deserved, a pregame ceremony involved visits from luminaries and concluded with a farewell speech from the honoree.

The "Say Hey Kid" would "say goodbye to America," but fans nationwide could get a few more glimpses in the coming weeks—so long as the rest of the Mets did their part.

Cleon Jones obliged by doing his best Mays impersonation at the plate with a sixth-inning home run that gave the Mets a 2–1 lead and then, with Montreal runners on first and second, ranging over the left–center field gap to haul in a potential hit to end the top of the seventh and preserve said lead.

Those plays most satisfied Jerry Koosman and Tug McGraw. The lefty tandem combined to hold Montreal to seven hits and one run. An even better result came in Pittsburgh, as the Phillies topped the Pirates to put the Mets one and a half games clear.

October 1 at Cubs

Salvaging a winning record and clinching the division are almost always mutually exclusive scenarios.

The Mets overtook their five Eastern Division foes. But with one series left, the lead was tenuous. Four clubs were separated by three and a half games. Even the Cubs, sitting one spot from last place, were mathematically alive at four back. Sweeping New York—and getting help elsewhere—was imperative.

The same day the vice president resigned, the Mets shook up baseball's power structure again. By beating Cincinnati, 7–2, they toppled a team with seventeen more regular season victories. But New York was riding a wave at its crest. Ed Kranepool (*second from left*), subbing for injured Rusty Staub (*far right*), delivered a two-run first-inning single. Cleon Jones, Wayne Garrett and Willie Mays authored timely hits. Tom Seaver (*far left*) nearly went the distance before giving way to Tug McGraw. As John Milner fielded a grounder and tossed to McGraw covering first for the clinching out, a sea of humanity flooded the Shea Stadium turf. *Jerry Coli/Dreamstime.*

This was not a time for patience, although Mother Nature wasn't helping. Two days of rainouts compressed the four-game set into consecutive Wrigley Field doubleheaders, beginning on Sunday, September 30.

With crowd turnout low due to maintained sogginess, it didn't feel like a pennant race–type atmosphere. The Mets might have been playing down to the level of the environment when they failed to score off Rick Reuschel and Bob Locker, making Jon Matlack a hard-luck 1-0 loser in the opener.

The offense redeemed itself later with a 9–2 win and a Jerry Koosman complete game. Chicago was officially eliminated.

Monday's scheduled twin bill and the Pirates-Padres matchup were the lone games on the docket, as the rest of Major League Baseball wrapped up its schedule. Still left was to see how the topsy-turvy East would shake out.

Cleon Jones's second-inning homer was his sixth over the past ten games. The Mets added two more in the fourth, two in the fifth and one in the seventh to build a 6–2 advantage for Tom Seaver.

But the eventual Cy Young winner tired—evidenced by Rick Monday's two-run blast over the ivy—as he gave way to 1973's late-year inspiration.

Tug McGraw didn't only save games. He saved the season. And when he got Glenn Beckert to pop softly to John Milner—who then stepped on first to double off Ken Rudolph, running on contact—for a game-ending double play, he ensured that this season would continue.

With the division locked up, game 162 was canceled. No nightcap was necessary. The Mets, at 82-79, were drinking champagne.

NL East Final Standings, 1973

	Wins	Losses	GB
Mets	82	79	
St. Louis Cardinals	81	81	1½
Pittsburgh Pirates	80	82	2½
Monreal Expos	79	83	3½
Chicago Cubs	77	84	5
Philadelphia Phillies	71	91	11½

REGULAR SEASON GAMES, 1986

April 24–27 at Cardinals

These Mets weren't strained by the burden of a pennant race.

Like department stores that hang Christmas decorations before Halloween, the preparations for postseason baseball were being made by the All-Star break.

Davey Johnson's spring training declaration of domination was most prophetic. But before New York could put it on cruise control in August

Keith Hernandez (*left*) was most responsible for pushing the Mets upward. Gary Carter (*right*) got them over the top. It's impossible not to think of one without thinking of the other. *Jerry Coli/Dreamstime.*

and September, it needed to slay the dragon that charred pennant dreams in 1985.

This four-game set at Busch Stadium began with a bang—a shot across the bow of Cards closer Todd Worrell courtesy of Howard Johnson, whose equalizing two-run homer came as the Mets were down to their final two outs. It took one inning for that momentum swing to carry over into a 5–4 victory.

The second game would eventuate into a laugher. Dwight Gooden went the distance on a five-hit shutout and was aided by an offense that broke open a late 2–0 lead with five eighth-inning runs and then two more in the ninth.

Things appeared to be heading in a similar trend the next day after New York registered a four-spot in the first against Danny Cox. But four is all they could get. St. Louis rallied to close the gap to a 4–3 ninth-inning deficit and threatened to come all the way back with two on and one out versus Orosco.

Jesse would be credited with the save, but Wally Backman played a major part in the rescue mission—diving for a Terry Pendleton grounder and initiating a 4-6-3 double play that was both rally killer and game-ender.

Bob Ojeda's complete game effort in the Sunday finale, his first as a National League pitcher, extended the Mets' win streak to eight. In totality, this series sent a direct message to the Cardinals as to who would be ruling the NL East roost.

Sweep complete. Tone set. Before long, Whitey Herzog was raising the white flag.

MAY 30 vs. GIANTS

Roughly five months before extra-inning comebacks aided by well-timed errors were made legendary, the Mets pulled the trick on visiting San Francisco.

Robby Thompson manned a role soon to be occupied by Dave Henderson—hitting a home run in the top of the tenth that broke a 6–6 tie, only to become one of the primary characters in an inglorious finish.

Keith Hernandez initiated a bottom-half rally by way of a leadoff single. Kevin Mitchell, with one out, followed suit. A wild pitch brought both runners into scoring position. Ray Knight brought home a head-first sliding Hernandez with a sacrifice fly to left field (his second on the night), and the score was even again.

The next batter, Rafael Santana, lifted an easy pop-up in Thompson's direction. Yet emblematic of the good fortune that resided with them from April through October, destiny proved to be on New York's side.

Taking a page out of the 1962 Mets playbook, shortstop Juan Uribe drifted over—and over—and collided into the second baseman. The ball landed beside Thompson's leg. Mitchell, running on contact, trotted home easily.

This was a victory, their thirty-first in forty-two games, gift-wrapped and slapped on with a pretty bow.

JUNE 10 vs. PHILLIES

Tim Teufel went from an everyday starter in Minnesota to platoon player in New York. Consequently, the chances to produce came few and far between. Teufel waited on the bench for the better part of eleven innings, then got an opportunity to bat with one out, bases loaded and the score tied at four.

A long fly ball would suffice, but Teufel—and his one home run to date—got much more than he, and the drawn-in Phillies infield, bargained for.

Tom Hume's pitch was sent to a place where no defender could catch it. Teufel maximized his pinch-hit occasion with a walk-off grand slam. While Teufel collected four RBIs on one swing, Gary Carter used three swings to drive in four.

First came a fourth-inning single that plated Darryl Strawberry. Then it was a two-run home run in the sixth that temporarily put the Mets on top. The Phillies regained the edge but would be done in again by Carter on a solo round-tripper. The peskiness displayed by Philadelphia, which would end up a distant second in the NL East, wasn't uncommon.

While nearly every National League foe in the Mets' 1986 path was laid to waste, the Phils were the only opponent to post a winning record against them.

JULY 3 vs. ASTROS

Trends are traced in many forms. Such was the case in the long-term development of Darryl Strawberry having yet to hit a home run off a left-handed pitcher since season's start.

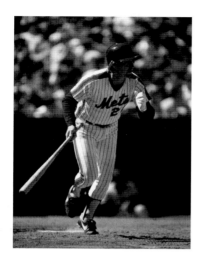

Eric Davis found out quickly, as did others who crossed him, not to mess with Ray Knight. The '86 Mets were remembered as much for their grit as their domination of the National League, and the former Golden Gloves entrant (who drove in seventy-six runs and packed a few punches, too) embodied that image. *Jerry Coli/Dreamstime.*

A more simplified instance, in the short term, was Ray Knight's incapacity to hit *anybody*. Both patterns had become old news by the time New York beat its eventual NLCS opponents in extra-inning, come-from-behind fashion reminiscent of the excitement level set to transpire in the postseason.

It also helped continue another tendency that progressed in '86: the Mets failing to accept defeat.

"Losing," Knight said postgame, "is a word we don't think of."

Their seventh straight victory almost never came to pass—when Phil Garner homered off Jesse Orosco, turning a tie after nine into a 5–3 tenth-inning lead for Houston. The gruff, gauche Garner in the top half gave way to the lean, sweet-swinging Strawberry with one on and none out in the bottom half.

He took southpaw Jim Deshaies deep with a fifth-inning flash that, for the moment, had New York on top 3–1. When his deep drive off fellow lefty Frank Dipino disappeared beyond the blue 410-foot center-field barrier, it was even.

Darryl's home run—the eleventh multi-homer game of his career—shook up Shea. Knight supplied the aftershock.

Leading up to his fifth at-bat, the Mets third baseman's row on the score sheet was laden with Ks—four of them. Turning repetition into retribution, the symbolic donning of a "golden sombrero" that represents such a dubious achievement was long forgotten when Knight (finally) made contact and sent the ball into the left-field bleachers for perhaps the finest of many regular season come-from-behind wins.

JULY 4 VS. ASTROS

On Independence Day, the Mets were relishing in their own kind of freedom—liberated from any NL East challenger. At thirty-two wins over .500 and less than half the season complete, the separation from second place was already twelve and a half games.

It was a different story in the West. Houston and San Francisco were neck-and-neck as the surprise contestants.

The two starting pitchers each contrastingly defied their birth certificates. Dwight Gooden, twenty-one, had fifty victories and more than six hundred strikeouts. Nolan Ryan, eighteen years his senior, was still managing to throw with breathtakingly similar velocity as he did when he was Gooden's age. He departed after five innings, down 1–0, in favor of a pinch hitter.

That plan by Astros manager Hal Lanier didn't pan out. Kevin Bass's turn at the plate in the top of the seventh, however, did. With one down, one swing by Bass brought Houston even.

The tie never made it past the seventh. After Rafael Santana walked and moved to second on a Gooden sacrifice, Lenny Dykstra doubled him in.

A bases on balls in the eighth and another free pass in the ninth were the only threats to Doc's 2–1 edge. His tenth win and eighth complete game was preserved by New York's eight-time Gold Glove winner.

Craig Reynolds's sharp grounder to the right side of the infield would elude just about any first baseman. But Keith Hernandez, who turned it into a routine putout, was no ordinary first baseman.

JULY 22 AT REDS

The Mets were the scourge of every other team and every other fan base. Partly because they were so damn cocky—with curtain calls, brawls and their own music video. And partly because they were so damn good—with a thirteen-and-a-half-game NL East lead at the All-Star break.

In the spotlight and under the microscope, the Mets' smooth road hit severe bumps in Houston. They dropped three straight, and a group of four players—Bob Ojeda, Tim Teufel, Ron Darling and Rick Aguilera—were arrested following a nightclub fight involving off-duty cops.

Another highly publicized scuffle took place in Cincinnati—with less legal consequences—and was the spice that made the pre–Fourth of July fireworks against the Astros feel like a tea party.

It would have been a routine 3–1 Reds win had Dave Parker held on to the lazy fly ball Keith Hernandez served. Parker, a two-time Gold Glover, developed stone hands. The drop allowed both base runners to cross home plate.

Then, things got *really* crazy. Ray Knight was in the middle of it again. Eric Davis slid hard into third base in the bottom of the tenth as the potential winning run. Unfortunately for Davis, he was met by someone who could retaliate such aggression in spades. Many ballplayers feign a fighter's mentality. Knight, a former amateur boxer, lived it.

Davis's jaw met Knight's fist and a melee broke out. When the dust settled, Knight and Kevin Mitchell (along with Davis and Reds pitcher Mario Soto) were ejected. Darryl Strawberry had been tossed in the fifth. Those departures, along with other substitutions Davey Johnson made before the fight, left the Mets manager short-handed.

Ed Hearn went in to catch. Gary Carter moved to third base. And with no everyday players left, Johnson put Jesse Orosco in right field and had Roger McDowell come in to pitch. The two relief pitchers would then spend the remainder of the game switching between the mound and right field—depending on the matchup.

The tie lasted until the fourteenth, when Howard Johnson pulled a three-run homer. It was back to the suddenly versatile McDowell, summoned from the outfield, to close out a game that best epitomized the Mets' resourcefulness.

AUGUST 3 VS. EXPOS

They won in just about every manner possible. But Bob Ojeda was attempting for a feat not accomplished in twenty-five seasons.

He held Montreal hitless through 6.1 innings. Several Mets—Tom Seaver and others—had sat in this spot before. And like Seaver and company, Ojeda wasn't able to bring it to fruition.

Even a victory would prove elusive. However, Ray Knight followed his tiebreaking two-run double in the eighth with a game-winning single in the bottom of the tenth that gave New York a 4–3 victory and a sweep of the Expos.

Eight outs from history, Luis Rivera—a twenty-two-year-old shortstop making his big league debut—became the culprit with a single to right. It was the first ball against Ojeda that made it past the infield.

George Foster (*left*), the 1977 NL MVP, came over via trade from Cincinnati five years later. He would be far from the player who once hit over fifty homers. By August 1986, he was released. Foster called the decision racially motivated, but a .149 batting average during July from the game's highest-paid player was a more logical reason. His departure opened up opportunities for young Kevin Mitchell and veteran Lee Mazzilli (*right*). The Brooklyn-born matinee idol, who was granted a second go-around with his home team, delivered key pinch-hits in Games 6 and 7 of the World Series. *Jerry Coli/Dreamstime.*

The no-hit bid was over. Before long, so was the lead, as Andre Dawson's two-out knock brought Rivera home and created a 1–1 tie.

After the Mets generated a pair of eighth-inning runs, Ojeda—not having lost in over two months—was seeking a seventh win since May 31.

Then, successive singles from Albert Newman, Rivera and Tim Raines made it 3–2 and ended Ojeda's day.

Just as Dawson would again produce a clutch hit—this against Roger McDowell—that knotted the score, Knight would eventually return to resume his part as tie-breaker.

When Wally Backman crossed the plate, Montreal ceded to Philadelphia as the Mets' closest pursuer. But at seventeen and a half out with sixty-one to play, this was small consolation.

AUGUST 6 AT CUBS

Dwight Gooden held a superior hand over Chicago. Building on his sterling one-hit tour de force in September 1984, he put together seven consecutive complete game victories over the past two years.

Doc was able to last nine innings again in a midweek afternoon matchup at Wrigley Field, but Keith Moreland's game-tying two-run homer pushed the finish line back—preventing an eighth straight.

This came as a surprise. Gooden apparently reached a supreme rhythm—having yielded two singles and a walk since the fourth. But no such thunderbolt could rattle a team 53-28 away from Flushing.

Keith Hernandez and Gary Carter reached base to start the top of the twelfth facing George Frazier. Mookie Wilson brought both around when he singled off Lee Smith. Roger McDowell, though, was almost generous enough to give it right back. With two outs to get, pre-managerial star Terry Francona and Jerry Mumphrey teamed up to make it 7–6 with the tying run on.

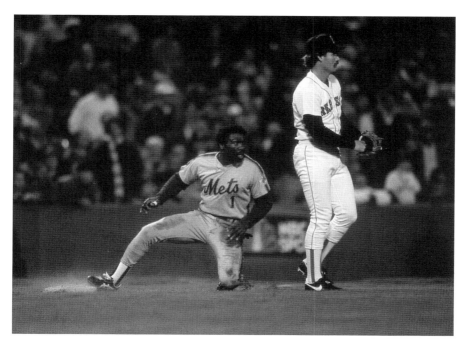

In contrast to the renegades on the roster, Mookie Wilson charmed fans with his thousand-watt smile. But he has as much hustle and spirit as anyone. *Jerry Coli/Dreamstime.*

Ryne Sandberg and Manny Trillo were the next two batters—and the last two. McDowell collected himself to cause a groundout and a fly out. The Mets worked overtime to get a victory, then worked an extra shift. By the same 7–6 margin, New York also prevailed on the back end of the Windy City doubleheader.

August 27 at Padres

To anyone in the New York area willing to combat tiredness and watch the week-and-a-half West Coast road trip in August, these were late nights well invested.

The Mets won eight of California nine—the wildest coming in the series finale in San Diego.

Gary Carter was on the disabled list due to a partial tear of the radial ligament on his left thumb, meaning it was Darryl Strawberry who occupied the cleanup spot. His first at-bat resulted in a single that drove in a pair and was part of a three-run first, to be followed up with a two-run second-inning homer.

Any thoughts of a stress-free night were put aside when the Pads rallied to tie by the eighth. The Mets withstood the comeback, managed to grab the lead back on Keith Hernandez's eleventh-inning sacrifice fly and then held it on a crazy final sequence.

With one out and Garry Templeton on second, Tim Flannery went up the middle for a base hit. Templeton had ideas of scoring. Lenny Dykstra short-circuited that plan—throwing Templeton out at home despite a nasty collision with catcher John Gibbons.

The mayhem at the plate gave Flannery the notion of trying to extend his double one base more. But Gibbons had the presence of mind to nail him before reaching third—8-2-5 if you're scoring at home. Or, "just your routine double play!" per the exclamation of announcer Tim McCarver.

September 17 vs. Cubs

The Mets couldn't have picked a better time for a four-game losing streak.

By dropping three straight in Philadelphia and one of two in St. Louis, they delayed their inevitable crowning as National League East champions—ensuring that victory party would be held at Shea Stadium.

Dwight Gooden fed off the air of anticipation as he tossed a complete game and struck out eight. But for all the established stars, young and old, who got the Mets to this point, it would be a rookie—Dave Magadan—who would shine. With Keith Hernandez suffering from the flu, his understudy filled in wonderfully in Mex's accustomed no. 3 hole—going 3-for-4 with two RBIs in the 4–2 victory.

"I had a pretty good year at Tidewater," Magadan said of his spell with the Triple-A affiliate, "but didn't even know if I'd come up. I was out there trying not to think about my other times at bat. So I didn't have a chance to think back on the game. I was trying to relax."

Hernandez was well enough to catch the final out from a ground ball to Wally Backman, which sent fans swarming on the field like bees to celebrate the first division title in thirteen years.

Step one of three complete.

NL East Final Standings, 1986

	Wins	Losses	GB
Mets	108	54	
Philadelphia Phillies	86	75	$21\frac{1}{2}$
St. Louis Cardinals	79	82	$28\frac{1}{2}$
Montreal Expos	78	83	$29\frac{1}{2}$
Chicago Cubs	70	90	37
Pittsburgh Pirates	64	98	44

REGULAR SEASON GAMES, 2000

MARCH 30 AT CUBS

Benny Agbayani was on the brink of learning baseball's harshest lesson.

With room for just a few more than the three starting outfielders, indications were Benny would be the odd man out of a congested depth chart jumble. That meant being relegated back to the minors—a spot in which he spent four years fighting to get his big break before the Mets called him up the year before.

While Agbayani fretted over a return to familiar territory, Major League Baseball entered unfamiliar terrain. The first-ever regular season series outside of North America came in front of fifty-five thousand at the Tokyo Dome.

In the second of a two-game set, and the Mets vying for a split, Valentine's starting lineup didn't have Agbayani included. It's hard to show you don't merit demotion when you can't play. But with the teams tied through ten innings, Benny was finally granted the opportunity to prove his worth with the bases loaded in the top of the eleventh.

The pitch from Chicago reliever Danny Young, making his first big-league appearance, went toward the 406-foot center-field wall. Damon Buford drifted as far as he could go. Sayonara.

Agbayani joyfully trotted 'round the bases—soon to be gifted with a replica shogun helmet and a $10,000 check from the welcoming country for being the star of the night. But of greater reward was what was to come: permanence on the Mets' roster for the rest of the season.

APRIL 24 VS. DODGERS

Cool early spring weather was failing to chill the red-hot offense.

From April 16 to 23, a stretch of seven games, New York exhausted the scoreboard with sixty runs. No surprise, the Mets won all seven.

But in a makeup contest against visiting Los Angeles, the Mets' bats finally took a night off. Fortunately, their pitchers were picking up the slack. Through 5.2 innings, starter Pat Mahomes allowed the Dodgers two hits and two walks before giving way to an equally effective bullpen.

Clutch hits, like runs, were nonexistent. The teams went 0-for-13 with runners in scoring position as Matt Franco stepped to the plate, batting for Dennis Cook, with the bases loaded and one out in the ninth.

His contact with an inside fastball hopped once as it went directly into the path of reliever Terry Adams. Hardly boasting a .118 batting average, Franco could use a favorable bounce.

"When I first hit it, I thought it was going to be a double play," Franco said. "Once I saw it tip off his glove, I knew we had won the game."

Melvin Mora raced home for the first and only run. What appeared to be an inning-ending grounder eventuated into a game-winning single—the Mets' eighth straight victory.

April 30 at Rockies

Each game at Coors Field can be accompanied by pinball music. Scoring runs in the mile-high air—even at forty-three degrees—is as easy as losing your breath in it.

Separated by a field goal, the Mets and Rockies threatened to drain the ink from a scorekeeper's pen—combining for twenty-five hits.

With a 14–11 final score, it's hard to believe there was a three-inning calm before a twenty-four-run storm. The only tally during the teams' initial six tries at-bat came when Melvin Mora used a sacrifice fly to right field to drive in Todd Zeile.

Mets starter Al Leiter and his opposite number, Brian Bohanon, were getting outs without a deluge of hits sandwiched in between. Then the rest of the game happened.

Zeile and Mora reappeared to produce dueling two-run homers. Leiter, meanwhile, gutted out seven-plus innings despite yielding five earned runs and departing with an 11–5 lead.

While the Rockies scored once in each of their next two tries, the Mets always had a rebuttal. A home run and sacrifice fly by Todd Pratt along with a two-RBI single from Edgardo Alfonzo made it 9–2.

Bobby Valentine called on the bullpen for resistance—to little avail. Colorado put up a six-spot in the eighth. No lead in Denver, even a five-run advantage with a top-flight closer, is secure. Armando Benítez gave up two ninth-inning runs. And in the offensively friendly atmosphere of Denver, that's tantamount to slamming the door.

May 20 vs. Diamondbacks

This was a game survived as much as won.

New York's indestructible 8–0 lead became endangered amid a bullpen demolition. Though, being a Mets pitcher of any kind proved quite painful.

Take starter Mike Hampton, for instance. He, like everyone else, waited out a three-and-a-half-hour rain delay. Then, he threw six shutout innings until a pulled back muscle forced his departure. That injury occurred while on the base paths during a five-run fourth in which Hampton laced a two-RBI single—the second time he reached base.

An Edgardo Alfonzo home run in the last of the seventh seemed like window dressing as the spread went up to eight. But with Hampton out of the picture, a walkover slowly turned into a nail-biter.

Pat Mahomes entered in the eighth, injured his ankle and gave up a two-run homer. Arizona then battered Rich Rodriguez and John Franco, who also fell prey to the sprained ankle epidemic, for five ninth-inning runs.

Armando Benítez came in with the tying run at second, struck out Erubiel Durazo and extinguished the fire.

Edgardo Alfonzo did the impossible: he became an under-the-radar standout in New York City—batting .324, driving in ninety-four, hitting forty doubles and making his only All-Star team. *Jerry Coli/Dreamstime.*

MAY 21 VS. DIAMONDBACKS

So much can change in eight months. However, when it came to the Mets and the D-Backs, not much did.

Elements that factored in New York's Division Series triumph the previous October were still alive the subsequent spring. Randy Johnson, on his way to his second of four consecutive Cy Youngs, found mortality similar to the NLDS opener. He came to Queens touting a 0.97 ERA. But that atomic number expanded when the first three batters doubled on consecutive pitches.

It started with Joe McEwing, standing a ruler's length shorter than the imposing presence on the hill. In this David-Goliath matchup, McEwing had more than one slingshot in the holster. Another double occurred four innings later, and a home run (his first of the season) came in the seventh.

The battle between "Super Joe" and "Big Unit" was quantified in inches. Mike Piazza's encounter was measured in feet—492 of them. His cannon blast reached the rarely entered territory of the left-field mezzanine seats.

Long balls from the expected, unexpected and Edgardo Alfonzo contributed to Johnson—despite thirteen Ks—being tagged with eight extra-base hits and five runs.

The Diamondbacks' bats came to Johnson's rescue—enough to take a 6–5 lead into the bottom of the eighth. Robin Ventura, though, came off the bench with a tying homer.

Then Derek Bell stepped up in the ninth with a liner barely afar from the glove of Travis Lee to score McEwing. Just like it was eight months ago, a D-Backs defender came up a hair short, and the Mets won three from Arizona.

JUNE 8 VS. ORIOLES

The Orioles' long road trip got a little longer. A rainout on June 6 added an extra workday to their ten-game sojourn away from Camden Yards.

After a hotel snafu in New York forced the team to spend a night in Baltimore, the O's trekked back up to Flushing with the hopes of washing away the previous night's 11–3 drubbing and avoiding a seventh loss in eight tries. But Baltimore's offense didn't appear too worse for wear. A six-run hammer dropped on Glendon Rusch through five innings—punctuated by home runs from Cal Ripken Jr. and soon-to-be-Met Mike Bordick.

The Orioles were doubling up New York by the bottom of the sixth. That's when the unlikely trio of Jay Payton, Kurt Abbott and Jason Tyner contributed run-producing at-bats.

Abbott's RBI—which came via a sacrifice fly to right field—was only his second in eighty-six plate appearances. The other was the result of a May 31 home run—not that anyone thought a featherweight shortstop had the muscle to double his long-ball total and triple his runs batted in aggregate over the span of a single game.

Jay Payton's round-tripper in the bottom of the eighth held up for only a few minutes, as John Franco and Armando Benítez allowed Baltimore to counter with an equalizing run.

Howie Rose has been a Mets broadcasting fixture spanning more than three decades. For nine years, including 2000, he did television play-by-play. Rose replaced the retiring Bob Murphy after the 2003 season and has been the radio voice of the team ever since. *Jerry Coli/Dreamstime.*

By the time the tenth inning rolled around, the Orioles might have had so little energy remaining that they were subject to hallucination when Abbott struck for a walk-off homer. But this was no nightmare.

Abbott sent the Shea Stadium fans home happy and the Orioles home thinking they would have been better off staying in Baltimore.

June 30 vs. Braves

For the considerable strides the Mets were making under Bobby Valentine, the Braves were always stomping on their toes. It wasn't a full hammer-to-nail condition, but New York could never measure up to Atlanta's prowess in the National League food chain.

With the All-Star game in the not-too-distant future, the Mets were looking good at 44-32. The Braves, as expected, were a tad better at 48-30.

For seven and a half innings on a late June evening at Shea, there was no indication New York would narrow the NL East margin. The Braves were ahead. And not barely. It was 8–1. Baseball logic suggests chipping away at such a large deficit and hoping your pitching staff can prevent the dam from bursting further.

But in the bottom of the eighth inning, there is no such time for such an imprudent strategy. Derek Bell began paving the Mets' comeback trail with a base hit. Edgardo Alfonzo flew out. Mike Piazza singled, and Bell advanced to third. Robin Ventura's ground ball to second base resulted in an RBI but elicited little hope—with two outs, the mountain steepened.

But Todd Zeile singled, driving home Piazza. And the line kept moving: Jay Payton, Benny Agbayani, pinch hitter Mark Johnson, Melvin Mora, Bell again and Alfonzo reached base to help draw the Mets even.

The comeback prophesy, forged by patient "small ball," was near complete. Now it was Piazza—the eleventh batter of the inning—to deliver the explosion he was so well suited for. With two on and two out, the crowd's anticipation was palpable—poised for its own release of noise with each upcoming pitch.

It took only one for Piazza to turn a Terry Mulholland offering into a heat-seeking missile aimed for the left-field corner. It didn't hook enough to travel foul. Instead, it struck the wall above and beyond the outfield fence in fair territory.

Piazza fiercely pumped his right fist as Shea went into a frenzy. The Mets had their most productive inning ever. The incredible 11–8 triumph wasn't the greatest comeback in team history, but it was the most thrilling.

July 14 at Red Sox

It took two games for Mike Piazza to alleviate any concerns.

The concussion induced by Roger Clemens's beanball to the head on July 8 kept New York's prized catcher out of the lineup for less than a week—the All-Star break included. The real concern, though, was not the length of his absence but if there would be any lingering effect when he returned for a weekend series at Fenway Park. As it turned out, there was nothing to worry about.

Playing it cautiously, Bobby Valentine penned in Piazza as the designated hitter. He had one job but doubled his efforts with

Al Leiter led the Mets' starting staff in victories (sixteen) and strikeouts (two hundred). *Jerry Coli/Dreamstime.*

two that cleared Fenway's fences—the latter putting the Mets on top for good in a 6–4 win.

Red Sox starter Pete Schourek, a Met from the dark ages, couldn't hold on to the lead granted by his offense. New York scored one in the fourth on the first of Piazza's homers and two the next. Boston countered with three unanswered runs.

The back-and-forth nature of this game swung for the last time thanks to the smack of No. 31's bat. With Edgardo Alfonzo on base, it was enough to reclaim the lead. They added insurance that proved necessary, as Armando Benítez created a ninth-inning distress.

A strikeout of Manny Alexander, posing as the potential winning run, put a kibosh on Red Sox comeback prospects.

JULY 29 VS. CARDINALS

The expansion of the playoffs made it slightly harder to foresee an October matchup—even with about two months of regular season remaining.

But St. Louis, five games ahead in the NL Central, and the Mets, with the second-best record in the National League, knew they could be seeing each other with much more at stake.

Both Andy Benes and Rick Reed sported nearly identical pitching lines: six innings and three earned runs being the primary figures. Games between quality opponents worthy of the postseason are decided by bullpens and timely offense.

New York's support staff, giving up just one hit, kept the Cardinals from breaking loose. The Mets, though, would do so in the bottom of the eighth. Appending an already splendid opening performance, Mike Bordick followed a third-inning homer with a seeing-eye single that put Robin Ventura ninety feet from taking the lead.

Lenny Harris, doing his usual splendid job in a pinch-hitting role, brought Robin the rest of the way with a single.

The eventual sweep of the Cards was a foretelling of future events. They went 20-9 in August, 6–3 against St. Louis in the regular season and 4–1 versus the Redbirds in the NLCS.

SEPTEMBER 13 VS. BREWERS

Through 144 games, little distinguished this year's Mets and the previous version—at least record-wise.

The year 2000 rode a much smoother path. New York was never challenged in the quest for the postseason by winning twelve out of the last eighteen contests.

Aiming for his fourteenth victory, Mike Hampton brought the stuff that merited it. Unfortunately, a first-inning Milwaukee run coupled with his lineup's incapacity to score put Hampton on the hook for loss no. 10.

Jeff D'Amico was responsible for the Mets' power outage, shutting them down to the tune of ten strikeouts through eight. But a wake-up call came in the ninth, when Curt Leskanic entered to close. Jay Payton led off with a double and was advanced to third on Edgardo Alfonzo's groundout to the right side of the infield.

Mike Piazza struck out, leaving the Mets down to their last breath. But Robin Ventura kept them alive— doubling down the left-field line to simultaneously end the shutout and Milwaukee's slim advantage. The Brewers failed to score in the tenth, meaning the Mets needed just one in the bottom half. Payton, being greedy, got three—on a two-out home run with two men aboard.

Come later in the month, for the ninth time in ten years, the Braves won the division title by a single game. But by losing to the Cardinals in the Division Series, it cleared the Mets' path toward National League supremacy.

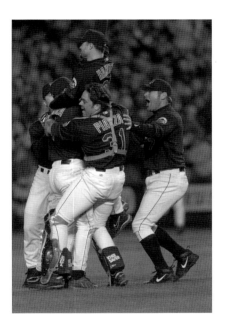

St. Louis held home-field advantage, but the Mets held the Cards at their mercy. New York won the NLCS opener 6–2, then took a back-and-forth affair at Busch Stadium to get a foothold on a commanding lead heading east. After dropping Game 3, the Mets used an extra-base hit barrage to capture Game 4 and the signature outing of Mike Hampton's short stay in Queens. His three-hit shutout earned him series MVP and sent the Mets back to the Fall Classic, where they awaited their nearby foes from the Bronx. *Jerry Coli/Dreamstime.*

NL East Final Standings, 2000

	Wins	Losses	GB
Atlanta Braves	95	67	
Mets	94	68	1
Florida Marlins	79	82	15½
Montreal Expos	67	95	28
Philadelphia Phillies	65	97	30

REGULAR SEASON GAMES, 2015

APRIL 27 AT MARLINS

The early inkling that things would be different this year than in any of the last nine surfaced in April.

Offsetting a 2-3 start, then tipping the scales favorably, the Mets put one win in front of another—stringing together eleven straight to match a franchise record set on three other occasions: in 1969, 1986 and 1990.

It was early in a season with so long to go that it was premature for anyone to think if this could-be omen would turn foretelling. But Terry Collins's club already showed the ingredients needed to cook up a title: beating divisional opponents and securing close victories. Both elements surfaced in Miami—albeit too late for comfort.

Jarred Cosart's eight shutout innings were making Dillon Gee's seven innings of one-run ball irrelevant.

Then the Marlins went to their bullpen, and the Mets couldn't have been happier.

Steve Cishek was the welcome sight, and New York reacted with a double and a walk. The tying and winning runs were there to be driven home. Michael Cuddyer couldn't do it—he flew out to right. Daniel Murphy, putting it into the same general area (except, you know, farther), could.

How would one describe Daniel's second home run and the seventh, eighth and ninth RBIs in the last four games, to give the Mets a 3–1 victory? "Murph-a-licious," according to Collins.

JUNE 15 VS. BLUE JAYS

Lucas Duda unconsciously heeded the advice of Wee Willie Keeler, a nineteenth-century standout, to "hit 'em where they ain't"—finding a flaw in a twenty-first-century innovation that became the focal point of an extra-inning victory.

Together since 2006, they have been regarded as the best local broadcast team in baseball. Coalescing a wealth of knowledge with sharp commentary and delightful chemistry, the trio of longtime play-by-play voice Gary Cohen (*center*) along with analysts Ron Darling (*left*) and Keith Hernandez make each telecast a must-watch—no matter how watchable the Mets are. *Marc Levine/SNY.*

One out from Toronto's twelfth straight victory, with Michael Cuddyer on first, the Blue Jays shifted its entire defense right—the modern way to combat a lefty pull hitter like Duda. The Met first baseman lofted a flare normally regarded as a routine fly to shallow left field. But with defenders nowhere to be found, it landed untouched—enough for both Cuddyer to chug around and Duda to reach second as the winning run.

No sooner could the tension be built before Wilmer Flores laced one up the middle—sending Duda home. The 4–3 victory cooled off the hottest team in baseball—a title once held by the Mets in mid-April.

Noah Syndergaard looked to have extinguished the Jays with the best performance of his young career. Facing his original organization, Noah limited the potent Toronto offense to one run, two hits, walked two and struck out eleven over six innings.

Just as the Mets should have lost it in the eleventh, they should have won it in the ninth. José Bautista ruined a regulation victory with a home run off Jeurys Familia—giving the New York closer his second blown save.

JULY 26 VS. DODGERS

A dormant offense received a bit of life. Juan Uribe and Kelly Johnson, a pair of reliable veteran hitters, were brought in from the Braves.

These certainly weren't transformative actions and could no doubt be compared to the acquisition upcoming. But relative to what the lineup produced during a summer drought, any halfway reliable bat would be a godsend.

Coming off a 2-for-5 night, which included a home run, Johnson got the start at second base and batted cleanup. His day at the plate was less eventful, while Uribe—sitting on the bench for more than nine innings—used his lone at-bat to put the finishing touch on a win the Mets desperately needed.

Three consecutive ninth-inning hits off Jeurys Familia turned a 2–0 lead into a 2–2 tie. More concerning than the potential for a loss that would keep them from gaining a game on the Nationals was the fact that this was the second straight blown save for Familia (who suffered only two through the All-Star break).

Uribe, though, arrived to bail out his new teammate. Pinch-hitting for Johnson with Curtis Granderson on second and Daniel Murphy on first, he hit a Kenley Jansen pitch on the screws that caromed high off the left–center field wall to easily plate Granderson and keep New York two games behind Washington.

JULY 31 VS. NATIONALS

In some parallel universe, Wilmer Flores and Zack Wheeler are playing for the Milwaukee Brewers. Carlos Gomez is back with the organization that drafted him. Yoenis Cespedes is not in Queens. And the Mets don't go on a run to the 2015 National League pennant.

Fortunately, the events unraveled in a different—yet torturous—fashion.

For a team that over the past three decades has tested its fan base with a Russian novel's worth of narrative twists, the week that led up to the opener of a showdown with Washington stretched the bounds of emotional whiplash.

Monday, July 27: Following a deal to nab veterans Juan Uribe and Kelly Johnson from Atlanta and the call-up of highly touted Michael Conforto, New York bolsters its bullpen by getting A's reliever Tyler Clippard.

Tuesday, July 28: The Clippard addition is validated after it is announced reliever Jenrry Mejía tested positive for the same steroid responsible for his 80-game suspension at the start of the season. The result: a new, 162-game ban.

Wednesday, July 29: Flores's own personal soap opera plays out in full view. The crying game that should have been avoided by a simple substitution instead adds to the club's reputation for mismanagement. It turns out to be nothing worth sobbing over, as New York's deal to acquire Gomez for Flores and Wheeler is ultimately nixed.

Thursday, July 30: Sadness turns to anger, as Jeurys Familia blows his third save opportunity since the All-Star break. The San Diego Padres complete a six-run comeback when Justin Upton goes deep with two outs and two on in the top of the ninth, a rally interrupted—*twice*—by ninth-inning rain delays.

All that heralded the happiest of endings: a date in which everything changed permanently for the better. July 31 began with the pursuit and eventual obtainment of Cespedes (without having to relinquish Wheeler) and ended in feel-good, storybook form: with Flores hitting a walk-off home run in the twelfth inning to give the Mets a critical series-opening victory.

The only tears on this night were joyous ones—a blissful atmosphere which permeated Queens through the rest of the summer and into the fall.

AUGUST 1 VS. NATIONALS

The second-largest crowd in Citi Field history simultaneously served as a welcoming party for Yoenis Cespedes and a celebration of renewed interest in a team that affirmed credibility.

While Cespedes's debut was relatively silent, save for the standing ovation he received on his first-inning at-bat, the star slugger was Lucas Duda. His one-man demolition of Washington pitching—concluding with a tie-breaking eighth-inning RBI double—sustained a personal hot streak, and a 3–2 win brought the Mets even closer to the trembling Nationals.

Jacob deGrom shook off the struggles of two first-inning runs and followed it with five scoreless frames—scuffling for a season-high 117 pitches to prevent Washington from scoring again. Duda took care of the

Fan-friendly and remarkably charitable, Curtis Granderson signs autographs during spring training. The 2016 Roberto Clemente Award recipient made generous contributions with the bat in the form of twenty-six home runs. *Courtesy of Jim Maggiore.*

scoring on the Mets' end. He erased the early two-run hole with a double dose of solo homers against an otherwise sufficient night for Washington's Joe Ross. That gave New York's first baseman seven round-trippers in the last seven games, preceding the go-ahead two-bagger influenced by the newest addition to the lineup.

Nationals manager Matt Williams eschewed pitching to the right-handed Cespedes in favor of a lefty-lefty matchup with Matt Thornton—a roll of the dice that came up snake eyes when Duda went to the opposite field and over the head of Jayson Werth.

The Mets stayed homer happy the next night, as three third-inning blasts (including another from Duda) led to a sweep of Washington and a virtual divisional tie.

AUGUST 27 AT PHILLIES

Carlos Torres, primarily a reliever, made like a goalkeeper. Jeff Francoeur's tenth-inning grounder eyed center field until Torres's reflexes—and the side of his foot—changed the ball's direction. It deflected to his left and in the area of Daniel Murphy, who bare-handed and blindly flipped to the pitcher covering first base.

If you wanted any visual proof that the rejuvenated Mets were steamrolling through August, en route to a 20-8 record, look no further than that play.

Torres's kick save brought about a win when the Mets blew open a long-standing 5–5 tie with four runs in the thirteenth—ensuring the bullpen's seven shutout innings of allowing seven hits and no walks. Torres actually started the winning rally with a leadoff single, augmenting his extended contributions on the mound.

Curtis Granderson moved him over to second and then Daniel Murphy transported both homeward on a double—marking the first score by either side since the fifth.

David Wright, recently removed from the disabled list, and Michael Conforto each had run-producing at-bats as well to polish off a 9–5 victory and a four-game road sweep of Philadelphia in which the Mets outscored the Phils 40–21.

SEPTEMBER 7 AT NATIONALS

On Labor Day, the Mets really had to work for it.

The five-and-a-half-game lead they built up through a galvanizing four-week stretch shrank to three after the first weekend in September.

Now, they encountered their toughest test yet. The sweep of the Nationals five weeks earlier proved the Mets were unafraid of the supposed division champs. But no longer would they enjoy the comfort of Citi Field. The support in D.C., strong as it might have been, wouldn't match the Flushing environment.

When Wilson Ramos unloaded a grand slam off Jonathan Niese to help tack on five fourth-inning scores to take a two-run advantage, the Nats—riding a five-game win streak—appeared ready to keep reeling the Mets in.

But it would be New York laying down the comeback trail. A run in the fifth and a run in the sixth—both against starter Max Scherzer—preceded the conclusive seventh versus a succession of four Washington relievers.

Yoenis Cespedes's double, which brought home David Wright from first with a relay-beating slide and an emphatic fist-pump toward the ground, was the exclamation point on a three-run frame that sent a portion of Nationals Park scurrying toward the exits.

While the Mets buried Washington's woeful bullpen, the Nats were held scoreless and managed only three hits following Niese's departure.

"What a game," Wright said afterward. "Just, what a game." But the best was yet to come.

September 8 at Nationals

Too often the minor leagues are the final resting place for major league dreams. In 2015, Kirk Nieuwenhuis went from the Mets across to the Angels, back to the Mets and down to Triple-A. Like any player in this position before, Kirk probably wondered if he would ever get called up again.

But when the major league rosters expanded on September 1, a spot was his. He economized his three home runs that year to a single game at Citi Field in July—and then created the latest surprise in the Mets' surprising turnaround.

Jonathan Papelbon, Washington's trade deadline addition, served an eighth-inning pitch down the heart of the plate that Nieuwenhuis cranked into the right-field stands for New York's seventh unanswered score.

The David Wright–Daniel Murphy–Lucas Duda round-the-horn double play in the ninth officially stamped one of the franchise's greatest rallies and, simultaneously, broke the backs of the Nats. Matt Harvey, eventually named NL Comeback Player of the Year, took a slight step behind. Washington tugged on the cape of "The Dark Knight" a few too many times for him to feel comfortable. He exited with one out in the sixth, down 7–1, and found a unique—if not unwelcome—method to solve the simmering innings limit debate between his agent and Mets management.

His coup de grâce came when a Michael A. Taylor bases-loaded single skipped under the glove of Yoenis Cespedes in center and allowed all runners to mosey around uncontested—creating that six-run separation.

But Cespedes atoned. He came up in the seventh against Drew Storen with a full supply of traffic on the base paths and roped a three-run double down the left-field line to cut the deficit to one. Storen was unable to locate the strike zone on three consecutive batters—forcing in the equalizer and setting up Nieuwenhuis's rare moment in the spotlight.

SEPTEMBER 9 AT NATIONALS

For the Mets, daggers drawn. For the Nationals, make or break. Two uplifting victories for New York and two dispiriting losses for Washington confirmed a power shift from the original NL East favorites to a team that had morphed swiftly into a powerhouse.

Stephen Strasburg, though, pumped some air back into his deflated team by retiring twenty-one of the first twenty-five he faced. Travis d'Arnaud's second-inning homer was the only New York run. Bryce Harper, the soon-to-be MVP, did everything he could offensively—going 3-for-4 and responsible for the entirety of the Nats' scoring.

The 2–1 lead for Strasburg and Washington heading into the top of the eighth was erased by a Kelly Johnson blast. The pick-up from Atlanta tied it. After, Curtis Granderson produced a one-out single that brought Cespedes up to the plate—a chance to add to his rapidly emerging Mets legend.

Nats manager Matt Williams, boos raining down, came to the mound and signaled for a still-harried Drew Storen. He might as well have been waving the white flag. All of the factors favored the Mets taking the lead on this matchup. After two pitches and one mammoth Cespedes swing, it came to fruition.

The Mets won 5–3. In a make-or-break affair, the Nats shattered. And Storen actually fractured his right thumb in a locker room tantrum.

New York officially completed its overthrow and clinched the division on September 26 in Cincinnati. But unofficially, the East was won this night in the nation's capital.

SEPTEMBER 13 AT BRAVES

Murphy magic, act two—just when the Braves thought, for once, they had them during this three-game series.

Atlanta punctured holes in the Mets bullpen to turn a 4–3 deficit into a 7–4 lead heading into the top of the ninth. New York's second baseman was due up fifth. His teammates would need to string together at least two productive plate appearances for him to try to atone for some earlier fielding faux pas.

It took until there were two outs before Juan Lagares doubled and Curtis Granderson walked to give Murphy the chance. The Mets remained backed against the wall until No. 20 lifted a Ryan Kelly pitch over it. A rather

Welcome to "Murph-tober." With each daily home run, Daniel Murphy sank the hopes of the Chicago Cubs. He went deep in each game of the four-game sweep—making him the first player in postseason history to homer in six straight playoff contests. The Windy City's wait for a Wrigley Field World Series would be put on hold for another year. *Arturo Pardavila III/ Wikimedia Commons.*

ordinary see-saw day for Murphy stayed on high when he drove in another run the next inning. It was with far less flair and of far less importance. The Mets had already been the beneficiary of a walk and an error that accounted for two earlier scores.

Murphy's extra contribution was merely window dressing for a team that saw the playoffs in plain sight. But a definite certainty was that the Mets had eighty-two wins, clinching their first over .500 season since 2008.

NL East Final Standings, 2015

	Wins	Losses	GB
Mets	90	72	
Washington Nationals	83	79	7
Miami Marlins	71	91	19
Atlanta Braves	67	95	23
Philadelphia Phillies	63	99	27

PART VIII

BEST OF THE BEST

TOM SEAVER SEASONS

10. 1974

Experiencing an unusual reversal of fortune, Seaver spent much of this season dealing with constant frustration rather than dishing it out.

Tom dropped four of his first five decisions, including a pair that saw him tagged for at least six runs in each. But the mental distress suffered was mild compared to tremendous physical discomfort. A nagging pain in his left buttocks resurfaced on July 7. He would be out for three weeks and, for the first time in his big-league career, was not included on the All-Star roster.

Seaver went winless—and yet not painless—over his final three starts, although the last turned out to be a tough-luck 2–1 loss to Philadelphia—which brought his record to 11-11. Deserving of a better fate, Tom struck out fourteen Phillies and gave up four hits over nine innings.

His 3.20 ERA—although the envy of less successful pitchers—was a career-worst at that time, even if his strikeout-to-walk ratio was a league-leading 2.68.

9. 1976

In many respects, this was the toughest year yet.

With the advent of free agency came player prosperity. Seaver—fresh off another Cy Young–winning campaign—sought his deserved share.

Consternation occurred on both sides, but the Mets gave Seaver a contract ensuring he'd be baseball's richest pitcher. Seaver got paid by his employers, even if he felt they didn't totally respect him.

Tom kept those feelings hidden, but the roots of frustration grew as the season played out. A 14-11 record—below his high bar of acceptance—barely came from individual struggles. He extended his record streak of seasons with at least two hundred Ks to nine and paced the NL in strikeouts for the fifth time. His 2.59 ERA amounted to a minimal increase from '75, and his WHIP actually decreased.

But he, like every Met who took the mound, was bothered by a lackluster offense that failed to feature an everyday .300 hitter and had just one player—Dave Kingman—with more than eighty RBIs and fifteen homers.

Seaver's insistence to pursue free agent bats—outfielder Gary Matthews, specifically—fell on deaf ears.

8. 1967

April 13—the beginning of something terrific.

Seaver started many Opening Days, but his personal opening day took place in the season's second game—on a Thursday afternoon against Pittsburgh.

Barely five thousand fans came out to Shea Stadium. Not every transformational moment is readily apparent from its outset. If we knew then what we know now, "standing room only" would have been the best way to describe the turnout.

Tom didn't win against the Pirates, but the Mets did. Seven days later at Wrigley Field, he went 7.1 innings, allowed six hits and two earned runs and (most importantly) attained victory no. 1. So many more were to follow.

7. 1968

Seaver didn't adhere to the sophomore slump.

His win-loss record from year one to year two was nearly identical (16-12 in '67 to 16-13 in '68). But every other vital figure enjoyed a change for the better.

Gaining 278 innings of mound experience (27 more than in his rookie season), Seaver shaved more than half a run off his ERA, dipped his WHIP to 0.978 (down from 1.203), doled out four fewer home run balls and tallied three additional shutouts. His strikeout total took a jump of thirty-five, and he even picked up a save, the only one on his extensive résumé, which came on the back end of a July 7 doubleheader in Philadelphia.

But of all the improvements made, the greatest boon to his betterment came before the year started, when the team hired Gil Hodges as manager. As Seaver asserted in his 1992 Hall of Fame speech, Hodges

Seaver called him "my catcher." The succeeding periods of Hall of Famers Gary Carter (*left*) and Mike Piazza (*center*) obscure the importance of Jerry Grote (*right*) to the Mets in the 1960s and 1970s. With Texas toughness, Grote cajoled stellar Mets pitching for eleven seasons. He was arguably the best defensive backstop of his time—an era that included Johnny Bench. A two-time All-Star, Grote improved his hitting to bat .295 in 1975 and was inducted into the Mets Hall of Fame in 1992. *Jerry Coli/Dreamstime.*

was the "one guy who taught me how to be a professional, to really be a pro…the most important man in my life from the professional standpoint of my career."

6. 1972

Seaver's fate charted a parallel path to that of his ball club.

As New York jumped out to a significant advantage in the NL East, their ace began 7-1. And like the Mets themselves, Seaver skidded through the summer—going 3-6 with 30 runs allowed in 70.2 innings from June 24 through August 2.

While a strong September was too little, too late for the club to get back in the division race, Tom's stellar concluding kick netted him another twenty-win campaign—even if his ERA (2.92) and WHIP (1.15) drifted above the impressive marks of 1971.

Seaver won nine of his last twelve decisions and gave up more than three runs in only two of those starts. A pair of complete-game gems against Pittsburgh were especially memorable. The first came on September 20 at Shea, in which he struck out fifteen. For the second, nine days later, he fanned thirteen more and pitched a shutout for his twentieth victory. He added one more on the season's final day.

Not too shabby for an off-year.

5. 1970

It would be impossible for the Mets and their ace to match—much less surpass—what was accomplished in 1969.

Although Seaver's 2.82 ERA was the highest of his four-year career, it was the lowest in the National League by season's end.

But the biggest improvement Seaver made for 1970 was in the strikeout category. With 283, it was 75 more than he registered the prior year. There were twelve starts in which he managed to fan at least ten batters.

Then there was the game where he nearly went twice as high. On April 22 against the San Diego Padres, the same afternoon he accepted his '69 Cy Young Award, Seaver's overpowering prowess reached a level unseen in big league history: a record ten straight strikeouts to end the game brought his total for the day to nineteen and a share of the National League mark.

4. 1975

Perhaps stimulated to avenge 1974's disappointment, Seaver enhanced his legendary status—both in Mets history and the annals of baseball itself—and silenced any thinly veiled notion of a decline.

Tom went 22-9 and attained two significant strikeout milestones. First came the 2,000[th] of his career—at the expense of Cincinnati Red Dan Driessen on July 24. The next occurred on September 1 against the Pittsburgh Pirates—leading the third-place Mets by five games in the NL East.

The pennant race, and a 3-0 New York lead, took a temporary back seat to what Seaver was on the verge of achieving. A home crowd, fully cognizant of the circumstances, watched as Manny Sanguillén went down swinging in the seventh inning. And, thus, Seaver became the only pitcher in major league history to have eight consecutive seasons of at least two hundred strikeouts.

Although the Mets limped toward the finish line, their ace ended the year on the highest of individual notes: a third Cy Young Award.

3. 1973

Surfacing from last place on August 30 to the division title on October 1, the Mets withstood numerous injuries and early disappointments to reach the World Series.

But their ace did not share his team's twists of fate. Steady as ever, Seaver posted a National League–best 2.08 ERA and major league–high 251 strikeouts—the primary figures that accounted for a second Cy Young plaque.

Only five runs were scored on him during April. His record through July was 13-5, in spite of New York's cellar-dwelling status. But as the Mets gained steam down the home stretch, Seaver delivered in those critical outings—spinning a complete game against Pittsburgh on September 22 to officially put New York atop the division. Less than two weeks later, he won the NL East clincher in Chicago.

Seaver stoutly handled Cincinnati's imposing lineup as the Mets captured the National League Championship Series to just three runs in almost two whole games. And in the winner-take-all affair at Shea, Tom avenged a tough-luck Game 1 loss to hold the Reds bats to one earned run in 8.1 innings.

2. 1969

By now, with two superb seasons of 16 wins apiece in his wake, Seaver had placed himself near the level of baseball's elite pitchers. By the end of '69, he had risen above every level—the entirety of his competition.

Of Seaver's 311 career victories, 198 came as a Met. *Jerry Coli/Dreamstime.*

If anyone else who took the mound wanted to make the claim that he had a better year than Tom, he wouldn't have much evidence to support it.

By winning twenty-five games, striking out 208, posting a 2.21 ERA and five shutouts, Seaver was awarded his first National League Cy Young plaque and granted the rare distinction of being *Sports Illustrated*'s "Sportsman of the Year."

By taking the Mets from annual laughing stock to division champs, pennant winners and the unlikeliest of World Championships, he became ingrained into the sprawling, but distinct folklore of New York sports.

This was the bedrock on which his Hall of Fame legacy was constructed.

1. 1971

The flawless mechanics of Seaver's rhythmic, drop-and-drive motion—an effortless, knee-scraping stride that became a staple of New York summers for more than a decade—never worked to greater effect.

His power, overwhelming—289 strikeouts a personal-high and a record for right-handed NL pitchers.

His precision, impeccable—a meager sixty-one bases on balls.

A 1.76 ERA, a 0.946 WHIP and 9.1 Ks per nine innings not only led the league, but they were also each his personal-best season-ending marks.

While personal summits were scaled in these season-ending statistics, the standard he surmounted with relative ease—twenty victories—didn't come as effortlessly, thanks to an offense not offering up much backing. Needing to win his last two outings to get there, Seaver retired eighteen straight batters and one-hit the eventual World Champion Pittsburgh Pirates on September 26. Then, in the season finale, he struck out thirteen and yielded one run against St. Louis—the twenty-eighth start in which he allowed two or fewer earned runs.

That pair of victories gave him a 9-2 mark over the final twelve starts along with fifty-eight hits allowed and 112 strikeouts in his last 107 innings.

Seaver did everything that measures up to winning the Cy Young Award—except actually winning it. Chicago's Ferguson Jenkins exceeded Tom by four in the win column and thirty-two in the vote total.

The lack of hardware, though, does nothing to diminish the brightest season in two shining decades. And if this here judgment doesn't suffice, you could ask the legend himself.

"I thought it was the best year of my career," he said in a 1988 book. Case closed.

ALL-TIME STARTING LINEUP

10. Designated Hitter: Howard Johnson (1985–93)

Upon moving from Detroit to New York before the 1985 season, "HoJo" probably wished the American League rules transferred too.

The Mets shuffled Johnson's fielding location so much—never to great effect—that it might have made him dizzy. He began at third base, moved between there and shortstop, was inserted in left field, spent thirty games of 1991 in right field and began 1992 as the starting center fielder. We'll do him a favor and spare him a glove. It'd be a shame not to use his bat or legs.

One who is fleet of foot isn't normally a power threat, and a player with power doesn't usually run the bases well. That's what makes thirty home runs and thirty stolen bases in the same season so distinguished.

Howard Johnson is more than just the name of a roadside motel—he became a household name in Mets history with his breakout 1987. Four years later, he took the National League home run and RBI title. *Jerry Coli/Dreamstime.*

Johnson swung and scurried into rarefied company three times: in his breakout season of 1987, when he became half of a 30-30 duet with Darryl Strawberry (the only time two teammates achieved the feat); in 1989, when he swiped forty-one bags and drove home 101 runs; and in 1991, when he led the National League in homers (38) and RBIs (117).

Twice an All-Star third baseman, Johnson bashed 157 home runs and stole 160 bags from '87 through '92.

9. Right Field: Darryl Strawberry (1983–90)

Boundless talents were capable of propelling Darryl into the pantheon of baseball legends. Only he could construct his limitations.

The sweet swing born of a thoroughbred build—poisonous for opposing pitchers who dared challenge him—unfurled into an uppercut that lifted 252 out of the park, which is at the crest of the franchise's home run list.

His 733 runs batted in remain second-most; 2,028 total bases rank fourth; 191 stolen bases are fifth. National League chart-topping figures like a .545 slugging percentage, .911 OPS, and thirty-nine homers helped make him the runner-up in the 1988 MVP voting.

His seven midsummer classic appearances in a Met uniform are second to Tom Seaver's nine. He easily makes the All-Time Mets team. But Strawberry should have been an all-time MLB great.

Self-induced controversies constantly engulfed him. Whether it be run-ins with teammates, contract disputes, off-the-field distractions, his questionable work ethic or his attitude, Darryl was his own worst enemy.

He's recently ditched the wayward habits that sent his life into a tailspin and prevented easy entrance into Cooperstown. But his career, both with the Mets and as a whole, will always be shrouded in disappointment.

8. Center Field: Carlos Beltran (2005–11)

Unfair as it may be, visions of Beltran—despite nearly seven seasons of top-notch production—are reduced to one game, one at-bat, one pitch.

The called third strike against him, which put a conclusion on the 2006 NLCS, detracts from the club records he set that year: 41 home runs, 127 runs scored and 80 extra-base hits.

The Mets would've never reached that point minus his presence in the lineup or his fluidity in patrolling the pivotal outfield position.

Beltran has rarely stayed too comfortable in one spot—having played with seven different clubs during a twenty-year career that ended after 2017. By his standards, seven years (the length of his Mets tenure) are almost an eternity.

With no other team did he produce more homers (149), runs batted in (559), doubles (208), or runs scored (551)—gaudy numbers that would have been bolstered if not for a series of injuries that kept him out for half of 2009 and most of 2010. Of his nine All-Star selections, five came with New York.

During his seven-season stay in Flushing, Carlos Beltran won three Gold Gloves and made five All-Star teams. *Jerry Coli/Dreamstime.*

Considering how his career totals approached Hall of Fame caliber, it wouldn't be so much of a stretch to say he'll be wearing a Mets cap—should such an honor be bestowed upon him.

7. LEFT FIELD: CLEON JONES (1963, 1965–75)

The enduring image—for him and the team he represented: a fly ball into his mitt, a knee down on the warning track and a miraculous World Series won.

Jones secured the final out against Baltimore and secured a place in Mets history with his .340 batting average. That would remain the highest ever in a single-season for three decades and was the third best in the National League (behind Pete Rose and Roberto Clemente).

For a while, until the arrival of Mike Piazza and David Wright, it could be argued that Cleon was the greatest Met hitter. He's certainly the franchise's first consistent offensive presence. In 1968, when the scales tipped far in favor of the pitcher, Jones hit .297 when only six other major leaguers could creep above .300. On top of boosting his average by more than forty points the next year, he finished fifth in on-base percentage, ninth in OPS and was an NL All-Star starter.

The '69 season was Cleon's best, but his finest ten days came during the stretch of an injury-riddled 1973. With New York fighting for the division, Jones produced six of his eleven homers and fourteen of his forty-eight RBIs after September 19.

Bitterly, he departed the Mets in a cloud of discontent—but not enough to obscure his significance in winning a championship and two pennants.

6. Shortstop: José Reyes (2003–11, 2016–present)

The rev in the Mets' engine, Reyes ratcheted up the excitement meter. Opposing pitchers and catchers, however, were a bit less thrilled.

Like Mookie Wilson before him, Reyes developed into another homegrown speed merchant. In 2005, he embarked on a three-year sequence featuring steal totals of sixty (to lead the NL), sixty-four (to lead MLB) and seventy-eight (a league-high and club single-season record).

The 2008 campaign also was the year Reyes passed Wilson and officially cemented himself as the team's premier base thief—an aggregate now above four hundred.

But the second-most prolific hitter in Met history couldn't cause disruption on the base paths without discipline at the plate.

José had more power than most leadoff hitters, averaging sixteen homers from '05 to '08. However, it was almost a letdown when he hit it out, because the thrill of watching Reyes emanated from gazing at a cleat-wearing gazelle swiftly turn a gap-filler into a triple.

There was no paucity of those. Four times he led the majors. Seven times he led the Mets. Reyes headed the triples category in 2011, and his .337 average made him the first Met to win a batting crown—one he took with him into the Citi Field dugout before the season finale concluded and then on to Miami.

Reyes discovered the grass wasn't greener in South Beach, Toronto or Denver. Three stops, five years and a domestic violence violation later, he came back to New York—excitement less frequent and reputation slightly tarnished.

5. Third Base: David Wright (2004–present)

Loyalty is hard to come by these days.

With regards to such stipulations, Wright remains a throwback—one who plays for the betterment of the team and for the love of the game.

It was true in 2004 at age twenty-one, and it remained true as he tried to conquer the distressing spinal stenosis and other ailments that have prevented his return to a field he occupied so consistently before.

Wright inherited the "face of the franchise" mantle from Mike Piazza, and he couldn't be a better representative. The leadership quality he exhibited on the diamond and in the clubhouse earned him captaincy in 2013. And the leadership he holds in nearly every vital offensive category ensures the retirement of No. 5 when the moment comes.

His legacy as a pillar of the Mets is secure.

DAVID WRIGHT MOMENTS

5. Returning in Style (August 24, 2015)

His influence pervaded, even if his presence in the lineup was nonexistent. Wright displayed qualities that teammates were made to follow. When he unloaded a mammoth shot into the far reaches of Philadelphia's Citizens Bank Park in the first at-bat since a 115-game stint on the disabled list, the rest obeyed that action in kind. The Mets established single-game club records for homers and extra-base hits in a 16–7 throttling of the Phils.

4. Becoming the Mets' Hit King (September 26, 2012)

An unassuming squibber toward third base can look like a line drive in record books. The way he got that infield single was less important than what it meant. Hit 1,419 made him the all-time leader in that category—surpassing Ed Kranepool's long-standing mark. David, in his usual self-effacing fashion, said, "It's obviously humbling, a little more exciting because we won today."

3. The Barehanded Catch (August 9, 2005)

Who said you need a glove? San Diego's Brian Giles bust a soft fly ball over David's head that was sure to be a cheap hit to left field—a challenging play with the glove, if he could even race back and do it. But David upped the degree of difficulty by sticking out his bare right hand while falling down. And he still caught it. It was one of the best grabs you'll ever see, by a Met or anyone else.

Jerry Coli/Dreamstime.

2. A Classic Smash (2015 World Series Game 3)

Wright banked on the future of the organization on November 29, 2012, by signing an eight-year, $138 million contract—effectively making him a Met for life. "I can honestly say I've never pictured myself in a different uniform. It wouldn't be as meaningful if I were to win somewhere else." Three years later, he would be rewarded with his first NL pennant. And his first home World Series at-bat produced a towering two-run blast that started the Mets onward to a 9–3 victory.

1. Walk-Off Hit off Mariano Rivera (May 19, 2006)

Queens's answer to Derek Jeter, Wright showed he also had a flair for the dramatic. Against Jeter's Yankees, no less, and against the greatest closer there's ever been, the budding star ended the opener of one of the most highly anticipated regular season Subway Series with a game-winning hit to deep center field.

4. Second Base: Edgardo Alfonzo (1995–2002)

Contrary to mainstream thought, Alfonzo proved it is possible to be overlooked in New York City. But even scouts failed to notice his capacity—something they're paid to do.

Whichever member of the Mets research group decided to ink "Fonzie" as an unsigned free agent back in 1991 retroactively deserves a raise. He never asked for publicity, nor did he ever seek it out. The greatest extent of his national recognition, outside of his games being on TV, is when *Sports Illustrated* featured him, John Olerud, Robin Ventura and Rey Ordonez on a 1999 cover—positing them as the best infield ever.

Alfonzo saved several runs with his glove (initially at third base before moving to the right side of the diamond), but what should have made him a star were the runs he produced—538 in eight seasons. He paced the Mets in on-base percentage twice and in hits three times. His 1,136 hits rank fifth on the franchise list.

As Mike Piazza's lead-in on the lineup card in 2000, Alfonzo got plenty of good pitches to hit. And with a .324 batting average, twenty-five homers, ninety-four RBIs and forty doubles, he put few of them to waste.

Piazza got more MVP votes that year, but Alfonzo had the better WAR (6.7).

3. First Base: Keith Hernandez (1983–89)

If you think intangibles can't be measured, you didn't notice the impression Hernandez made. Delivering a swift organizational attitude adjustment, Keith possessed a sheer force of personality that instilled confidence in his teammates. His uncanny power of leadership held the ear of those around him. And in 1987, he was appointed as the Mets' first-ever captain.

Before Hernandez, the Mets thought they *might* win. After Hernandez, they *knew* they would. The visceral franchise change bared itself in his first full season. New York's 1984 performance was a direct reflection of Keith's words being put into action. He hit .311, smacked fifteen homers and thirty-one doubles and drove in ninety-four—often using his cerebral plate knowledge to generate a key hit at will.

In turn, the Mets poked at the division-winning Cubs for much of the year, and Hernandez was the runner-up for NL MVP.

At .297, "Mex" enjoys the highest batting average among hitters with more than three thousand at-bats. But what made him a unique first baseman was the manner in which he maximized and expanded the capabilities of a position rarely regarded as a bastion for exemplary defense.

Keith charged toward the plate on potential bunts—directly affecting the way opposing teams would sacrifice. He displayed range rarely (if ever) seen and turned infielders' bad throws into outs. During his first six seasons in New York, Hernandez claimed a Gold Glove—which added to his record-setting sum of eleven straight.

Hernandez parlayed that intuitive baseball knowledge and generally acerbic wit into a broadcasting career that has enhanced his popularity further—if his legendary *Seinfeld* cameo didn't already do it.

2. CATCHER: MIKE PIAZZA (1998–2005)

A sixty-second round draft pick to the Hall of Fame, Piazza is an unlikely journey better saved for fables. Stardom formed in Los Angeles, but it was New York where his case for Cooperstown was cemented.

From 1999 to 2002, his four healthiest full seasons with the Mets, Piazza averaged 37 homers while leading the team in RBIs and OPS. Statistics aside, he gave Queens's baseball team a clear-cut identity. And in supplementing his Hall call in 2016, the Mets made sure they'd immortalize his legacy as well—with "31" joining the short list of retired numbers.

TOP FIVE MIKE PIAZZA STATISTICS

5. .348 Batting Average (1998)

Mike's noted power stroke didn't immediately transfer over to New York—with five home runs in his first forty-three games. But never was there a lag in his batting mark. During that same eight-week stretch, it was .331. And he improved with each passing month—ultimately erupting to .378 over his final eighty-two at-bats.

---

4. Forty Home Runs (1999)

With a full season in the Big Apple and a hefty contract extension, Piazza never looked more comfortable. As the Mets won ninety-seven games and made the postseason for the first time in eleven years, the biggest slugging star since Darryl Strawberry launched twenty-one homers during the second half and eleven in August.

3. Twenty-Four-Game Hitting Streak (1999)

The Mets have had dependable middle-of-the-lineup hitters. Few, if any, occupied their spot longer than Piazza. He was never steadier than from May 25 through June 22, when he matched a club record previously set in May 1984 by Hubie Brooks. It would eventually be overtaken by Moises Alou in 2007.

Jerry Coli/Dreamstime.

2. 124 Runs Batted In (1999)

During a season of explosive offense, Piazza's total ranked only seventh among NL batsmen. But in terms of Mets' lore, it's the highest single-year total ever. Like he did in his home run accumulation, Mike saved the bulk of his production for the latter half of the schedule, when his bat escorted seventy-nine to the plate.

1. Fifteen Consecutive Games with an RBI (2000)

When can fifteen be more impressive than twenty-four? Starting on June 14 and ending on July 2, Piazza was a model of run-producing consistency. This streak came two short of the all-time mark and was dramatically kept alive with a three-run homer on June 30 against the Atlanta Braves to cap a stirring eighth-inning comeback from seven down. The Marlins brought it to a close on July 3—a string in which Piazza had hit safely in each game, knocked out eight homers and drove in twenty-eight.

1. STARTING PITCHER: TOM SEAVER (1967–77, 1983)

Preceding Piazza among Mets who strode through the hallowed gates in Cooperstown—and doing so by the highest voting percentage at the time—is the touchstone by which greatness within this organization will be judged.

But truthfully, "Tom Terrific" is beyond compare.

His entries in the team record book should be written in permanent ink. When you have more strikeouts, more wins, more complete games, more shutouts and the lowest ERA among pitchers who have thrown at least three hundred innings, you have no equal—worthy of being judged among the all-time greats.

ALL-TIME SECOND-TEAM

10. DESIGNATED HITTER: DAVE KINGMAN (1975–77, 1981–83)

Rarely has a player ever fit the "feast or famine" expression better than the man they called "Kong."

When the opposing pitcher's ball connected with his bat, there was no park that could contain him—not Shea Stadium and maybe not even Yellowstone.

On thirty-six occasions in '75, Kingman tested the limits of National League stadiums. His single-season Mets home run record stood for a mere twelve months, because he broke that mark the next year with thirty-seven (overcoming a thumb injury that limited him to 123 games).

Kingman's towering drives were as majestic and remarkable to watch as his many misses. Kingman whiffed 288 times over those same two years.

After his return during a strike-shortened 1981, Kingman brought back more moonshots (22) and more cool breezes (an NL-high 105)—while maintaining a boorish, moody behavior and defensive ineptness.

In '82, he held the league lead in both round-trippers (37) and strikeouts (156). And he batted .204—a lower average than that of Cy Young winner Steve Carlton. It took a mere 664 games for Kingman to slot at 154 home runs, which remains fifth on the team's all-time list.

9. RIGHT FIELD: RUSTY STAUB (1972–75, 1981–85)

Gil Hodges's last personnel move was one of his best. Adored in Montreal, the man born as Daniel—acquired from the Expos as part of a March 1972 swap—would be embraced by New York in short order. And the Big Apple still hasn't let go.

Being the first Met to tally a one-hundred-plus RBI season (doing so in 1975), hitting three homers in the 1973 NLCS, driving in five of the team's six runs in a must-win World Series Game 4 that same year (despite a badly injured right shoulder), coupled with toughness and affability, engendered a high mark of sustained gratitude.

Rusty exited—although not by his doing—shortly before the roof caved in during the late 1970s. He returned in 1981, shortly before the franchise was escaping the doldrums and returning to legitimacy.

The second act saw Staub reinvent himself to take on a far different role. Occasionally at first base, Rusty sparingly saw outfield action and appeared mainly as a pinch-hitter—where he became one of the best at that function.

His 1983 collection of twenty-four sacrifice hits led the major leagues. And his twenty-five pinch-hit RBIs that season matched a major league record.

8. Center Field: Tommie Agee (1968–72)

The debate about the greatest catch in World Series history could last forever. But when considering the *two* best, there's no debate.

Two out and two on in the fourth inning of Game 3. Elrod Hendricks is sure to have an extra-base hit, except Agee races and makes a backhand grab short of the 396-foot marker in left-center field. The crowd had barely stopped buzzing before a seventh-inning bases-loaded encore—robbing Paul Blair with a diving catch on the right–center field warming track. Those plays collectively prevented at least five Oriole runs in what eventuated into a 5–0 Mets win and a 2-1 series lead.

Agee stopped Baltimore's scoring while jump-starting New York's attack. A leadoff homer punctuated a season that started with him hitting the longest long ball Shea ever saw—coming a long way from the depths ventured one year earlier. Even if the Mets did go from basement to penthouse, there was little chance Agee would be part of it.

On the heels of being traded from the White Sox, the 1966 American League Rookie of the Year and two-time All-Star experienced immense difficulty acclimating to the National League—including a woeful 0-for-34 stretch at the plate.

But the awakening from his slumber coincided handsomely with the Mets' rise to prominence. Agee earned his stay at the leadoff spot and turned in team bests in runs scored, homers and RBIs. The outfield range he so prominently showcased on the national stage would be recognized with a Gold Glove in 1970.

7. LEFT FIELD: MOOKIE WILSON (1980–89)

If you think the credit he reaped for a "little roller up along first" that found its way between the legs of Bill Buckner is solely the product of good luck, you don't know the whole story.

Two of Mookie's finest superlatives made the culmination of the Mets' most iconic comeback possible. His steadfast resolve—fighting off pitches and working the count against Bob Stanley long enough for the Sox reliever to throw one past he and catcher Rich Gedman—allowed Kevin Mitchell to race home and tie Game 6 at four.

His breakneck speed—which helped him gain the all-time stolen base mark at 282 (until José Reyes surpassed it in 2008)—might have beaten Buckner to first base anyway, even if it was fielded cleanly.

While a summarization of his Mets career could be boiled down to a five-minute, season-on-the-line situation, Mookie's immense popularity—which rivals that of Seaver and Piazza—spawned from maximum effort, regardless of the circumstances, while never departing from his optimistic beliefs.

Such an endearing quality evident in the mid- to late 1980s—when the Mets were fighting for division titles, pennants and World Championships—was equally apparent in the early part of the decade—when the Mets were fighting for respectability. No. 1 in your program, no. 1 in your heart.

6. SHORTSTOP: BUD HARRELSON (1965–77)

The measurements for what constitutes a premier shortstop oscillate depending on team and time.

Harrelson's value would lessen had he been on a club with success less contingent on pitching and defense and more dependent on offense—or perhaps not. Few players of any era could live up to the determination and fortitude Derrel McKinley Harrelson brandished on the field.

With a .236 average and seven homers, Harrelson hardly portrayed much of a hitting threat—a notion to which he would openly

More impactful with the leather than the lumber, Bud Harrelson was critical to the Mets' defensive-minded focus. *Jerry Coli/Dreamstime.*

attest. But the Mets cherished a glove that could pick as equally as a bat that could pop.

"Having him playing at shortstop every day is like having a top-notch pitcher," Tom Seaver said. "It keeps you out of a losing streak."

As the glue that kept the infield together, his steady hand up the middle contributed to a lifetime fielding percentage of .969. He set a then–major league standard of fifty-four consecutive errorless games at his position in 1970—the same year he earned a selection to his first All-Star team. Bud made it again in '71 and enhanced his season's honors with a Gold Glove Award.

Harrelson's staying power with the organization extended into an assortment of Met ventures—from coaching and managing to broadcasting and scouting.

5. Third Base: Robin Ventura (1999–2001)

Unlike an enormity of free agents the Mets rued, Ventura's entrance to New York instantly resulted in a career year.

As an occupant of the White Sox hot corner for a majority of the 1990s, he amassed five Gold Gloves while exceeding thirty home runs once and one hundred RBIs twice.

Ventura maintained his fielding prowess, rewarded in '99 with a sixth award symbolic of individual defensive excellence. But it was his offense that took an appeasing upturn. The .301 batting average and 120 RBIs were each his loftiest season-ending total, 38 doubles matched a career-high and the 32 homers were just two less than his best. And he actually garnered more MVP voting points than Mike Piazza.

These contributions did, however, come at a price. Battered and bruised, Ventura played hurt and through a struggle of a postseason. But any pain suffered both in physical condition and in the stat sheet (a .120 batting average) was alleviated with the legendary NLCS "Grand Slam Single" that forced the series with the Braves to head back to Atlanta.

Although Ventura's production regressed over his other two years, he still managed better than twenty homers and twenty doubles in each.

4. SECOND BASE: DANIEL MURPHY (2008–2015)

He was an elevator ride of emotion unto himself.

One moment, he comes through with a big hit or a dazzling play. And before you know it, he's committed an egregious, head-scratching base running or fielding gaffe. Take your pick.

But the good certainly outweighed the bad.

Murphy performed above the level initially expected in the forty-nine games following his call-up from the minors late in 2008. And during the 2015 postseason, he went out of his mind—beyond even the most historical comparisons.

Seven home runs over the course of the Division and League Championship Series—six in consecutive games—carried the Mets to a pennant and temporarily converted Murphy (with a .529 batting average in four victories versus Chicago) into a delicious concoction of Babe Ruth and Reggie Jackson.

This was a turn of power both timely and stunning. Murphy hit fourteen homers in all of '15 and averaged nine in the five full seasons preceding it.

Compensating for curious base path judgments and questionable defensive decisions, his steadiness at the plate was exemplified by averaging a .288 batting mark, 36 doubles, and 154 hits. The 228 two-baggers logged remain the third-highest output among Mets.

3. FIRST BASE: JOHN OLERUD (1997–99)

Here is the best example of substance outweighing style.

Flashiness was foreign to Olerud, unless you believe wearing a helmet in the field constitutes a fashion statement and being fundamentally sound should earn air time on highlight shows.

Originally drafted by the Mets in the twenty-seventh round of the 1986 MLB Amateur Draft out of high school before deciding to attend (and become one of the greatest college players ever) Washington State, Olerud's delayed—albeit welcome—entrance came after eight years, two World Series titles and a batting crown in Toronto.

During the bludgeon ball phase of the late 1990s, home run totals of twenty-two, twenty-two and nineteen are extremely modest in comparison. But an on-base percentage of .425 over those same three years is monumental.

When batting in front of Mike Piazza, as he did for the majority of '98 and pretty much the entirety of '99, finding a way to reach was paramount to Mets success.

Olerud did it about as well as anyone in the National League, and his .354 batting average in '98 is the high-water mark for a single season in club history. Although each of his three Gold Gloves are of the AL variety, his fielding percentage rates with that of Keith Hernandez in his heyday.

2. Catcher: Gary Carter (1985–89)

Gary Carter was inducted into the Mets Hall of Fame in 2001 and the Baseball Hall of Fame in 2003. *Jerry Coli/Dreamstime.*

He was someone you hated to play against but loved to play with.

Those who observed Carter from afar and even those who shared a clubhouse with him thought the player they called "Kid" resembled something of a phony. The fair-haired, can't-wipe-the-smile-off-if-you-tried backstop, who spent seven seasons with the Expos, was—as detractors put it—too good to be true.

But it's hard to be fake when you're like that all the time. And you'll never find a testimonial stating otherwise.

Carter shared Keith Hernandez's tenacity and guidance but stood out with his abundant supply of enthusiasm.

Gary also possessed a dominant clutch gene. He was a man for the moment—several coming in the 1986 postseason. Carter broke out of a rare slump with the walk-off hit in Game 5 of the NLCS, took advantage of the inviting "Green Monster" at Fenway Park with two home runs in Game 4 of the World Series and pioneered the indelible rally in Game 6.

Carter statistical performances in New York, during which his aching body got the better of him, aren't on par with the Hall of Fame–worthy numbers achieved in Montreal. Yet the input he had in pushing the Mets over the top and doing so as an exemplar for others to follow, is irrefutable.

It's hard to comprehend that for the many players on the '86 team who lived so perilously, the one who lived so decently was the first to depart.

As the painful reality of brain cancer ultimately took him in February 2012 at age fifty-seven, there's no doubt he maintained that vivacious preponderance of spirit and a smile. Gary Carter wouldn't know any other way.

1. STARTING PITCHER: DWIGHT GOODEN (1984–94)

Captivating, mesmerizing, awe-inspiring. No pitcher or player captured those descriptions better than Doc over his first two seasons. He was that good.

The 1982 no. 5 overall draft pick nearly was a unanimous choice for Rookie of the Year in 1984. There was no "nearly" in 1985 when it came to Cy Young Award voting.

A year older, a year wiser, a year more dominant. At twenty, he equaled his age in victories on August 25—becoming the youngest to reach that milestone. He then bettered it by four. He lost just four times. His ERA was a microscopic 1.53. And he struck out 268 to complete the pitching Triple Crown. It's the best season on the mound in Mets history and one of the greatest of all-time.

It would be near impossible for Gooden to match such success, even with almost an entire career supposedly ahead of him. He remained the staff ace for the better part of the next nine seasons, even as injuries sapped a portion of his power.

He won seventeen games in '86; eighteen more in '88; nearly attained twenty in 1990; became a four-time All-Star and started the Midsummer Classic twice. But his tenure in New York is forever marred by his own foibles.

A failed drug test shortly before 1987 brought questions about his well-being. In the end, those demons never deserted him. Another positive cocaine test in 1994 led to a suspension for 1995 and a close to his Mets career.

Doc is second to Tom Seaver in wins (157) and strikeouts (1,875). But, like Darryl Strawberry, who knows what could have been had not personal torments intervened.

POSTSEASON GAMES

10. 1973 World Series Game 2

It had the length of an epic, the thrills of a drama and the pratfalls of a comedy—supplied with catching fails, errant throws, missed calls and botched grounders.

These dotted the four-hour, thirteen-minute landscape of a contest in which both sides received and gave back victory until the Mets emerged 10–7 winners in twelve innings to even a series against the prohibitive favorite on its home field before heading east.

New York's 6–4 ninth-inning lead withered under the late afternoon sun as aching Willie Mays, at the last stage of his brilliant career, showed why not even he, at age forty-two, could beat Father Time. His stumbling attempt to snag a fly ball that he used to basket catch in his sleep began an A's rally that concluded with Gene Tenace's tying single.

Bud Harrelson tried to put a quick end to the tie in the tenth, but home plate umpire Augie Donatelli ruled him out on an attempt to score on a fly out to left fielder Joe Rudi. Slow-motion replay showed that catcher Ray Fosse missed the tag. Willie Mays, on both knees, and manager Yogi Berra—among others—furiously (and fruitlessly) contested the call.

The controversy abated two innings later, when Mays atoned with an RBI single to center—the final hit of his career. Three additional runs came across with the help of errors from Mike Andrews on two consecutive plays.

Weary Tug McGraw, working his seventh inning, couldn't finish, as another Mays misplay let Reggie Jackson triple.

George Stone prolonged the drama, as the tying run reached the plate. But no more generosity. The Mets took this win, regardless how it was done.

9. 1986 NLCS GAME 5

Reprising their July 4 matchup, the generation-spanning mound duel between Dwight Gooden and Nolan Ryan lived up to its billing.

Doc overcame nine Astro hits to limit visiting Houston to one run in ten innings, while Ryan yielded two hits and one run over nine. The first thirteen Mets failed to reach base. The fourteenth, Darryl Strawberry, had enough distance and hook to sneak a homer into the right-field corner.

A 1–1 stalemate held up for more than six innings, as both teams sought control of the series.

Charlie Kerfeld—the bespectacled, brash and bulky right-hander in his third inning of work—couldn't maintain his control on a pickoff attempt of Wally Backman. The errant throw allowed Backman to move to second.

With one out, that open base would soon be occupied by Keith Hernandez via an intentional walk in favor of pitching to Gary Carter—carrying the burden of a 1-for-21 slump.

The weight of Carter's drought departed as soon as his hit went past the mound, between the second baseman and shortstop and into center field. Backman beat Billy Hatcher's throw home, and the Mets took a 3–2 series lead back to Houston.

"I kept telling myself, 'I'm going to come through here,'" Carter said postgame. "I knew it was just a matter of time. I'm not an .050 hitter."

8. 1999 NLDS GAME 4

The Mets lived September on the edge. Eight losses in nine games put them in a most precarious spot. Entering the final three of the regular season two behind the Reds for the Wild Card, they needed to sweep the Pittsburgh Pirates and a bit of help from the Brewers—who were hosting Cincinnati.

New York did their part—highlighted by a pair of walk-off victories. Milwaukee did its share by taking two and creating a one-game playoff at Riverfront that Al Leiter and some early runs made victorious.

On to Arizona and a split of the first two Division Series games. Back at home, New York took Game 3 easily, putting the Mets in control and the D-backs in the desperate spot. But by letting two separate leads slip away and trailing by a run in the bottom of the eighth, the screws tightened once more.

To the victors go the spoils. The championship trophies emblematic of the 1969 (*left*) and 1986 (*right*) World Series triumphs are on display at the Mets Hall of Fame Museum inside Citi Field. *Author's collection.*

The Mets, though, scratched for one. As a tenth inning awaited, it was an idyllic occasion for their catching star to provide timely power. If only he could. Not even the adrenaline of October could heal Mike Piazza's thumb. Luckily, Todd Pratt, with vastly less power, had just enough.

To straightaway center field, headed for the 410-foot mark. As Steve Finley came down from his leap with a resigned look and an empty glove, it signaled the newly famed catcher, the Mets and Shea Stadium to go crazy. From total obscurity, Pratt became the fourth player to end a playoff series with a home run.

7. 1988 NLCS GAME 3

If ever a playoff game went through the rinse cycle and air dried at a mist-filled forty-three degrees, this was it.

For over three and a half hours, the Mets and Dodgers competed for the series edge on a Shea Stadium turf that served as a forty-thousand-square-foot slip 'n' slide and showed why baseball won't be considered as a winter Olympic sport.

Sure-footed athletes were reduced to ice skaters in cleats as the once-postponed contest was given a full go the following afternoon. This wasn't the ideal scenario for Los Angeles' next-to-invincible Orel Hershiser—given the start on three days' rest.

So, if the Mets bats couldn't thwart dominance, perhaps Mother Nature's devious ways could.

Both elements worked against the eventual Cy Young winner—as six hits, four walks and two errors produced three runs over seven innings.

But up until the eighth, it hadn't been enough. The Dodgers broke a 3–3 tie with a bases-loaded walk, but would soon be victim to the Mets' paranormal postseason touch and Davey Johnson's brand of gamesmanship.

Johnson had been informed that Jay Howell, who came in to pitch the eighth, used pine tar on his glove. Umpires heeded Johnson's call for Howell's mitt to be inspected in search of the illegal substance. Davey's suspicion was validated. The judges ruled guilty and Howell was ejected. And the Mets were able to extricate themselves from their own sticky situation.

Wally Backman, eclipsed in the wake of Gregg Jefferies's emergence, delivered a two-out hit into the right–center field gap that scored Howard Johnson. And the line kept moving—a base path conveyor belt that manufactured four more runs and an 8–4 win in a game far less artistic than critical.

6. 1986 NLCS Game 3

That year, 108 victories in the regular season would mean nothing without 8 in the postseason.

The Houston Astros lacked warm feelings about the first playoff game at Shea Stadium since 1973, especially Bill Doran, who did his best to eradicate the exuberance. A two-run second-inning homer compounded Ron Darling's frustration after he allowed a pair of first-inning scores.

Bob Knepper, holding a 4–0 advantage, was about to discover how quickly a lead can disappear. The Mets sprang in the sixth with a skill that distinguishes good teams from great ones: an innate ability to come back through timely bursts of offense.

New York chipped away with a Kevin Mitchell single to left, a Keith Hernandez single to center and a Gary Carter grounder past shortstop Craig Reynolds that drove in Mitchell. Quivering Shea was waiting to burst—a good time for a Strawberry shake. As Knepper tried to get ahead in the count with a first-pitch fastball, he didn't have the velocity to throw it by Darryl's quick bat. The towering drive over the right-field wall signaled a power shift. But as quickly as the Mets harnessed momentum, the Astros—by scoring one in the top of the seventh—got it back.

The Mets, though—in their weird, sadistic fashion—began to relish this comeback role. Wally Backman's successful drag bunt to start the bottom of the ninth against Houston closer Dave Smith—in which the Astros unsuccessfully claimed he stepped out of the baseline—put the tying run on. He moved to second base on a wild pitch and stayed there when Danny Heep flew out.

Lenny Dykstra, who (like Backman) had a penchant for starting rallies, now finished one—while finishing the Astros' prospects of taking a 2–1 series edge with his lead-changing, game-ending swing.

Honorable Mention

1969 World Series Game 4

The remarkable outfield plays didn't end with Tommie Agee in Game 3. Ron Swoboda (known more for what he couldn't do on defense) stretched out parallel to the ground on a Brooks Robinson liner to right field in the ninth inning—a ridiculous catch that kept Tom Seaver and the Mets from falling behind. Tied at one in the tenth, J.C. Martin's bunt to the right side of the infield was taken by O's lefty reliever Pete Richert. His throw to first nailed Martin in the arm, allowing pinch-runner Rod Gaspar to score the game winner from second base.

1973 World Series Game 5

Two wins from another World Series title, there was no better time to believe. Jerry Koosman, who had long since shaken his early season struggles, threw with renewed conviction. Similar to his series clincher four years previous, Kooz came through—and even better than before. Collaring the Oakland A's for 6.1 innings, he passed the baton to Tug McGraw with shutout faiths unbroken. Tug would preserve the 2-0 lead and the Mets ventured back to the Bay Area on the brink.

1988 NLCS Game 1

Unyielding Orel Hershiser picked up where he left off. With fifty-nine consecutive scoreless regular season innings firmly in the all-time annals, he blanked the Mets into the ninth as the Dodgers maintained a 2-0 lead. Then with one out, Darryl Strawberry doubled home Gregg Jeffries to mark Orel's exit. Gary Carter, down to his last strike against Jay Howell, got a short looping liner to drop short of center fielder John Shelby. Strawberry and no-holds-barred Kevin McReynolds—bowling over catcher Mike Scioscia—scored the winning runs.

2000 NLDS Game 2

Armando Benítez and John Franco differed in look and delivery, but each shared a common trait of testing fans' patience. Down a game, but up 4-1 on the Giants, Benítez served a tying bottom-of-the-ninth homer to J.T. Snow that snuck inside the right-field foul pole. Now in danger of digging an 0–2 hole, the Mets recovered to score once in the tenth. Franco entered in the bottom half and got Barry Bonds looking on a 3–2 changeup—bailing out Benitez and breathing new life into New York.

2015 NLDS Game 5

As decisive as Daniel Murphy's sixth-inning homer off Zack Greinke turned out to be, it wasn't as crucial as the steadfastness Jacob deGrom displayed. Four consecutive first-inning singles—resulting in two runs—put him in danger of an early hook. DeGrom limited the damage and allowed the Mets to tie it in the fourth and take the lead on Murphy's blast to right field. Noah Syndergaard and Jeurys Familia overpowered Dodger bats the rest of the way.

5. 1969 World Series Game 5

Six months earlier, such a scenario defied comprehension. For a civilization recently witness to such an otherworldly event as a moon landing, the Mets—cellar dwellers for most of their first seven years—were on the brink of an accomplishment registering as much awe as what took place 239,000 miles from earth.

Even 100 regular season wins and a sweep of the Atlanta Braves in the inaugural NLCS could not convince skeptics that the Mets could conceive of toppling the 109-win Orioles when the World Series began.

Despite dropping Game 1 in Baltimore, the magic refused to dwindle. Three straight wins turned skeptics into believers. And just one win away, the elements bringing the Mets to this juncture—superb starting pitching and timely hitting—carried them over the top.

But one last touch of fate intervened in the bottom of the six, down 3–0 and the Orioles attempting to take the series back to Baltimore.

Cleon Jones claimed he was hit in the foot by a Dave McNally pitch. Home plate umpire Lou DiMuro wasn't convinced until Gil Hodges brought DiMuro the ball—which skipped toward the dugout—bearing a smudge of shoe polish. DiMuro reversed his decision and awarded Cleon first base. The next ball was promptly vaulted airborne by Donn Clendenon. 3–2, Orioles.

Al Weis, starting the bottom of the seventh, then hit his first Shea Stadium home run to draw even. Two doubles and two Oriole errors in the eighth elicited a 5–3 Mets lead.

Jerry Koosman, four hits and three runs permitted over the first two innings, yielded one hit over the final seven. The final pitch was sent to deep left field. Jones, on the warning track, began to kneel as he secured the clinching out—almost as if to acknowledge the heavens for a title distinguished as providential.

The Mets, hundred-to-one odds to win it all when the season began, were World Champions. Amazin'.

4. 1986 World Series Game 7

The postscript to the epic theater of some forty-eight hours earlier was anything but a fait accompli—even if the divine plan was for the Mets to win and the Red Sox curse to be prolonged.

This page: Jesse Orosco (*right*) lets loose after striking out Marty Barrett to end Game 7 of the 1986 World Series. Soon, the rest of his teammates engulfed him in a mob by the pitcher's mound. As the celebration unfolded, Bob Murphy proclaimed on the radio: "The dream has come true." *Jerry Coli/Dreamstime*.

Sunday rains let Boston manager John McNamara give Bruce Hurst the starting nod, and he proceeded to reinforce credentials for series MVP—an award in his possession before the Mets' emergence from mortality.

Once Ron Darling evidenced that he couldn't match the Mets' latest encounter with a red-hot hurler, they called on their own lefty savior, Sid Fernandez, to limit the damage by retiring seven straight and fanning four.

Like 1969's clincher, the Mets spotted their opponent a 3–0 lead. And again the sixth inning was the turning point.

Lee Mazzilli and Mookie Wilson built the rally with one-out singles. Tim Teufel walked, arranging a ready-made moment for their clutch-hitting first baseman. Keith Hernandez similarly delivered an ultimately Game 7–winning hit for the Cardinals in 1982. This time, his single to center field brought home Mazzilli and Mookie and the Mets to within a run.

On the next pitch, Gary Carter's looping fly ball to right field landed in front of a diving Dwight Evans—allowing pinch-runner Wally Backman to score the equalizer. The Mets' charge steamed forward. Ray Knight had his MVP moment in the seventh with a homer to left center against Calvin Schiraldi.

New York scored twice more—so did Boston. But Darryl Strawberry's leadoff homer in the bottom of the eighth, followed by another run and then Jesse Orosco's three up, three down ninth ensured Saturday's dramatics were more catalyst than footnote.

By winning 8–5, the Mets did what they were supposed to do from the outset. But the method by which they did it showed that for all their dominance, they had character and resolve when it mattered most.

3. 1999 NLCS Game 5

The two-and-a-half-week tightrope the Mets walked—placing one wobbly foot in front of the other—began to fray.

Walt Weiss scored on Keith Lockhart's triple in the top of the fifteenth—breaking a 2–2 tie maintained since the fourth.

A five-and-a-half-hour taut trek through the late afternoon and into a rainy evening was three outs from reaching resolution—as was the hypnotic, thrilling journey of Bobby Valentine's team.

The Atlanta Braves thought they had the Mets dead and buried by crushing them in late September, when taking a one-run lead into the bottom of the eighth of Game 4 and again tonight.

But then came another encounter with ghosts of miracles past. Shawon Dunston led off the bottom of the fifteenth and worked young Kevin McGlinchy for twelve pitches before singling up the middle. Matt Franco drew a walk. Edgardo Alfonzo, in his ever-understated way, sacrificed both runners ninety feet farther.

With a base open, John Olerud—responsible for the entirety of the Mets' scoring by way of his two-run homer eons ago—got an intentional pass.

Todd Pratt somehow had the chance to reprise the dramatics of eight days earlier. Yet his effort was minimal. The rattled McGlinchy walked in the tying run.

Bases were still loaded for someone comfortable with this RBI-rich situation. Robin Ventura, pained yet not sidelined, could send everyone home (and both teams south) with an addition to his eighteen career grand slams.

From the crack of the bat to the ball landing beyond the right-center field fence and in front of the massive scoreboard, it was a grand slam in the most classic sense of the description and visualization.

Except his over-exuberant teammates wouldn't allow Ventura to savor his home run trot—instead mobbing him in the path between first and second base.

The result of the play, forever a "Grand Slam Single," was of little significance to the joyous Mets. Whether the final score was 4–3 instead of 7–3 didn't matter. They rose from the dead once more and lived to play another night.

2. 1986 NLCS Game 6

Among the dramatic fulcrums from the 1986 postseason, one stands out.

What if the Mets lost Game 6 of the NLCS and were forced to face a pitcher who owned them twice before in a deciding Astrodome showdown?

Jesse Orosco's sixteenth-inning strikeout of Kevin Bass made certain that scenario wouldn't come to pass—ending a playoff epic with as much sustained tension as any before. But the conclusion can't be told without context.

Even though New York held a 3–2 series lead, the specter of Mike Scott—the pitcher who made the Mets look mortal in Games 1 and 4 and was scheduled to go in Game 7—loomed like a grim reaper in the opposite dugout.

If ever a team leading a series faced a must-win situation, *this* was that situation.

Houston starter Bob Knepper was turning that possibility into probability with each passing inning. Given three early runs, the lefty assumed total command—barely breaking a sweat with a two-hitter through eight.

But before the space separating them from Scott closed completely, the Mets offered a swift renouncement. Lenny Dykstra muscled a triple beyond the reach of center fielder Billy Hatcher. Mookie Wilson singled barely over second baseman Bill Doran's mitt. Keith Hernandez followed with a double to force Knepper's ouster. But Dave Smith couldn't stem the tide.

Two walks preceded Ray Knight's sacrifice fly. The narrow escape from defeat raised a tension level already on high. It would get higher. After Roger McDowell went five remarkable shutout innings, Wally Backman drove in Darryl Strawberry in the top of the fourteenth.

The Mets were now counting down the outs—and a Saturday night date in Queens with the American League champs—until Billy Hatcher spoiled it. He towered Orosco's offering deep down the left-field line and into the screen substituting a foul pole.

New York, though, retained as much resilience as its opponent—not letting the back-breaking moment serve as the momentum to carry Houston into tomorrow.

Knight's opposite-field single in the top of the sixteenth scored Strawberry. Two insurance runs came across, which turned out to be invaluable security, as the Astros continued to disregard relent.

They answered with two runs and put two runners on with two outs and Bass coming up. Orosco's heater receded to batting practice effectiveness.

"If you throw another fastball, I'm going to knock you out" is how a one-way mound conversation went between Hernandez and the on-fumes reliever—or something to that effect.

Tired arm but lucid mind, Orosco ran the count full before getting Bass to swing and miss on a 3-2 breaking ball.

The Mets finally extinguished the Astros' competitive fire and exhausted their last-gasp try while simultaneously exhausting themselves. It was a Game 6 for the ages—to be outdone ten days later.

1. 1986 World Series Game 6

"Congratulations World Champions Boston Red Sox."

Although not official, it was likely that the message prematurely displayed on the scoreboard at Shea Stadium would become a reality.

Down 5–3, with one out to spare and nobody on base in the bottom of the tenth, even outrageous believers who witnessed miracles from '69 and '73 could not be convinced that this team, which prevailed 115 times dating back to Opening Day, could rescue its season and avoid a disheartening resolution to a year that had championship aspirations.

The rowdy, raucous, rambunctious Mets—who resoundingly sped past National League challengers with bullhorn in hand—were about to go quietly into the night.

As Wally Backman and Keith Hernandez each flew out to put the Mets on the brink of defeat, the visitors' clubhouse of an otherwise sullen Shea donned the appearance of a soon-to-be celebration.

Preparations were set for Boston to purge its haunted past and win the first title since 1918. The Commissioner's Trophy sat in the Sox locker room. Bob Costas was tuning his microphone and adjusting his earpiece for the winner interview and trophy presentation, cellophane draped over the lockers to shield from the spray of champagne.

What ensued was a sequence of events that created memories inimitable in the long history of baseball and the iconic franchise moment. It's replayed both too often and never enough, a religious experience for the most devout Mets devotee. The Immaculate Conception, Noah's Ark and the parting of the Red (Sox) Sea rolled into one.

Gary Carter, who tied the score at three with an eighth-inning sacrifice fly, started it by lacing a single to left field against Calvin Schiraldi. Then Kevin Mitchell—rumored to have been in the locker room undressed/making travel plans/drinking a beer or all of the above—delivered a base hit to center.

Ray Knight, tailored for goat horns for his seventh-inning throwing error leading to a Red Sox go-ahead run, fought off an inside 0-2 pitch and placed it in center field—bringing in Carter to make it 5–4 and moving Mitchell to third.

Mookie Wilson, batting from the left side and facing new pitcher Bob Stanley, held the responsibility of staving off the hairbreadth potential of elimination. Any swing could be the last. He fouled off four of six pitches, working the count to 2-2 before Stanley let one get away. The pitch avoided

Mookie's feet and catcher Rich Gedman's glove. It scooted to the backstop. Mitchell scored. Knight advanced into scoring position.

An incredible occurrence. It paled by what happened next.

With pressure lessened, Mookie continued to swing freely—spoiling two more pitches. Finally, he hit a fair slow roller toward first base, a ground ball fitted with destiny's eyes.

Around the glove and through the legs of Bill Buckner it went—allowing an astonished Knight to touch home amid a mob of teammates and dispatching Shea into its most exultant state.

SOURCES

GENERAL

Baseball Reference. www.baseball-reference.com.

Blatt, Howard. *Amazin' Met Memories*. Tampa, FL: Albion Press, 2002.

Ferry, David. *Total Mets: The Definitive Encyclopedia of the New York Mets' First Half-Century*. Chicago: Triumph Books, 2012.

Honig, Donald. *The New York Mets: The First Quarter Century*. New York: Crown Publishers, 1986.

Kalinsky, George. *The New York Mets: A Photographic History*. New York: Macmillan, 1995.

Lang, Jack, and Peter Simon. *The New York Mets: Twenty-Five Years of Baseball Magic*. New York: Henry Holt and Company, 1986.

Samelson, Ken, and Matthew Silverman. *The Miracle Has Landed: The Amazin' Story of How the 1969 Mets Shocked the World*. Hanover, MA: Elm Street Press.

Silverman, Matthew. *New York Mets: 50 Amazin' Seasons*. Minneapolis, MN: MVP Books, 2011.

Ultimate Mets Database. www.ultimatemets.com.

EARLY METS

Anderson, Will. "Carl Willey." Society for American Baseball Research. Accessed July 13, 2017. https://sabr.org/bioproj/person/1cd9a765.

Kearney, Seamus. "Richie Ashburn." Society for American Baseball Research. Accessed June 30, 2017. https://sabr.org/bioproj/person/cda44a76.

Pruden, Bill. "Jack Fisher." Society for American Baseball Research. Accessed July 26, 2017. https://sabr.org/bioproj/person/533d1612.

Debuts

Curry, Jack. "Jones Puts Finishing Touch on Trammell's Magic Moment." *New York Times*, July 31, 2000.

Jenkins, Lee. "Smashing Start for Mets Begins on the First Pitch." *New York Times*, April 7, 2004.

Keh, Andrew. "Left in Hands of Mets, Sparkling Debut Is Lost." *New York Times*, August 23, 2012.

———. "One-Two Punch Looks Dominant as the Mets Sweep." *New York Times*, June 18, 2013.

Martino, Andy. "Harvey K's 11 in Debut, Leads Met to 3–1 Victory Over Dbacks." *New York Daily News*, July 27, 2012.

Tayler, Jon. "Steven Matz Makes Historic MLB Debut for Hometown Mets." *Sports Illustrated*, June 28, 2015. https://www.si.com/mlb/2015/06/28/steven-matz-debut-new-york-mets-mlb-history.

Rookie Seasons

Metropolitan Baseball Club. *Accent on Youth*. Film, 1977.

Paine, Neil. "The Mets' Rise and Fall With Doc Gooden and Darryl Strawberry." FiveThirtyEight, July 14, 2016. https://fivethirtyeight.com/features/the-mets-rise-and-fall-with-doc-gooden-and-darryl-strawberry.

Single-Game Pitching Performances

Belock, Joe. "Mets vs. Giants in NL Wild Card: The Rivalry's Best Moments." *New York Daily News*, October 4, 2016.

Brown, Thomas J., Jr. "Mets' Tom Seaver Strikes Out 19 Padres Batters." Society for American Baseball Research. Accessed May 25, 2017. https://

sabr.org/gamesproj/game/april-22-1970-mets-tom-seaver-strikes-out-19-padres-batters.

DiComo, Anthony. "One-Hit Wonder: Dickey Brilliant in 10th Win." MLB. com. June 14, 2012. https://www.mlb.com/gameday/mets-vs-rays/ Invalid%20date/Invalid%20date/Invalid%20date/318666#game_ state=final,game_tab=,game=318666.

Southpaw Starters

Augustine, Bernie. "Jon Niese Take Shot at Mets Defense After Trade to Pirates." *New York Daily News*, December 10, 2015. http://www. nydailynews.com/sports/baseball/mets/jon-niese-takes-shot-mets-defense-trade-pirates-article-1.2461329.

Prince, Greg. "Al Jackson." Society for American Baseball Research. Accessed November 26, 2017. https://sabr.org/bioproj/person/9bc53b1d.

Relief Pitchers

Costello, Rory. "John Franco." Society for American Baseball Research. Accessed June 11, 2017. https://sabr.org/bioproj/person/2966ede2.

Single-Game Hitting Performances

Battista, Judy. "Alfonzo Knocks Out Astros." *New York Times*, August 31, 1999.

Diamos, Jason. "Ochoa Hits for the Cycle to Spark Mets." *New York Times*, July 4, 1996.

Durso, Joseph. "Revamped Mets Win to Stop the Streak at 7." *New York Times*, August 2, 1989.

Frey, Jennifer. "For Mets, Big Fall but Sweet Recovery." *New York Times*, August 6, 1993.

Karpin, Howie. *162-0: Imagine a Mets Perfect Season*. Chicago: Triumph Books, 2012.

VILLAINS

Pearlman, Jeff. "At Full Blast." *Sports Illustrated*, December 27, 1999.
Weintraub, Robert. "Reflections of a Mets Killer." *New York Times*, September 7, 2012.

DISAPPOINTING TEAMS

Carig, Marc. "Sources: Mets Owner Fred Wilpon Protected Terry Collins from Getting Fired." *Newsday*, September 28, 2017.
Klapich, Bob, and John Harper. *The Worst Team Money Could Buy: The Collapse of the New York Mets*. New York: Random House, 1993.

DEVASTATING LOSSES

Major League Baseball Promotion Corporation. *The 1973 World Series*. Film, 1973.

WORST TRADES

McCarron, Anthony. "Stung by Trade, Rick's Finally a Good Reed." *New York Daily News*, May 22, 2010.
Verducci, Tom. "The Amazin' Collapse of the Mets." *Sports Illustrated*, December 20, 1993.

INTERNAL FEUDS

Berg, Ted. "Matt Harvey Looks Terrible in Sudden Drama Over Innings Limit." *For the Win*, September 6, 2015.
Boswell, Thomas. "Strawberry Takes a Club to the Club." *Washington Post*, March 13, 1988.
Callan, Matthew. "Jordany Valdespin: Worse than Everyone Ever, Apparently." SB Nation. Accessed May 17, 2013. https://www.amazinavenue.com/2013/5/17/4331850/new-york-mets-jordany-valdespin-worse-than-everyone-ever-apparently.

Daily Stache. "Throwback Thursday: 12 Years Ago Today, Wilpons Buy Out Doubleday." August 14, 2014. http://dailystache.net/throwback-thursday-12-years-ago-today-wilpon-buys-doubleday.

Kernan, Kevin. "Jefferies Leaves Embattled Mets Past Far Behind." *New York Post*, January 30, 2010.

Klapich, Bob. "Darryl Strawberry Takes a Swing at Keith Hernandez in 1989." *New York Daily News*, March 1, 2016.

Waldstein, David. "Regretful Phillips Takes Blame for Feud with Valentine." *New York Times*, November 30, 2011.

Wulf, Steve. "Taking the Rap." *Sports Illustrated*, July 13, 1987.

Yorke, Aaron. "Mets' Jordany Valdespin Reportedly Called Manager Terry Collins a Cocksucker, Demanded to Be Placed on Disabled List." SB Nation. Accessed July 14, 2013. https://www.amazinavenue.com/2013/7/14/4523784/mets-jordany-valdespin-terry-collins-cocksucker.

Subway Series Victories

Bradley, Jeff. "As Mets Met Yankees in 1997, Dave Mlicki Stole Show When Spotlight Was Brightest." *Newark Star-Ledger*, May 21, 2011.

Chass, Murray. "Wells Has the Cure for Vaughn's Woes," *New York Times*, June 17, 2002.

Diamos, Jason. "Mets Find Consolation in a Strange Series Finish." *New York Times*, June 29, 1998.

Jenkins, Lee. "Wright's Body Language Says It All for Mets." *New York Times*, May 20, 2006.

Keh, Andrew. "Mets Beat Yankees and Rivera with Two Runs in Ninth." *New York Times*, May 29, 2013.

Olney, Buster. "Pure Storybook: Mets Win One to Remember." *New York Times*, July 11, 1999.

Shpigel, Ben. "Mets Salvage Finale of Subway Series." *New York Times*, July 4, 2011.

———. "Mets Win 2 of 3 Against Yankees in Subway Series." *New York Times*, May 24, 2010.

REGULAR SEASON GAMES, 1969

Chicago Tribune. "The Cubs' Collapse of 1969: An Oral History." October 17, 2015. http://www.chicagotribune.com/sports/baseball/cubs/ct-cubs-mets-1969-spt-1018-20151017-story.html.

Delcos, John. "This Day in Mets History: Hodges Pulls Jones for Not Hustling." Mets Merized. July 30, 2012. http://metsmerizedonline.com/2012/07/this-day-in-mets-history-hodges-pulls-cleon-jones-for-not-hustling.html.

REGULAR SEASON GAMES, 1986

Durso, Joseph. "Finally, the Mets Achieve the Inevitable Title." *New York Times*, September 18, 1986.

———. "Mets Win on Error in 10th." *New York Times*, May 31, 1986.

Huber, Mike. "Mets Win Extra-Inning Slugfest with Brawl and Home Run." Society for American Baseball Research. Accessed June 2, 2017. https://sabr.org/gamesproj/game/july-22-1986-mets-win-extra-inning-slugfest-brawl-and-home-run.

SportsChannel/Rainbow Home Video. *1986 Mets: A Year to Remember*. Film, 1986.

Yannis, Alex. "Mets Win on 2 Homers in 10th." *New York Times*, July 4, 1986.

REGULAR SEASON GAMES, 2000

Curry, Jack. "Round Trip Ends Orioles' Long Trip." *New York Times*, June 9, 2000.

Kepner, Tyler. "Grounder by Franco Bounces Right Way." *New York Times*, April 25, 2000.

Marchand, Andrew. "A Simply Amazin' Night: Down 8–1, Mets Rally to Stun Braves." *New York Post*, July 1, 2000.

Vecsey, George. "Against the Odds, Agbayani Gets Mets Home Even." *New York Times*, March 31, 2000.

Regular Season Games, 2015

Associated Press. "Daniel Murphy's 3-Run Homer in 9th Lifts Mets over Marlins." April 27, 2015.

Puma, Mike. "Unbelievable! Flores Dries Tears for Walk-Off HR in Thriller." *New York Post,* July 31, 2015.

Rohan, Tim. "Mets' David Wright Says It All: 'What a Game.'" *New York Times*, September 7, 2015.

All-Time Starting Lineup

DiComo, Anthony. "After Signing New Deal, Wright Bullish on Future." MLB.com. December 5, 2012. http://m.mlb.com/news/article/40518804.

Ehalt, Matt. "David Wright Sets Mets Hits Record." ESPN. September 26, 2012. http://www.espn.com/new-york/mlb/story/_/id/8429423/david-wright-breaks-new-york-mets-record-hits-1419.

All-Time Second-Team

Metropolitan Baseball Club. *You Gotta Believe: 1973 Mets Highlights*. Film, 1973.

Postseason Games

Anderson, Dave. "Sports of the Times." *New York Times*, October 15, 1986.

ABOUT THE AUTHOR

Brian Wright has been featured in *Bleacher Report* and the *Washington Examiner* and on NESN.com, SB Nation and The Cauldron. For three years, he was the lead MLB writer for *The Sports Daily*.

Brian is the managing editor for a book published by the Society for American Baseball Research (SABR) encompassing the greatest games in Mets history. He has also contributed to a SABR book on the greatest games at Wrigley Field.

He currently resides in Arlington, Virginia.